CW01304308

Endorsements

"Julie Saad has written a must-read guide for the contemplative path, impressively furthering the work of Fr. Thomas Keating. Inviting and accessible, filled with personal stories, useful practices and wise teachings, this book is a valuable resource for anyone drawn to Centering Prayer or the desire to be transformed by contemplation in life, beyond the meditation cushion."

—**David Frenette**,
author of *The Path of Centering Prayer*
and one of the creators of the Contemplative Living Experience teachings

"In this book Julie Saad has embodied Thomas Keating's foundational teachings on Centering Prayer as well as his explanation of the Human Condition and the influence of the unconscious on our daily living. The awareness and comprehension of these teachings is essential to our spiritual growth. The additional contemplative practices that Julie describes so well in her book serve to feed and indeed nourish the commitment to dispose ourselves to the transformation of our very lives. This book is a gift to everyone open to developing connection to the Spirit in everyday living. Isn't this what Father Thomas's teaching is all about?"

—**Rose Meyler**,
former coordinator of the Contemplative Living Experience program,
and volunteer and board member of Contemplative Outreach of Colorado

"This book brings out Father Thomas Keating's teachings in clear, concise, and remarkably systematic ways. It not only points to the glory and majesty of God, but unlike really any other book I have ever come across, makes the divine mystery accessible. That is an extraordinary feat; one that feels inspired. This is a book to be read with a contemplative tempo—like a delicious meal, savored, chewed with the intention of experiencing every bite/word. The subtle weaving of Julie's experience throughout the text keeps the whole thing fresh, interesting, and relevant to the reader. This is truly a post-modern spiritual text in its applicability to those who may be religious, or just call themselves spiritual but not religious."

—**Dan Davis**,
friend and spiritual seeker

"The power of this book is that it is coming out of Julie's lived experience of many years of living and teaching this material. She is passionate in wanting to share it. Establishing a firm daily routine is essential in maintaining a fruitful and intimate encounter with the Lord."

—**Father Carl J. Arico**,
a founding member of Contemplative Outreach

Contemplative Life

Discovering Our Path into the Heart of God

J U L I E   S A A D

BALBOA.PRESS
A DIVISION OF HAY HOUSE

Copyright © 2021 Julie Saad.

All rights reserved. No part of this book may be used or reproduced by any means, graphic, electronic, or mechanical, including photocopying, recording, taping or by any information storage retrieval system without the written permission of the author except in the case of brief quotations embodied in critical articles and reviews.

Balboa Press books may be ordered through booksellers or by contacting:

Balboa Press
A Division of Hay House
1663 Liberty Drive
Bloomington, IN 47403
www.balboapress.com
844-682-1282

Because of the dynamic nature of the Internet, any web addresses or links contained in this book may have changed since publication and may no longer be valid. The views expressed in this work are solely those of the author and do not necessarily reflect the views of the publisher, and the publisher hereby disclaims any responsibility for them.

The author of this book does not dispense medical advice or prescribe the use of any technique as a form of treatment for physical, emotional, or medical problems without the advice of a physician, either directly or indirectly. The intent of the author is only to offer information of a general nature to help you in your quest for emotional and spiritual well-being. In the event you use any of the information in this book for yourself, which is your constitutional right, the author and the publisher assume no responsibility for your actions.

Scripture texts, prefaces, introductions, footnotes and cross references used in this work are taken from the New American Bible, revised edition © 2010, 1991, 1986, 1970 Confraternity of Christian Doctrine, Inc., Washington, DC All Rights Reserved. No part of this work may be reproduced or transmitted in any form or by any means, electronic or mechanical, including photocopying, recording, or by any information storage and retrieval system, without permission in writing from the copyright owner.

Cover art: Photograph by Evie Shaffer

Print information available on the last page.

ISBN: 978-1-9822-7574-7 (sc)
ISBN: 978-1-9822-7572-3 (hc)
ISBN: 978-1-9822-7573-0 (e)

Library of Congress Control Number: 2021920932

Balboa Press rev. date: 11/04/2021

*To my beloved cousin, Jay Walljasper (1955–2020),
whose encouragement and support midwifed this book into being.*

CONTENTS

Foreword ix
Introduction xiii

PART I: CONTEMPLATION AND TRANSFORMATION

Chapter 1   Cultivating a Contemplative Life................................. 1
Chapter 2   The Human Condition...13
Chapter 3   Introduction to Centering Prayer 35

PART II: CONTEMPLATIVE LIVING EXPERIENCE

Chapter 4   Introduction to the Contemplative Living
                  Experience Program...51
Chapter 5   Awareness of God's Presence and Action:
                  Logging and Spiritual Reading.....................................61
Chapter 6   Intention and Consent in Relating to God:
                  Lectio Divina and The Active Prayer 81
Chapter 7   Letting Go and Receiving True Life:
                  The Welcoming Prayer 115
Chapter 8   Rest and Sabbath-Keeping...135
Chapter 9   Contemplative Discernment...147
Chapter 10 Addictions, Attachments, and Aversions 161
Chapter 11 Forgiveness 177
Chapter 12 Contemplative Life..197
Chapter 13 Community 217

Afterword...231
Acknowledgements 241
Notes 249

FOREWORD

I met Thomas Keating a few years after I moved to Colorado in 1987. I knew very little about him except that he was a Trappist monk who had been instrumental in bringing Centering Prayer, an ancient Christian contemplative practice, into the 20th century. The United Church of Christ clergy were holding a retreat in a rustic church camp, and he was our speaker. I have no memory of what he said, but I do remember his deep contemplative presence, his kind and sparkling eyes, and the red wool hat perched on his head atop his tall frame.

I had been asked to be part of a panel to respond to his talk. My opening sentence was "I'm not a contemplative, but……" This memory is lodged in my mind and heart thanks to the words of a colleague who challenged me later. "Why did you say you're not a contemplative? You're one of the most contemplative people I know." My response was disbelief. "How could I be a contemplative when I don't have a regular practice of Centering Prayer?"

My friend's comment stayed with me long after I left the retreat. I began to explore Centering Prayer and other methods of contemplative prayer. As my understanding of these practices expanded, the narrowness of my previous image of a contemplative person was revealed.

At that time, I was teaching prayer and spiritual formation at the Iliff School of Theology in Denver Colorado. In my work there I recognized others who held the same limited view idea of contemplation. When I asked class members to form a picture in their minds and hearts of a contemplative, the image they painted was some version of a silent, introverted, serious person. They filled this out further with more words like alone, never smiling, wearing a long robe, ignoring the world, grim, never plays, and boring. We agreed that if this description were accurate, it would be hard to imagine why anyone would want to live a contemplative life.

Like me, these students needed to expand their understanding and experiences of the contemplative life. I decided to ask them some questions about their engagement with a variety of contemplative practices. "Are you examining your spiritual life?" "Do you enjoy periods of silence?" "When have you been amazed at the beauty of creation?" "Where in your life do you experience the presence of God?" "What are you longing for?" "Do you read poetry?" Many of them identified with some of these activities and became aware of the many ways to engage the contemplative life. They began to think of themselves as being much more contemplative than they had thought.

The stereotype of a contemplative was not the only thing that had some students resisting that identity. "I can't be a contemplative; I'm an activist!" they argued. Just as I had them create a picture of a contemplative, I invited them to create a stereotypical portrait of an activist.

What they came up with was a person who was often angry, loud, challenging authority, marching, extroverted and with very strong opinions. "How many of you identify with that definition and claim yourselves to be an activist?" I asked. A few said they did, but the majority of the students talked about being a different kind of activist that didn't match the description. They realized there are many ways to be an activist just like there are different ways of being a contemplative. We entered into a lively discussion of whether we could be both. We played with a combination of the identities. What about becoming a contemplative activist? Or an active contemplative? Must we be either one or the other? They decided the answer to that question was a resounding "no."

I share these examples from my teaching life because I imagine some of you have had a similar experiences with these identities and are wondering if a book on the contemplative life is for you. I urge you to continue reading.

Julie Saad studied with Thomas Keating and over the years became a teacher of Centering Prayer and other practices that lead toward a contemplative life. The teachings of Thomas Keating are at the heart of this book. She has added to his wisdom by telling stories of her own experiences of learning to live a contemplative life. Her lively writing offers you guidance for your own journey while making it clear that the contemplative life will be experienced differently by each person.

Julie makes no promises as to what will happen to us on this path. She knows the contemplative life is an ongoing journey that unfolds before us as guided by the Spirit. Her wisdom can offer encouragement and assurance as we discover the path toward the heart of God. She warns us that pursuing the path will be a transformative experience no matter where it takes us. Are you ready?

Rev. Jane E. Vennard, July 2021

Reverend Jane E. Vennard, ordained in the United Church of Christ, is a spiritual director in private practice in Denver who leads workshops and retreats throughout the United States and abroad. She is the author of eight books, including *Fully Awake and Truly Alive: Spiritual Practices to Nurture Your Soul.*

INTRODUCTION

"This is what you are to do:
lift your heart up to the Lord,
with a gentle stirring of love..."[1]
The Cloud of Unknowing

CONTEMPLATIVE LIFE BEGINS WHEN WE TAKE THE FIRST STEP INTO the silence of our heart. It's a pilgrimage—a journey that takes us first to the inner reaches of who we really are, and from there, into the life we were meant to live. We don't usually start a journey like this unless we're searching, even longing, for a different way of life. The search often begins when we experience an existential crisis, a trauma, a loss, or sometimes just a weariness with the way life is. It may be a search for purpose or meaning, or a desire for a deeper connection with the Ultimate Mystery. As any spiritual pilgrim knows, the journey is one of mystery and discovery. It's a different path for every person with one experience common to all: every person who embarks on the journey will be changed by it. It doesn't matter where you are on your life's path, whether you're young or old, experienced in prayer or a novice, religious, spiritual, agnostic, or none of the above. What matters is that something deep in the silence of your heart called you to take the first step.

This book is a guide to a formation program called the Contemplative Living Experience (CLE). The CLE program's foundation is based on the Christian contemplative practice of Centering Prayer, along with other contemplative practices. It first teaches us how to grow in the life of the Spirit, and then how to integrate our spiritual experiences into daily life, thus cultivating a contemplative life. We all have been formed by our life experiences. Engaging with a formation program like CLE gives us the opportunity to be intentional about entering into a process that fosters transformation. When we enter into this process, we're simply consenting to be transformed. We commit to the program and the practices it teaches, but we're not expected to change ourselves. Transformation is the work of the Spirit. Formation is a lifelong process, a journey that starts in the silence of our heart and leads us into the heart of God.

Historically, this program and the program from which it is derived, the Practice of Contemplative Living (formerly known as the Nine-Month Course), have been held in person in Denver and New York for one weekend per month over a period of nine months. It's a big commitment! Many people who take the program consider it for a long time before they finally get to the point where they decide this is the year they are ready for it. A couple of months before the program begins, the CLE program facilitators hold interviews with participants to give them detailed information about what's involved so they have a better idea of what to expect and what they're committing to. Usually, by the end of the interview people are even more excited and ready to get started. They often ask, "What do I need to do to prepare? Is there anything I should be reading?" The truth is nothing can prepare you for what God has in store for you in a program geared towards transformation. This is why I encourage people to "come as you are." This is your journey, your life. As in all of life, God meets us where we are. I have no idea what your transformation will look like. The only thing I know for sure (from watching people go through this program for many years) is that if you commit to a program designed to help you live a more contemplative life, you will be changed by it.

So, I wonder where you are today on your journey. What interested you about this book? When I first heard about the Nine-Month Course in the early 2000s, I had been practicing Centering Prayer for about ten years and was looking to go deeper. We talk about that in Contemplative Outreach from time to time: how important it is to share the prayer and the teachings with those who haven't heard about it, but also, how do we help people who already have a regular practice of Centering Prayer go deeper? And what exactly does it mean to go deeper?

I love the notion of living with questions, and I encourage you to live with some of the questions you'll find posed in this book, and others you will find yourself asking as you engage with this material. Were you drawn to this book from a desire to go deeper? What does it mean to you to go deeper? In the first few chapters of this book, you'll learn more about my spiritual journey and what it means to me both to live a contemplative life and to go deeper. My hope in sharing my own journey is that it will encourage you to think about your journey: the things along the way that were important to you; how God has been working in your life; how you've struggled with language, concepts, religion; what gives you hope and meaning;

what you're being called to. These are the things that move us in the direction of going deeper.

I hope you will consider taking the CLE journey. In fact, I decided to write this book because I wanted to make the benefits of the CLE program available to people who don't live near New York or Denver, where it has been hosted in person. To get the most benefit from this book, you will need to spend time with the practices and teachings. Exactly how much time will be up to you. But remember, people who go through this program in person do so over a period of nine months. We've discovered that nine months is an ideal time frame to immerse yourself in a formation program like CLE. Reading this book from cover to cover without spending time immersed in the practices will provide you with a lot of information, and that may be all you're looking for at this time. However, if your intention is to enter into the process of formation in contemplative life, that takes time to unfold. My natural inclination is to hurry through things, get so busy I don't have time for practice, or at times, even think I don't need to slow down and practice anymore. The difference may be (and I really do mean *may* be) that I decided a long time ago that I wanted to live a contemplative life. So, when I fall into the trap of being hurried, busy, or thinking I already know it all, I catch myself pretty quickly, return to prayer and practice, and restore the interior silence and experience of God's presence I have come to treasure.

My intention in writing this book is to give you a window into living a contemplative life. Part One (Chapters One through Three) provides a foundation for the rest of the book. Chapter One is about contemplative prayer—the definition, its history in the Christian contemplative tradition, and how it became a way of life for me. Chapter Two is about "the human condition" as taught by Thomas Keating, one of the co-founders of Contemplative Outreach and one of the principal architects of the Christian contemplative practice of Centering Prayer. I have been a student of Thomas Keating's since 1994. His teaching on the human condition—what causes human beings so much suffering and how we can heal and be free of what holds us back in life—had the most profound effect on my spiritual life. It underlies much of the rest of Keating's teaching as well as the teaching of the practices in this book that bring about our healing and transformation. I think it is a brilliant marrying of the Christian contemplative path with leading-edge science that makes it relevant for our time and the future. Chapter Three is a primer on the method of Centering Prayer. The CLE program is based on a foundation of Centering Prayer so it's important to first establish a Centering Prayer practice if you are not already practicing daily. In addition, it is strongly recommended that if you are not doing Centering Prayer twice a day that you start doing that regularly before you begin with the other practices. The practice of Centering Prayer helps us to deepen our relationship with God so that whatever we experience in this program we are experiencing with God, not on our own.

Part Two is made up of what I call the practice chapters, which contain the actual teaching of the CLE program. Chapter Four introduces the program, the same information participants in the in-person program would experience in the initial interview and the first weekend of the program. Each of the practice chapters that follow (Five through Thirteen) contains the teaching about the practices, the methods for the practices, and a "Going Deeper" section that helps you establish the practice in your life throughout the month (or however long you decide to spend on that chapter and the practices it contains.) The end of the Going Deeper section provides a suggestion for integrating the practices into daily life.

If you're used to doing spiritual work on your own, as I know some people are, you should be able to work through this book at your own pace. My hope for you is that you will find a group who is interested in journeying with you. I think most people go deeper with the work when they do it within a community that bonds over time. You may already have a community, a prayer group, a Contemplative Outreach chapter, or spiritual friends that would relish the opportunity to do something like this together. How ever you decide to use this material, my prayer for you is that it moves you deep into the heart of God—into the heart of love.

Come as you are. All of your life experiences have brought you to where you are today. Nothing more is needed.

PART ONE

Contemplation and Transformation

CHAPTER ONE
Cultivating a Contemplative Life

*"I will give you a new heart, and a new spirit I will put within you.
I will remove the heart of stone from your flesh
and give you a heart of flesh."*
Ezekiel 36:26

THE EARLY DAYS OF MY SPIRITUAL JOURNEY WERE A ROLLER COASTER of experiences and beliefs, but like most young people I was searching for purpose and meaning. While my route was circuitous, once I found the path of contemplative prayer I stopped searching for a path and started the journey of discovering who I am and who God is. I think this is true for most of us: once the path is found the rest of life's journey is a continual unfolding of who we are and who God is for us. I always had this expectation that the journey had a particular destination, but the further I traveled the more I began to realize that contemplative life is more about being open to the mystery—the mystery of life and the Ultimate Mystery—and surrendering to it.

I came to this realization through a regular practice of Centering Prayer. Early on, I found it difficult at times to remain faithful to a practice, to find the motivation to do it every day, and to persevere when sometimes what I discovered about myself was painful. Having a community to journey with made all the difference for me—a community that prays together, studies contemplative teachers, goes on intensive retreats, and talks about what we are experiencing. Community makes the path lighter, more meaningful, and even joyful. It helps us make sense of what we are doing and experiencing. One of the experiences on my path that seemed to contain all of these ingredients was the Contemplative Living Experience program. The CLE program was the linchpin that helped me understand the difference between merely having a contemplative practice and truly living a contemplative life.

Julie Saad

What is Contemplative Prayer?

The verb "to contemplate," according to the dictionary definition, means to think about, to reflect on an idea or mystery, to meditate, or to think profoundly or deeply. In the Judeo-Christian tradition contemplation and contemplative prayer hold almost the opposite meaning. It's less about thinking, reflecting or meditating, and more about simply being. In other words, it's less about using our mental faculties than it is about letting go of them. When the psalmist tells us, "Be still and know that I am God" in Psalm 46:10, we're invited to still our faculties and allow our spiritual senses to awaken to the presence of God in the silence of our heart. As I practice the stillness that begins the movement into contemplative prayer, I recognize that thinking about God and experiencing God *as God is* are not the same thing. My idea of God is not God. When I can let go of my idea of God, I'm closer to experiencing the presence of God *as God is*.

My desire to cultivate a life of contemplative prayer started with my desire to deepen my relationship with God. While we may think of prayer as the words we use to speak to God, most relationships deepen when we discover a common language and engage in a dynamic exchange, rather than a one-sided monologue. Thomas Keating, the Trappist monk, theologian, and author who helped revive the Christian contemplative tradition in modern times and who served as one of the founding members of Contemplative Outreach, often says that God's first language is silence. Some say he's quoting the Persian poet Rumi; some say Saint John of the Cross. The point is that the stillness and silence of contemplative prayer are the common language that move us closer to experiencing the dynamic presence of God. In his book *Open Mind, Open Heart*, Thomas Keating describes contemplative prayer as "a pure gift of God." He continues,

> "It is the opening of mind and heart—our whole being— to God, the Ultimate Mystery, beyond thoughts, words and emotions. Through grace we open our awareness to God whom we know by faith is within us, closer than breathing, closer than thinking, closer than choosing— closer than consciousness itself."[2]

Thomas Keating is part of a long line of Christian mystics and teachers who have shed light on the practice of contemplative prayer. To get a sense of how steeped in the Christian tradition contemplative prayer is, let's look at some of the teachings from Scripture and the wisdom of the mystics, both ancient and modern-day. Jesus offered a teaching about how to pray in his Sermon on the Mount: "But when you pray, go to your inner room, close the door, and pray to your Father in secret, and your Father who sees in secret will repay you" (Matthew 6:6). Most of the people in this region during Jesus's time lived communally, mostly in caves, tents, or one-room houses that didn't have private rooms with doors. John Cassian, a fifth-century monk and theologian who studied and wrote about the Desert Mothers and Fathers of Egypt, interpreted "inner room" to mean the spiritual level of our being where we are not preoccupied with our ordinary everyday life. Thomas Keating says the inner room is not so much a place as a state of consciousness and when we close the door, we are not only closing out the external world with all its distractions, but also the inner distractions of interior dialogue, commentaries, judgments, and emotional reactions that are part of our ordinary stream of consciousness. This opens the door to the prayer in secret where we begin to experience interior silence—the awareness of the presence of God within.

Many other teachers in the Christian tradition contributed to our understanding of contemplative prayer. Saint Evagrius Ponticus, a fourth-century Christian monk, described prayer as the "laying aside of thought." Saint Gregory the Great, a sixth-century Benedictine monk (and later, pope) who established the monastic practice known as the Gregorian chant, called contemplative prayer "resting in God." The fourteenth-century anonymous author of *The Cloud of Unknowing*, the book said to be a primary inspiration for the practice of Centering Prayer, wrote that the work of contemplation is "lifting our hearts to the Lord with a gentle stirring of love."[3] Saint Teresa of Ávila, a Carmelite nun who was part of the Catholic reformation in the sixteenth century and who is a Doctor of the Church, referred to contemplative prayer as "the prayer of silence" and described it as an act of love with words being unnecessary.

In more contemporary writings, twentieth-century monk and mystic Thomas Merton called contemplative prayer "an attentive, watchful listening with the heart."[4] *Into the Silent Land* is a beautiful book on contemplative prayer by Martin Laird, an Augustinian priest and professor of historical theology at Villanova University. He uses poetic, metaphorical language to aptly describe something that is difficult to put into words:

> "We are built for contemplation… Communion with God in the silence of the heart is a God-given capacity, like the rhododendron's capacity to flower, the fledging's for flight, and the child's for self-forgetful abandon and joy."[5]

This is the definition of contemplation I most resonate with. We are indeed built for communion with God in the silence of the heart. Just as a rhododendron needs the sun and rain to flower, the fledgling needs a nudge out of the nest, and a child needs a parent's love, so we need to dispose ourselves to nurturing, nudging, and divine love. We experience this through the many contemplative practices at the heart of all the world's religious traditions. Two such practices have emerged in modern Christianity: Centering Prayer, which is the foundational practice of this book, and Christian Meditation as taught by John Main and The World Community for Christian Meditation (WCCM).

An important lesson I learned about contemplative prayer is that we can do nothing to achieve it. For me, this is a very freeing concept because, like a lot of people, I sometimes think I can do anything I put my mind to if I just work at it and keep trying harder. This mindset simply doesn't apply to contemplative prayer. It's not about accomplishing some goal; it's about letting go of our desires and attachments and realizing that we already have what we seek. We can open ourselves to receiving the gift of contemplative prayer through the practice of Centering Prayer, which helps dismantle the obstacles that make us feel as if we are separate from God. Saint Teresa of Ávila said the problem most people have with prayer is that we pray as if God were absent. Centering Prayer is about consenting to the presence and action of God within, reminding us that God is always present.

When I was a child, I was taught to pray to a God outside myself, but I didn't learn how to experience God's presence within me. I was taught that I was made in the image and likeness of God based on the creation story found in Genesis 1:27, but I didn't really believe it because I felt separate from God. The practice of Centering Prayer allows us to cultivate an intention to consent to the presence and action of God within us. When I first began my contemplative journey, I still wasn't sure this "God within" existed, but thankfully, I was willing to be open to the possibility that this prayer of consent might have something to teach me. Before I became involved with Contemplative Outreach, I had participated in Al-Anon, a twelve-step program for friends and family of alcoholics, where I learned the importance of willingness. That's how I approached Centering Prayer. I was willing to explore how willingness might lead to manifesting intention and consent. My experience with Al-Anon started me down the path of developing a relationship with God, but it has been over the course of many years of practicing Centering Prayer—being still, praying in secret, silence, resting in God, the gentle stirring of love, attentive listening, opening my whole being, communing with God in the silence of my heart—that I came to experience this God within me.

Looking back, I can see that many of the things that are present in any intimate, close relationship helped me experience God in a very real way deep within my own being, as well as in all of creation. Many of us who were raised in a traditional Christian denomination were taught that creation was an event: God first created the heavens and the earth, then human beings, and then rested from all this work. But through my spiritual journey, I've come to see creation as a process that is ever unfolding, ongoing, and occurring in the present moment. Franciscan Sister and evolutionary theologian Ilia Delio helped me develop my understanding of this in her book *The Unbearable Wholeness of Being*, where she says,

> "God is not the prime mover of a static cosmos but the dynamism of love swelling up in space-time through the process of evolution and the rise of consciousness... Creation, therefore, is not so much a past event as a present becoming that is oriented toward new being up ahead... Love is generative and divine love longs to become more visible in the fruitful flowering of life."[6]

We are invited to participate in this fruitful flowering of life, to be co-creators with God in this present becoming. Experiencing this dynamism of love is what the contemplative life is all about. The deep, abiding relationship that develops through contemplative prayer leads to participating with God in a life of service in the name of love. Consenting to God's active presence in our lives is just the beginning of the journey.

Julie Saad

The Evolution of a Contemplative Life

As I walk this contemplative journey every day, I find it helpful to stop periodically and ask myself this question: what does it mean to me to live a contemplative life? I like the notion of living with a question like this because the answer keeps changing, leaving room for me to grow. When I first began to ask myself this question, my answer was very different than it is today. And I expect the answer to continue to evolve for me as I enter new phases of my life.

In the Introduction to this book, I said I hoped that sharing my journey would encourage you to reflect on your journey and what brought you to where you are today. What has been important to you along the way? How has God been working in your life? What have you struggled with, or do you continue to struggle with? What gives you hope and meaning? What are you being called to? Like most of us, I had spiritual experiences in my early life, some through religion, school, and family, some through nature, but it wasn't until I was in enough pain in my life that I knew I needed help creating a different kind of life. Help for me came in the form of Al-Anon, a twelve-step program for friends and family of alcoholics that became an integral part of my spiritual journey. You may or may not be familiar with twelve-step programs, and so I want to be clear: this is part of my story, not necessarily the norm for others on the contemplative path. My purpose in sharing this part of my life with you is to show the development of my awakening to God calling me to contemplative life. This can happen in countless ways; Al-Anon just happened to be the first step for me. I hope you will reflect on what was the first step for you.

When I was in my early thirties I was in a very dark place in my life. I had become an obsessive, controlling enabler—a very painful, neurotic behavior pattern. I had no idea what alcoholism was, but I knew something was very wrong in my marriage. I was blessed to have a close friend who did understand some of the dynamics of an alcoholic family system and advised me to see an intervention counselor at an alcohol and drug treatment center. The counselor read me a list of fifteen questions that changed my life. It included questions like, "Are you preoccupied with your spouse's problems? When your spouse acts inappropriately in public do you feel guilty and try to cover it up? Are you hyper-vigilant about your spouse's moods?" I answered yes to thirteen of the fifteen questions. (The two questions I didn't answer yes to were about children and we didn't have children.) The counselor then told me that if a person answers yes to five or more of these questions it indicates that alcoholism likely exists in the family and that it is affecting the person living with the alcoholic. I was stunned, but ready to accept my reality. About the same time, I also discovered I had been suffering for many years with untreated depression.

The counselor suggested I start going to Al-Anon meetings. Before I left that fateful counseling session, he asked me if I believed in God. I said yes, although I can't say why I said yes. I was born into a Catholic family and went to Catholic schools from kindergarten through high school. This was during the 1960s when the Church and the country were rapidly changing. It was the era of Vatican II, the Beatles, the war in Vietnam, Apollo 11, assassinations, Woodstock, demonstrations and riots, birth control, the Civil Rights Act, and Jesus Christ Superstar. It was a revolutionary time and a very confusing time to be a teenager. I came through it peripherally involved in the Church only because my family still participated, but I never thought much about God and certainly didn't have a relationship with God. So, when the counselor asked me if I believed in God, it's a mystery to me why I said yes. That night, when I was out for a walk after dark, I felt God taking me by the hand. It was an indescribable feeling. And here's what became clear to me in that moment: sometimes all we have to do is say yes.

I started going to Al-Anon meetings as the counselor had suggested and felt very much at home with people who understood my life circumstances and with whom I could begin to share my secrets. In other ways I was uncomfortable with Al-Anon being a spiritual program and all the talk about God, even if it was *"God as we understood him,"* as it states in the Al-Anon third step. But over time something started to change in me. I started feeling okay when I was at an Al-Anon meeting. I did not feel okay anywhere else in my life. My feelings were so shut down I could only identify with either feeling okay or not okay. I started going to a meeting every day because it was such a relief to feel okay. I knew somewhere deep down that I needed to heal, that I needed to change—to embrace what in Al-Anon is called recovery. I also started going to some open Alcoholics Anonymous (AA) meetings because "the program," as it is called, is approached from a life and death perspective in AA. The painful, neurotic behavior I had become accustomed to and was suffering from felt like life and death to me. I was blessed to find an Al-Anon home group that emphasized the importance of "working the program," which included studying the twelve steps and

Julie Saad

applying them to my life. I joined a step-study group and put my heart and soul into working the steps. I came to believe that a power greater than myself could restore me to sanity (step two). I was able to find a higher power that I chose to call God, as I understood God, and became willing to turn my will and my life over to God (step three). I wrote a moral inventory, admitted my shortcomings to God, to myself, and to my sponsor (steps four and five). When I got to step eleven, "Sought through prayer and meditation to improve our conscious contact with God, as we understood him, praying only for knowledge of his will for us and the power to carry it out,"[7] I came to my first awareness of a desire to live a contemplative life. As I began seeking to improve my conscious contact with God, even though I didn't yet know what contemplation meant, I now recognize that a more contemplative life is what I was seeking.

I prayed every day, using a little *One Day at a Time* daily reader published by Al-Anon. My sponsor told me that I was doing fine with that part of the eleventh step, but that I really needed to start meditating. My knowledge about anything spiritual or religious was limited to my Catholic upbringing, where meditation was never a topic discussed. The only exposure I had to meditation was a brief encounter with a Nichiren Buddhist group when I was nineteen, about twelve years before I started going to Al-Anon, when I was still living in Chicago. I was approached by a young woman while walking in a neighborhood known as New Town who invited me to this Nichiren Buddhist gathering. I was lonely and looking for young people to hang out with, so I spent about three months with this group of chanting Buddhists. I learned and practiced the chant, but I never really felt at home in the community, so I stopped going to their gatherings. In some ways, Buddhism was a welcome change from my experience with religious or spiritual gatherings, but the teaching was too far outside my religious upbringing for me to feel comfortable at that time in my life. But at least it gave me some exposure to something outside the Catholic Church. So, twelve years later, when I went to the bookstore looking for a book to learn how to meditate, which in those days led you to the section on Eastern religions, I was open to finding a book by Eknath Easwaran, a spiritual teacher from India. In fact, I consider myself fortunate because I found my first inter-spiritual teacher, and I developed a deep respect for his teaching and became more open to other faith traditions. He seemed very comfortable talking about Hinduism,

Buddhism, and Christianity. Through his book *Meditation*, I learned a Buddhist meditation practice that I was able to add to my other spiritual practices in Al-Anon. Because Al-Anon does not preach any doctrine or dogma, the method of meditation I discovered was perfectly acceptable. I very quickly became attracted to a daily meditation practice because I experienced immediate benefits in the slowing down of my obsessive thinking. I was still living with my husband at the time and still very much caught up in my codependent behavior, but I could feel a change subtly taking root in my psyche and in my daily life.

AA and Al-Anon slogans function like active prayers or mantras to help with improving conscious contact with God, leading toward living a more contemplative life. "How important is it?" "Let go and let God." "One day at a time." "Keep it simple." I remember a prayer that I found in the AA Grapevine magazine: "God, please remove my fear and direct my attention to what you would have me be." In the midst of the almost constant fear, anxiety, and worry, these slogans and prayers, repeated over and over again, helped to stop my obsessive thinking, much like the Active Prayer practice you'll learn in Chapter Six. The fellowship, the steps, the slogans, and especially the prayer and meditation taught me how to live a new way and start to heal my wounds. For so many of us it is our woundedness that brings us into relationship with God. I have often said that my experience in Al-Anon triggered a paradigm shift in my life—a fundamental change in how I live my life and what's important to me. I started to recognize that "having had a spiritual awakening as the result of these steps" (step twelve) was just the beginning of the spiritual journey. I had been living my life self-reliant and alone, but through Al-Anon I became part of a community of spiritual seekers, learning to rely on God. The spiritual awakening I experienced comes with responsibility, also part of the Al-Anon step twelve, to "carry this message to others and to practice these principles in all our affairs." Carrying the message is about helping others—giving back from a place of having integrated the twelve-step teachings into my daily life and being a part of something bigger than myself.

For eight years I continued my participation in Al-Anon and my Buddhist meditation practice. In the meantime, I became a professional drug and alcohol counselor specializing in working with families. It became difficult to continue to participate in Al-Anon because I would sometimes see family members of patients at meetings and didn't feel I could be completely open and honest about my own recovery. At about that time I was introduced to Contemplative Outreach and Centering Prayer. My meditation practice had become dry, and I didn't have a meditation community with whom I could discuss what I was going through. I was likely experiencing what's known as a dark night of the soul, but I had no knowledge of or context for the experience. The dark nights are often thought of as hard times or times of depression, but that's not really accurate. What Saint John of the Cross described as the "Dark Night of the Soul" in his epic poem by the same name is an integral part of the spiritual journey, what in the Christian tradition is called purification. Certain aspects of our personality and sense perceptions block us from a more intimate relationship with the divine. In a dark night, what is blocking us is being revealed. We may feel that we are going backwards on the journey or that God has abandoned us, which is what I meant when I said my practice had become dry. This is a time when some people abandon the spiritual journey altogether. It was during this time that I first heard about Centering Prayer, and I knew right away it was for me. Because it comes out of the Christian tradition, the language and concepts were more familiar and easier for me to grasp—more comfortable for me than Buddhism had been. I also found a sense of community within Contemplative Outreach that I was missing since I had stopped going to Al-Anon meetings.

When I first started in Al-Anon I was struggling with it being a spiritual program and what that meant to me. I remember someone asking me about my image of God. My answer was "an old man in the sky." I wonder sometimes if there isn't still an element of that in my psyche. One of the hardest things for me to put into words has always been my image of God. I should clarify that while today I'm quite comfortable using the word God to refer to what Thomas Keating often calls the Ultimate Mystery, this wasn't always true for me. Being brought up in the Catholic tradition with the doctrine of the Trinity, we learned about God the Father, God the Son, and God the Holy Spirit, and God was always referred to as "He." I struggled to make meaning out of this concept of God. Being a woman, I couldn't reconcile the male images of God. I always thought of the Holy Spirit as gender neutral or maybe genderless and often used Spirit when referring to God. One of my struggles was the notion that we were created in the image and likeness of God, as written in Genesis 1:27. How could I be created in the image of God if God is male? Some people may think this isn't a big deal, but

Contemplative Life

for me it caused a cognitive dissonance that as a child and young woman I wasn't able to reconcile. This feeling of disconnect was part of what caused me to throw out God entirely in my late teens and twenties.

A few things have helped me over the years with my disharmony with male images of God. One was in Raimon Panikkar's book *Christophany*, where he encourages the reader to think of the Father and Son not as male images, but as roles in relationship, i.e., parent and child. I could reframe Father and Son into Parent and Me. Another is where Martin Laird says, "The Creator is outpouring love, the creation, the love outpoured."[8] I think this is a beautiful image of the Trinity with the creator (Father), the created (Son), and the love outpouring and outpoured (Holy Spirit). Maybe even more helpful to me was something I read in Episcopal priest and spiritual teacher Cynthia Bourgeault's book *The Meaning of Mary Magdalene*. Bourgeault talks about becoming fully human, which in modern psychology might mean the integration of opposites within oneself—the masculine and feminine. But she says what is more important is "the integration (that) takes place on a cosmic scale and is accomplished through learning how to anchor one's being in that underlying unitive ground: that place of oneness before the opposites arise."[9] I don't necessarily think of men and women as being opposites, so to me this refers more to that place of oneness before we become differentiated in any way. If I think about this in the context of cosmology, it means even before human beings were differentiated from God. Today this is what I think of as the source of all life and the ground of my being.

In *Invitation to Love* Thomas Keating wrote, "Whatever we experience of God, however exalted, is only a radiance of his presence."[10] Human beings tend to anthropomorphize God. How else can we find words to describe our experience of the energy of the universe, "existence itself" as Meister Eckhart says, Divine Love, the Ultimate Mystery? Thomas Keating's words remind me that whatever I think of God, whatever my image of God may be, that is not really God, but it might be the radiance of God's presence. When I reflect on how my image of God has evolved over my life, I realize that I'm part of something that my human mind cannot fully comprehend and yet it draws me forward, it longs for me as I express my longing, it "searches my heart and knows me" as Saint Paul wrote in Romans 8:27, and it seems that all I can do is desire being open to the mystery. I can't even open myself to the mystery by my own will power; I can only let it be my heart's desire.

CHAPTER TWO

The Human Condition

> *"What I do, I do not understand.*
> *For I do not do what I want, but I do what I hate."*
> Romans 7:15

IN *THE MYSTERY OF CHRIST*, THOMAS KEATING GIVES US THE KEY TO understanding what causes human beings so much suffering and unhappiness. Understanding starts to unlock how we can be healed and be free of what holds us back in life:

> "The Gospel calls us forth to full responsibility for our emotional life. We tend to blame other people or situations for the turmoil we experience. In actual fact, upsetting emotions prove beyond any doubt that the problem is in us. If we do not assume responsibility for our emotional programs on the unconscious level and take measures to change them, we will be influenced by them to the end of our lives."[11]

This is the passage from Keating's writings that I probably have quoted and reflected on more than any other. I can't think of anything else in my life that I have resisted more or benefited from more than taking responsibility for my emotional life and stopping the endless blaming of everyone and everything outside myself for what didn't go right in my life. Not taking responsibility is what led me to feeling powerless for so much of my life. I couldn't see what was within my power to change so that my life could be more peaceful, fulfilling, and free. This reminds me of the Serenity Prayer that was adopted by twelve-step groups but was actually written by a twentieth-century American theologian, Reinhold Niebuhr. Here's the excerpt from that prayer that has become a central part of the twelve-step lexicon: "God, grant me the serenity to accept the things I cannot change, the courage to change the things I can, and the wisdom to know the difference." When we begin to accept responsibility for our emotional life, it becomes clearer to us what we can and cannot change.

Martin Laird's classic *Into the Silent Land* warns,

> "We do not journey far along the Spiritual path before we get some sense of the wound of the human condition, and this is precisely why not a few abandon a contemplative practice like meditation as soon as it begins to expose this wound; they move on instead to some spiritual entertainment that will maintain distraction."[12]

The contemplative life is not a panacea. The journey is long and full of ups and downs, with bumps along the way that sometimes seem insurmountable. Contemplative practice gives us a roadmap that has been used by many who have journeyed before us. If we can trust that the road is sure, we will be buoyed with the confidence to persevere.

No matter how long we are on the spiritual journey, no matter how deep our healing and transformation, we continue to face our human condition every day. The healing and transformation we experience doesn't erase our woundedness, but our wounds no longer control our lives. The human condition may be what Saint Augustine referred to when he introduced the concept of original sin in the late fourth century. After many years of grappling with the concept of original sin as I understood it—that by our very nature we as individuals are sinful and need to be redeemed—Thomas Keating's teaching helped me to reframe the meaning of the concept. My understanding today is that we all have a basic core of goodness but are born into this human condition and need to be healed from what holds us back in life. We are born into the evolutionary process wherever it happens to be at the time of our birth, into a culture whose conditioning we can't escape, into a family that has likely suffered, into circumstances over which we have no control. Even those who had a happy, balanced childhood struggle with what life brings and with figuring out how to live to their full potential. More often than not, when we are frustrated or upset, a person or event or even a thought is setting off something buried deep in our unconscious. What happens next will either be a conscious choice

Contemplative Life

we make or an unconscious reaction we may end up regretting. I realize that I am simplifying something that many teachers explain in great detail, but sometimes it really is as simple as that.

One of Thomas Keating's greatest contributions to the Christian contemplative tradition is his teaching on the human condition. He recorded about seven hours of video on this teaching for *The Spiritual Journey Series* video course offered by Contemplative Outreach. He also included the teaching in his book *Invitation to Love: The Way of Christian Contemplation*. And in 1997 he delivered the Harold M. Wit Lecture on Living a Spiritual Life in a Contemporary Age at Harvard Divinity School, the transcript of which was published in a classic little booklet called *The Human Condition: Contemplation and Transformation*. In 2017 he made it known to Contemplative Outreach how important he felt this teaching was and requested that *The Spiritual Journey Series* video course be made more widely available and accessible. His request resulted in the creation of a year-long online course known as "The Spiritual Journey: Formation in the Christian Contemplative Life." His vision was for the course to start with his teaching on the human condition. I was a part of the Contemplative Outreach team that facilitated the online course. In the early days of formulating how we would carry out Thomas Keating's wishes, I heard that he repeatedly said he wanted us to start the course with Part Two of *The Spiritual Journey Series*, "Models of the Human Condition," and that he didn't want us to edit it. After hearing this repeated by several people, I finally decided to call Thomas Keating at St. Benedict's Monastery to let him know that we had heard his request. He seemed very pleased to hear from me and, as often happens when talking with him, I received a wonderful teaching on his perspective of what he called "The Philosophical Model of the Human Condition" and how he felt it reflected the perennial tradition, which points to truths held by all the world's religions.

Some will find Keating's teaching on the human condition challenging. I encourage you to take your time and as you read, reflect on why—of all the teachings he shared over the course of his life—when developing the conceptual background of the practice of Centering Prayer, this teaching was so important to him. In my own experience, this is the teaching that drew me into the Christian contemplative path. It seemed to speak directly to what I was interested in and what I was struggling with in life. It made me want more—more of this God of love, more healing, more understanding of the Christian tradition and how it could continue to be relevant in my life, more freedom from being so trapped in the unsatisfying life my mind and emotions were creating.

It is within this context that we come to recognize the journey of Christians throughout the ages as *our* journey, because Keating puts it in today's language, thought, and scientific understanding. He took what the mystics knew intuitively, and what Saint Paul wrote about over 2,000 years ago in Romans 7:15, "What I do, I do not understand. For I do not do what I want, but I do what I hate," and applied modern science to make sense of what we all experience on this life journey.

Keating starts his teaching on the human condition with the evolution of human consciousness work done by Ken Wilber, most notably in his classic book *Up from Eden*, and adds to it what we know from modern anthropology, psychology, sociology, philosophy, and theology. Before we move into the teaching on Centering Prayer and the other contemplative practices, it's important to understand the healing work of contemplative prayer, what Keating calls "divine therapy." We will first explore what needs to be healed and why we would need or want healing.[13]

Levels of Consciousness

Drawing on Ken Wilber's integral theory work, Thomas Keating maps the levels of consciousness that span over six million years of human evolution. In an evolutionary model based on the idea that the human species (which Keating calls "the human family") becomes capable of higher levels of consciousness as the human brain evolves, he shows how each of us in our development, starting in infancy, recapitulates the evolutionary experience of the entire species. As we grow from infancy to adulthood, our brain develops along with our ability to move to higher levels of consciousness. How we resolve psychological conflicts and pre-rational emotional perceptions influences how much we suffer as adults. Keating's existential model reflects what happens when, developmentally, we reach full self-reflective self-consciousness feeling separate from God. Here is where the human condition rears up, causing roadblocks or obstacles in our ability to experience divine union. Understanding how this happens is the first step in recovering our full potential in life.

Before we go any further, I want to acknowledge that some of this teaching is generalized so that it applies broadly but may not apply to each person specifically. For example, some have suffered at the hands of someone else's abuse, whether physical, sexual, or emotional. Some carry generational wounds that went unresolved in their ancestors' lifetimes and were passed on to them. Some have experienced the loss of a loved one or had a traumatic experience that significantly impacts their psyche. Others have a physical or mental condition that may go untreated or cause them ongoing suffering. All of these things can have a profound impact on a person's life, and each may require treatment. It's important to seek whatever help is available and appropriate in these situations. I certainly needed therapy and medication to treat chronic depression. But after a long time undergoing clinical treatment, I found that western medicine's model of treating depression, while helpful, wasn't enough for me. I also needed what Thomas Keating calls "the divine therapy." I've experienced divine therapy as something God initiates as we consent to God's presence and action within through a regular practice of Centering Prayer.

By the time I discovered Centering Prayer I had long been a student of the natural and social sciences—psychology, history, anthropology, sociology, comparative religions, and evolutionary biology. My degree is in Human Services and these subjects were largely what I studied. The first thing I did after attending an introductory workshop on Centering Prayer was take *The Spiritual Journey Series* video course. When I discovered that Keating's teaching modernized the Christian contemplative tradition by using the language from modern science, I was drawn in. Christian teaching finally made sense to me in a way it never had before. I thought I was taking a course to learn a meditation practice, but I found myself in a course on the evolution of consciousness and the human potential for transformation and divine union. To learn that this was a way to deepen my relationship with God was life-changing for me. Keating says in order to become fully human we need to rediscover our connectedness to God, which we repressed in early childhood. His teaching on the human condition, particularly the evolutionary and existential models, culminating in what we experience as "energy centers" or what he calls "emotional programs for happiness," provides a clear understanding of what blocks us from being fully human.

The first part of Keating's teaching on the human condition addresses the levels of consciousness—uroboric, typhonic, mythic membership, and mental egoic—which leads into developing an understanding of the energy centers and how they become our emotional programs for happiness or what Keating refers to as the "false-self system."

The Uroboric Period—Security Center

The first level of human consciousness in Thomas Keating's evolutionary model—the uroboric period—began about five million years ago and is sometimes called the era of reptilian consciousness. Humans who lived during this stage of evolution were hunters and gatherers and were instinctually connected to nature. Their primary concern was attaining food and shelter as a means of survival. They did not have a sense of a separate self because they relied heavily on each other to meet their common needs. Without self-consciousness, they didn't distinguish their inner experience from their environment.

The more primitive developmental levels of the brain, commonly called the reptilian brain, control the vital functions of the body and the activities required for survival, as you might notice in an infant. The reptilian brain, often associated with the brainstem, was the first part of the modern brain to develop. Functioning outside of our conscious awareness, it constantly scans the environment for potential threats and reflexively reacts into fight or flight. This is the part of the modern human brain that registers stress and anxiety when our reactions come from unconscious motivations.

As the human family progressed through the uroboric period, concerned primarily with fulfilling needs for food and shelter, so the modern-day infant must go through a period of learning how to get its security and survival needs met. When an infant's biological needs are not immediately met, the infant will have an emotional outburst, which creates a memory or perception. Any parent, no matter how attentive to the infant's needs, will inevitably fail to meet every single desire the child has, leading to numerous daily outbursts, each reinforcing the infant's experience of unmet needs. Memories of these times can create wounds that reside deep in the unconscious of the developing infant (much more so when abuse or neglect is involved). I once worked with a man who was an adult child of an alcoholic. What his life might have been like as an infant was unknown to him, but throughout his life he struggled with interpersonal relationships. He was afraid of people, especially those in authority or who were angry, and he had an overdeveloped sense of guilt and shame. I remember an experience he described as an adult that seemed reflective of what he might have experienced as an infant. While in a grocery store he dropped a jar of spaghetti sauce on the floor and it broke. He panicked and froze. Most of us would have been somewhat embarrassed and looked for an employee to help clean it up. He couldn't describe what he was feeling beyond being unable to move. We can only imagine what survival instinct kicked in for him that held him captive in this way. Security and survival become hidden values—perfectly appropriate for an infant—but once the survival system is established, need to be integrated so the infant can move on to the next value. In other words, the infant needs to be reassured in some way and trust that survival and security needs will be met by caregivers for the child's emotional life to continue to grow. Otherwise, the emotional life becomes fixated at the level of the perceived deprivation. In the case of the man in the grocery store, the inability to trust that accidentally breaking a jar of sauce was not a shameful event or that he would not be shamed by others resulted in a moment of physical and emotional paralysis.

The Typhonic Period—Sensation Center and Power Center

About 200,000 years ago, the second level of consciousness emerged, known as the typhonic period. In mythology the typhon was half-human, half-animal. You might think of toddlers who are very connected to the animal world—they play with animals, imagine animal friends, love movies about animals, and often dream of animals. Humans in the typhonic period began to realize a body-self that is separate from nature, but they do not distinguish the self from the body. They are still very much immersed in nature and the instinctual anxieties that accompany day-to-day survival. Along with this sense of body-self comes an awareness of their mortality and the fear or terror associated with death. Their mental functioning is limited to magical thinking with limited ability to distinguish imagination from reality. Their everyday life would have been similar to what we experience in dreams. In the Typhonic period, language developed, as well as magical religious rituals aimed at pleasing the gods.

As in the case of the earliest development of human infancy recapitulating the early development of human consciousness in the uroboric period, the toddler years recapitulate evolutionary features associated with the typhonic period. As the two to four-year-old child begins to experience his or her own body as separate from mother and father, the magical thinking of the typhonic consciousness is expressed in the child in make-believe, imagination, and games. Who hasn't been lured into the play of a child at this age? The awareness of mortality and fear of death characteristic of this level of consciousness manifests in the child as fear of the dark, monsters under the bed, or any number of things the child's imagination can conceive. I remember as a child I was always careful to not have any part of my body extend over the edge of the bed while I slept to keep myself safe from whatever scary thing might have been under the bed. The inability to distinguish the self from the body translates to a child who seems to have insatiable desires for pleasurable or perceived-pleasurable food, toys, experiences, games, etc. This is the time of "just one more..." This is also a time when a child asserts the independence needed to explore the world and, to that end, learns how to control and/or manipulate family, friends, pets, and the environment. Emotions continue to develop, and moods can change rapidly. As the child learns to talk and develops vocabulary, the movement into socialization accelerates.

At this stage esteem and affection and power and control can become hidden values. These are normal needs and desires for a toddler at this stage of development and integration of these values translates to a healthy self-esteem and sense of self along with an understanding of what is within one's control and what's not. When these values are not integrated, the toddler carries the never-ending search for approval and attempts to control itself and its environment into the next level of consciousness.

Mythic Membership Period—Cultural Conditioning

Around 12,000 years ago, with the advent of a farming culture, the mythic membership level of consciousness started to develop. Advances in agriculture led to surplus in the food supply, which allowed for some leisure time and the ability to plan for the future. City-states began to appear, providing a sense of belonging, protection from outsiders, and a longer lifespan. The body-self was, for the first time, seen as separate from the environment. A social self emerged with a greater sense of identity with a group, and less connection with nature. Social hierarchies developed, along with a need for a military. The continuing evolution of the brain provided the ability to think logically (though still not abstractly), reflect, and become more self-conscious.

As children, conforming to the norms and values of social groups, such as family, religious groups, school, peers, clubs, sports teams, etc.

gives us a sense of belonging. It also reinforces our feelings of security and survival, affection and esteem, and power and control developed in earlier stages. Our desire to belong and meet these instinctual needs may sometimes cause us to behave in ways that are contrary to our forming consciences. I can relate to this, having grown up in the 1950s and 1960s in Chicago in a time of much racial conflict. I repeatedly heard racial slurs in my family, neighborhood, and school. Although I was deeply disturbed by the use of this language, my loyalty and identification with these groups, and my fear of being made an outcast, kept me from voicing my concerns and instead caused me to suppress my feelings. Because we are influenced by the culture in which we live, unconsciously taking on values from the culture that may not reflect our individual conscience can cause an interior dissonance. The human psyche has the ability to transcend this level of consciousness, but the power of cultural conditioning sometimes holds us back.

Mental Egoic Period—Age of Reason

A dramatic leap in human consciousness took place about 5,000 years ago and continues to unfold today, along with the development of the human faculty of reason. Anthropologists call this era the mental egoic period. Before this time, the human family was driven by self-centered emotions and instinctual drives. Increased ability to reason provided human beings with more freedom, and along with that came a greater responsibility to behave in ways that considered the well-being of others. This marks the beginning of moral development within the human family. This is also where the sense of self becomes separate from the body, wherein individuals begin to identify primarily with the mind. This greater development of the intellect had many benefits, but one of the disadvantages of expanding the capacity for reason is a concurrent tendency to repress emotions. Since the body is the warehouse of the emotions, this decrease in emotional awareness can also cause a disconnect with the body.

The age of reason for a child starts at around the age of eleven or twelve. While this may be a time of greater awareness of a feeling of separation or being disconnected from God, the ability for rational and abstract thinking allows the child to weigh the values handed down through the expectations of social groups they belong to and begin to develop moral values and a conscience. At the same time the child will start to assert even more desire for independence and autonomy, looking more to peers and the larger world for validation. When the values of this level are integrated, the child will feel a greater sense of responsibility for others and for the earth, have less of a need to control or dominate others and learn to cooperate rather than compete. Some of these values open the door to reclaiming the seemingly lost relationship with God. When the son of some friends of mine was this age, he became very concerned with the earth and the environment. He cried when his father cut down a diseased tree because he could somehow feel the pain of the tree. He had a strong sense of doing what he perceived as being right, just, even healthy. He openly explored what God was for him, one time pointing to his arm and saying "this is God" because he knew God was in everything.

The Continuing Evolution of Consciousness

The levels of consciousness of the human family continue to develop, expand, and evolve. In his teaching on the human condition, Thomas Keating combines what we have learned from modern science with what the mystics throughout the ages have described as the development of a life of contemplative prayer. Some of the higher, or more developed levels of consciousness and of prayer that Keating describes include the following three levels of consciousness:

1. The intuitive level of consciousness, where we start to experience a sense of oneness and belonging to God, the human family, and the universe.
2. Unity consciousness, what today is sometimes called non-dual consciousness.
3. Union with God, our ultimate state.

Each of these levels access the spiritual level of our being where we come to know our true self.

Before we can understand and move to these more developed levels of consciousness, we look first at where we are today in our own development, not with judgment, but in the spirit of knowing that God is revealing what we need in order to bring us closer to divine union. As the human family moves through evolution and each of us move through our own development, the values and limitations of the previous stage linger and need to be integrated. How well we do that is a barometer of how much we suffer in life. In one of *The Spiritual Journey Series* videos Keating says,

> "The unconscious is filled with the emotional pain of early life, with both values that are limited and also potentials that we don't know yet."[14]

What follows is Thomas Keating's seminal teaching on the false-self system and our "programs for happiness that can't possibly work." I have heard so many people express what I experienced when I was first exposed to this teaching. It was as if my eyes were opened as to why my life was so difficult and wasn't working despite my best efforts. And it gave me hope that by the grace of God I could be healed and transformed.

The Energy Centers

In the evolution of the human family, emotional and behavioral patterns known as "energy centers" developed for the survival of the species. They are biologically programmed in our brain, nervous system, and senses to respond to our physical world, and are largely instinctual, not requiring conscious thought. Thomas Keating developed an understanding of how these patterns influence our spiritual lives in his work relating to the human condition. He speaks of them as a state that has become distorted by the circumstances of early life. Inspired by Ken Keyes, Jr.'s work (much of which is detailed in Keyes's 1973 book called *Handbook to a Higher Consciousness*), Keating focuses on the "lower" three energy centers and relates them to the first stages of the evolution of consciousness—the uroboric and typhonic. These lower three centers are: the security center, the sensation center, and the power center. The security center corresponds to the uroboric level, related to the primary focus on acquiring food and shelter and whatever else we associate with security and survival. The sensation center relates to the typhonic level which has to do with pleasurable sensation and activities that, on an emotional level, meet our need for esteem and affection. The power center also relates to the typhonic level and has to do with our safety and boundaries, often expressed by dominating people, events and circumstances to increase our self-importance. It reflects how out of control we may feel and affects how much control we attempt to exert in our lives.

The energy centers develop when our brain is not yet capable of rational thinking, generally before the ages of five to seven, and we are still very much immersed in emotions and imagination. Nothing is wrong or bad about the energy centers. They start with instinctual needs that we are trying to meet as best we can. Because children are naturally self-centered, most people's early lives are characterized by ongoing emotional reactions that create our perceptions. From our perceptions we create stories we tell ourselves repeatedly, using our imagination to embellish the story in the retelling. Because children are not yet capable of rational thinking, the stories tend to be irrational and emotional, but we think they're true. They become what Keyes refers to as our "emotional programming" and what Keating calls "emotional programs for happiness."

When something becomes programmed into the unconscious, we don't really think about it anymore. It becomes automatic. Think of your morning routine. When I get up in the morning, I open the doggie door, turn on the coffee pot, go to the bathroom, brush my teeth, take my coffee to my prayer chair where I do spiritual reading before practicing Centering Prayer. This is, without fail, my morning routine. I am habituated to this routine, and I don't think about it, I just do it. It has been relegated to my unconscious. Changing any part of it interrupts the routine because I have to think about it. The same thing happens with our emotional programming. There was a time in my life when I had very little self-confidence and often felt inadequate. Any hint of criticism—from a boss, coworker, friend, my mother, even a stranger—would set off a cascade of thoughts, emotions, and commentaries: fear, dread, self-loathing, sadness, not good enough, she doesn't like me, I'm never going to learn how to do this, I can't get anything right, I don't know why I thought I could do this, I should just keep my mouth shut. It didn't matter what the person said to me even if it was harmless, or at least unintentional, I created my reaction in my body, mind, and emotions because it touched on something unknown or unresolved in my unconscious—something that touched into one or more of the energy centers.

You can usually tell if an energy center is being triggered because it starts with an afflictive or upsetting emotion. Each energy center triggers automatic emotional responses that affect our thoughts, commentaries, and behavior. Often associated with the security center are emotions related to fear, worry, and anxiety. With the sensation center it's usually disappointment, frustration, and boredom. With the power center it's generally anger, resentment, hostility, irritation, and hate. As we grow out of childhood, we have the ability to move to higher levels of consciousness, but most of us get trapped, at least in part, by automated responses to which we have become habituated, triggered by the energy centers.

As we grow through childhood into adulthood, not only do we become capable of higher levels of consciousness, but also higher levels of rational thinking. The influences of the emotional programs co-opt our capacity to mature emotionally and spiritually. Instead of evolving into healthy adulthood, we use these increased abilities of the brain to reinforce the emotional programs in our attempts to find even more security, esteem and affection, and power and control.

The influence of the energy centers exaggerates our loyalty to groups we are or have been involved with through our cultural conditioning. We become over-identified with these groups and their values that we have accepted and haven't discerned as our own. They become hidden values that we may not even be aware we hold. For example, when I was in my 20s, I was married to someone who was addicted to drugs and alcohol, was unfaithful to me, and contributed very little to taking care of our household. I had an over-exaggerated sense of responsibility and so I took control. I was very unhappy and in a constant state of worry and obsessive thoughts of how to manipulate my husband and my circumstances. In all likelihood any modern-day priest would have agreed that this marriage was not a sacrament, in other words, was not a commitment to a lifelong partnership. Yet I had a hidden value about marriage being a permanent commitment—no matter what—instilled in me by my Catholic upbringing and perpetuated by my loyalty to my family. Divorce was simply not an option within the framework of my cultural conditioning. Even after my heart told me this marriage was over, it took me three years to say it out loud and take steps to dissolve it. My over-identification with my cultural conditioning, in this case the church and my family, led me to believe that if I got a divorce, I would be a failure. Before I ever made the decision to get a divorce, I already felt the shame of my failure. It wasn't that anyone actually said this to me; it was what my mind had conjured up. In fact, my family was relieved when I finally made the decision, and the Church granted me an annulment.

By the time we reach mental egoic consciousness in adolescence, we are already so entrenched in our pre-rational emotional programs and our identification with cultural groups that we use our capacity to reason to rationalize, justify, and glorify our hidden values. Before I completed a fourth step in Al-Anon I valued being seen as a "good girl" over being honest. The fourth step required me to do a searching and fearless moral inventory of myself. Honesty is the key to benefitting from this work on the fourth step. I found it interesting that the fourth step work started by making a list of my resentments, usually related to my feelings that someone had wronged me. And then I learned to look for my part in the dynamic. By the time I was working on the fourth step I was so unhappy and disillusioned with life that I would have done anything to heal whatever was causing my suffering. Looking at the part I played in my own suffering was extremely painful for me and completely shattered my illusion about the value of being a "good girl." Every resentment contained the thread of my dishonesty in either what I said and did or didn't say or do. The cost to my self-esteem and my integrity was so high it was almost unbearable. That's where God took me on this journey—to the point where it was almost unbearable so that I could awaken to the ways these programs for happiness were really programs for misery. This awareness showed me that no amount of rationalizing, justifying, or glorifying my behavior was worth the cost of my soul. Of course, I didn't start a fourth step until I completed the third step by turning my will and my life over to the care of God. That was the only way I could become honest enough to face this reality. I knew I wasn't doing it alone. This, for me, was the step I needed to take to have that attitudinal shift into the mature use of the abilities of mental egoic consciousness. I started to be able to move beyond self-centered concerns and turn my attention to the greater concerns of life.

Once this attitudinal shift takes root, it opens up the possibility to move to higher levels of consciousness. The intuitive level is where our spiritual faculties are opened and we begin to sense our connection to the human family, nature, the universe, and of course God. We are now ready, or perhaps just becoming willing, or maybe even just willing to be willing, to go through what the Christian tradition calls the purification of the unconscious. This is where we begin to have the ability to distinguish between the workings of the emotional programs and the movement of the Spirit.

Some years ago, I took a nine-month writing course called "Writing to Heal" with author/teacher Mark Matousek. The first month's topic,

"Touching the Wound," started with some thought-provoking questions such as this:

> "Describe precisely and economically what happened to you (the cause of your wound). What is the story you tell yourself about this event and its effect on your life? How might memory have betrayed (or tricked) you into believing a false version of what happened to you? How has the story about the wound helped you to survive?"[15]

Until I took this course, I hadn't really thought of myself as having a wound. I wrote many 1,000-word essays trying to answer these questions, trying to find one wound. I was looking for the one thing that someone else did to me that caused me to have depression, issues with food, low self-esteem, and troubled relationships. What I discovered was that there wasn't one thing that someone else did to me. What caused my woundedness was my perception of what happened on a pre-rational level of consciousness that I kept recreating into a pattern of emotions and behavior. I was looking for someone to blame. But no one is to blame. This is why we call it the human condition. We all go through it in varying degrees. Our spiritual work in life is first to discover that we have a human condition and second, to allow it to teach us how to live full and meaningful lives.

What's in the Unconscious?

> "What I do, I do not understand. For I do not do what I want, but I do what I hate… Now if I do what I do not want, it is no longer I who do it, but sin that dwells in me. So, then, I discover the principle that when I want to do right, evil is at hand. For I take delight in the law of God, in my inner self, but I see in my members another principle at war with the law of mind, taking me captive to the law of sin that dwells in my members. Miserable one that I am! Who will deliver me from this mortal body?" Romans 7:15, 20-24

In Chapter Six we will study Lectio Divina, an ancient contemplative prayer practice that involves praying with Scripture to reach deeper levels of meaning. One of the things I love about Lectio Divina is that it teaches me to ponder Scripture and allow the Spirit to reveal the relevance of the passage in my life today. This passage from Saint Paul's letter to the Romans speaks to me of the human condition. At the time the passage was written the unconscious had not yet been named by modern psychology. Yet Saint Paul knew from his own human experience something that felt out of his control was running his life, causing him to do what he did not want to do. Anyone who has struggled with addiction or any compulsive behavior will relate to this. How many times was I going to quit smoking tomorrow and when tomorrow came, I found myself doing what I did not want to do. And then there was the conviction that I was going to quit trying to fix myself because I wasn't broken, until Amazon suggested the newest self-help book that had just the remedy I needed. Can you think of a time in your life when you were convinced something you were doing wasn't good for you and yet you were unable to stop?

Saint Paul's words were translated as "sin" and "evil," which for me trigger thoughts of shame and unworthiness. But when I reframe those words in the context of the human condition and the unconscious, I can relate to Paul's frustration with the discrepancies in his life. The unconscious is more powerful than most of us realize, and as Thomas Keating says in *The Mystery of Christ*, we will be influenced by the unconscious to the end of our lives unless we start awakening and taking responsibility for it. It was difficult for me to embrace this concept of taking responsibility because it felt like everything that was wrong with me, or that wasn't going as I thought it should, was someone else's fault. I learned somewhere along the line to look for someone or something to blame. The point of this is not to excuse anyone who has been abusive or intentionally caused harm, or to diminish circumstances and events outside of our control. The point is that my reaction, whether it appears in the form of thoughts, emotions, or behavior, is largely, if not wholly, influenced by unconscious motivations.

Thomas Keating says repeatedly in his teaching in *The Spiritual Journey Series* video course that we should repent in the true meaning of that word, which simply means change the direction in which we are looking for happiness. It doesn't mean we should beat ourselves up with guilt-filled remorse, the message we may have received from early religious training. This simple reframing of my perspective was truly liberating for me. How much of my life did I spend thinking my life would be better and I would be happier if he would just do this, or she would do that, or I moved there, or I had this job, or I had more money, or my mother loved me more... yada, yada, yada? But I really did think that way! And that is a very painful, disappointing, unfulfilling way to live. I'm not saying that my life was horrible by any stretch, but there is a difference between surviving and thriving that I wasn't aware of until I took responsibility for my emotional life. The key to that awareness for me was a consistent Centering Prayer practice that drew me into the divine relationship and opened my heart.

One of the treasures that's buried in the unconscious (and often remains there when we are not open to awakening) is our gifts and our goodness. I remember what an impact a Marianne Williamson quote had on me some years ago:

> "Our deepest fear is not that we are inadequate. Our deepest fear is that we are powerful beyond measure. It is our Light, not our Darkness, that most frightens us."[16]

Could it be that I was more afraid to face my inner goodness than any so-called bad thing I had done? If so, I wanted to be free of that psychological and spiritual burden.

Psychological healing helps us to feel better and to live a more fulfilling life. But spiritual healing allows us to live a life more aligned with the will of God. Thomas Keating says that as we heal, we move towards using less and less of our own energy and as we become empty of that, the divine energy quickly moves into that space so that, truly, our action is God's action in us. In Matthew 5:15-16 Jesus says, "Nor do they light a lamp and then put it under a bushel basket; it is set on a lampstand, where it gives light to all in the house. Just so, your light must shine before others, that they may see your good deeds and glorify your heavenly Father." As we heal, we come out from under the bushel basket so that our light shines.

When I first started going to Al-Anon I struggled to speak up in meetings. I was lucky if I could put one sentence together. I was overwrought with trying to put on a good face, not airing my dirty laundry in public, being a "good girl." I was always grateful that it was perfectly acceptable to just say "pass" if I didn't want to share. I may not have been able to keep going to meetings without that option. As time went on and I started to heal I started being able to say more than one sentence. Pretty soon I was chairing meetings, which means opening the meeting and facilitating it. As I allowed myself to become known, I was asked to share my story at Al-Anon meetings, and then also at combined AA/Al-Anon meetings. After participating in a step-study group, I led a step-study group. I started an Al-Anon meeting at the treatment center where my ex-husband went through treatment so families would have support like the patients had with their AA meetings at the treatment center. I went back to school and became an addictions counselor so I could help families understand and survive post-treatment. I learned how to help families talk to each other, do their own work in recovery, and live their own lives regardless of what the alcoholic/addict did. I began to see the healing work we do in life is never just about us feeling better and living more fulfilling lives. It's about uncovering our gifts, letting our light shine, and serving. Why does that scare us so much? I'm not sure I was ever able to answer that question, but I lived with it for a long time until finding an answer was no longer important.

Why would it be important for us to become aware of our goodness, to let our light shine, to awaken to the gifts we so often keep hidden, usually unknowingly? You'll hear me repeat more than once in this book what Thomas Keating tells us throughout his teaching: that our journey in contemplative life is not merely a personal journey; what we are doing is affecting the world. I think this is difficult for most of us to believe, especially in the early days of practice. South African Archbishop Desmond Tutu helps to make this clear:

> "We are fundamentally good. When you come to think of it, that's who we are at our core... What difference does goodness make? Goodness changes everything... Goodness changes how we see the world, the way we see others, and most importantly, the way we see ourselves. The way we see ourselves matters. It affects how we treat people. It affects the quality of life for each and all of us. What is the quality of life on our planet? It is nothing more than the sum total of our daily interactions. Each kindness enhances the quality of life. Each cruelty diminishes it."[17]

When we ask ourselves what needs to be healed and why we want or need healing, we begin to face some difficult questions. I ask you to consider your own experience. How in touch are you with your goodness? Are you aware of and are you using your gifts? How do you see yourself? When you have a personal interaction that you don't feel good about, can you see your part in it? Are you living with an intention of kindness and compassion? Centering Prayer and other contemplative practices taught in the Contemplative Living Experience (CLE) program help us to be willing to live with these questions until we begin to discover our responses.

One of the things I heard Thomas Keating say repeatedly that has been most helpful to me is that the divine therapy is about making the unconscious conscious. Neuroscientists agree that about 95% of our life is run by unconscious programming, which is how we perceive and interpret what we experience. Because we are so young as a species in terms of the evolution of consciousness, we are still mostly programmed in the fight or flight mode, with a tendency towards fear and negativity. Our gifts and our innate goodness have a formidable obstacle up against this powerful programming. Healing of the human condition starts with becoming aware of the negative programming that our unconscious minds run unchecked and seemingly out of our control. It might be out of our control, but it's not out of God's control. If you are drawn to Centering Prayer, to living a contemplative life, to deepening your relationship with God, God will reveal to you what needs to be healed and either heal it or show you the path to healing.

Part of the soul's healing journey is what Saint John of the Cross describes as the "Night of Spirit" from his epic poem the "Dark Night of the Soul." The dark night is a process we undergo during one of the traditional stages of contemplative prayer known as purification. Its purpose is twofold: illumination or the awareness of the presence of God, and union, what we also refer to as contemplation. Thomas Keating helps us understand this process in the context of the contemplative life. In *Manifesting God*, he says,

> "The goal of the Night of Spirit is to bring us to the permanent and continuous awareness of God's presence and of our abiding union with him. Our emotional programs for happiness based on the instinctual needs

of the child have finally found their true home: God is our security, God is our Beloved, God is our freedom."[18]

Over the years as I have thought about what it means to live a contemplative life, what Keating says about the night of spirit in this quote is the closest to what I have experienced (albeit fleetingly) and what has motivated me to continue on this path. The two things he refers to: the permanent and continuous awareness of God's presence, and our abiding union with God, have become my heart's desire. It's not something I can achieve. I can only open myself to receive this gift. The practices and experiences offered in this book that are part of the CLE program can only dispose us to this open receptivity. We practice and we let go.

When I say that this CLE program is built on the practice of Centering Prayer, that Centering Prayer is the foundation, I hope you can see why more clearly now that you've learned about the human condition and what typically leaves us feeling separate from God. The feeling of separation is not what God intends for humanity. I have a sense that all of my life God has been bugging me to come closer. Pursuing me. Relentlessly. I often prefer to stay unconscious in all the many ways my false self has created for me—smoking, depression, watching TV, solitaire on my phone, overeating, engaging in relationships with people who didn't love me, reading voraciously about how to fix myself, oversleeping. You get the idea. None of it worked, none of it every made me happy or soothed my wounds. It took me years to understand what Keating means when he says repent—change the direction in which you're looking for happiness. When I started doing Centering Prayer, I hadn't quite changed direction, but I began to see the path more clearly.

A Centering Prayer practice opens the door to contemplative prayer, an incredible gift that this God of love is offering us if we would only say yes. It starts the process of the divine therapy, the healing of what obscures our awareness of God's presence and our abiding union with God. With the door to contemplative prayer opened, even just a little, we can begin to explore the mystery of contemplative life.

What is your heart's desire? Are you ready to take that first step into the silence of your heart? Before we move into the teachings of the CLE program, let's explore this life-changing practice of Centering Prayer in the next chapter. Even if you are experienced in Centering Prayer, Thomas Keating always encouraged us to go back to basics. Please read on with a beginner's mind, as if you're encountering this material for the first time.

CHAPTER THREE
Introduction to Centering Prayer

"Be still and know that I am God."
Psalm 46:10

THOMAS KEATING WROTE IN HIS CLASSIC TREATISE ON THE contemplative dimension of the Gospel, *Open Mind, Open Heart*,

> "The term *contemplative life* is the abiding state of divine union itself, in which one is habitually and continuously moved both in prayer and action by the Spirit. Centering Prayer is an entrance into the process that leads to divine union."[19]

The Contemplative Living Experience (CLE) program is based on a foundation in the practice of Centering Prayer. On that foundation, using the teachings of Thomas Keating and other contemplative teachers, we begin to build a contemplative life using other contemplative practices for daily life. Together with our lived experience with the practices, we cultivate a contemplative life that awakens our "abiding state of divine union."

We often describe Centering Prayer as being a Christian meditation practice, but the use of the word "meditation" can cause some misinterpretation of what the practice really involves. I prefer to call it a contemplative practice, which is less about concentrating, focusing, or "stilling" the mind, and more about letting go of all thoughts and resting in God. I mentioned in Chapter One that when I was searching for a meditation practice in the 1980s, I was led to the section on Eastern religions in the bookstore. The only books I could find back then taught a concentrative method of meditation. Focus or attention was put on a mantra, a prayer, an image or the breath. Whenever the mind wandered, the attention was returned to the mantra, prayer, image, or breath.

The method I learned at that time came from the Buddhist tradition and, interestingly, used the prayer ascribed to Saint Francis of Assisi that begins "Lord make me an instrument of your peace…" The instruction was to silently say each word or phrase while imagining a pearl dropping into a pool of water. If the mind wandered, we were instructed to start the prayer over again from the beginning. In some ways this felt like punishment to me because in a twenty-minute period I had to start over again so many times I rarely reached the end of the prayer. Yet this type of meditation was very helpful to me in calming down my neurotic, obsessive thinking. It helped me to realize that my experience in the meditation period, even if frustrating at times, was indeed impacting my daily life in positive ways. But I struggled to understand some of the language and concepts in the books I read because they came out of a tradition I was not familiar with. I didn't have a teacher and I didn't know how to take it further on my own.

After eight years my practice had become dry, and I became bored with it. I had no idea that this could actually be a sign of progress on the spiritual journey, such as happens in what Saint John of the Cross calls the Dark Night of the Soul. We reach a point where the consolations we may have experienced in the early days of practice disappear and we think God has disappeared with them. This is what is referred to as dryness. The experience of God's absence is a movement to the experience of God *as God is*, rather than our idea of God. I was close to dropping my practice altogether, and yet I couldn't deny the fruits the practice had manifested in my life. It was at this time that two people I knew and respected told me about Contemplative Outreach. The Center for Contemplative Living in Denver, a part of Contemplative Outreach, was founded in 1987 and held its first annual conference in 1994. That was the first event I attended, even though I didn't yet know how to practice Centering Prayer. Shortly after the conference, I attended an introductory workshop that taught the method of Centering Prayer and, as a result, was quickly able to shift my practice from a concentrative method to the receptive method that is Centering Prayer. I started taking classes at the Denver Center on the conceptual background of Centering Prayer and on the human condition as part of Thomas Keating's *The Spiritual Journey Series* video course.

Thomas Keating's interreligious dialogues support the idea that all meditation practices, including Centering Prayer, ultimately take the practitioner to the same place—toward higher levels of consciousness and oneness or unity with the Ultimate Mystery and all of creation. For me, the concentrative method had been like holding on tight with fists and jaws clenched trying hard to still my mind. Centering Prayer was more like taking a deep breath. I could open my hands, palms up, unclench, and offer it all to God. And with open empty hands I was able to receive something in return. I could rest in God (which is one of the ways we describe this practice) and let go of all effort. I don't think I realized how much of an effort life was until I started to truly let go. In twelve-step circles one of the slogans you hear a lot is "Let Go and Let God." With all my being I wanted to do that, but until I started practicing Centering Prayer I didn't know how. I'm reminded of a prayer I learned at a treatment center where I worked. I don't know the source or even if I have the words exactly right, but it made a lasting impression on me:

> *As children bring their broken toys with tears for us to mend,*
> *I brought my broken dreams to God because he was my friend,*
> *but then instead of leaving him in peace to work alone,*
> *I hung around and tried to help with ways that were my own.*
> *At last, I snatched them back and said, "How could you be so slow?"*
> *"My child," he said, "What could I do? You never did let go."*

The image of God I grew up with made it difficult for me to let go. Letting go requires unmitigated trust, and that kind of trust requires a loving relationship. The God I was introduced to when I was a child was not a God I particularly wanted to have a relationship with. But Centering Prayer taught me how to have a relationship with God. It was tentative at first, just as any human relationship would be. It took time and practice. Prayer wasn't something that came easily to me because it had always been focused on communicating with words and I was never sure who or what I was supposed to be communicating with. It never occurred to me that words were not required until I heard Thomas Keating say that silence is God's first language. I also learned that you don't get to know someone when you do all the talking. In fact, some of the most satisfying times I have spent with loved ones have been in that space of intimate silence where words are not necessary. The exchange of the energy of love is often best held in silence.

Religion has a place in some people's lives; it certainly did in mine—up to a certain point. What I didn't learn in my religion was how to go directly to God without any intermediary. It was always hard for me to believe what someone else told me I had to believe in order to belong. But through it all I never stopped longing for God. I remember hearing one time that our longing for God is really God's longing for us. In my human experience I never felt particularly "longed for" until I started doing Centering Prayer and developed a direct relationship with God. That's when I started to experience what Divine Indwelling means.

The experience of Centering Prayer is rarely blissful, and most practitioners have difficulty describing what the experience is like. My humble attempt to describe it goes like this: I am wrapped in the arms of God's embrace and the energy of divine love is pulsing in my heart space. For me, it happens in the heart. But the difficulties many of us experience in Centering Prayer—as you'll see, often have to do with the mind.

Centering Prayer

Many of the Eastern religious traditions have had uninterrupted structures in place from their beginnings to support those who have meditation practices. In the early days of the Western Christian tradition, contemplative prayer, which is similar to what Eastern traditions refer to as meditation, was practiced by lay persons and monastics alike in the form of Lectio Divina. This was a practice that started with listening and reflecting on Scripture, moving into deeper listening in the interior silence of the heart, culminating in resting in the presence of God. The Middle Ages brought more attention to teaching and practicing methods of prayer rather than the more spontaneous prayer that came from this deep listening. Even though contemplative prayer was no longer commonly practiced by all Christians, it remained very much alive in monasteries. It's no surprise that the Christian contemplative heritage was reintroduced in modern times by monastics. Three Trappist monks—Thomas Keating, William Meninger, and Basil Pennington—led the charge to revive the contemplative tradition. A grassroots movement emerged and grew into an organization called Contemplative Outreach, founded to support individuals and small faith communities in living the contemplative dimension of the Gospel in everyday life. Contemplative Outreach is the extension into the world of the spirituality of a Catholic monastic order known as the Trappists.

The programs offered by Contemplative Outreach provide the structure—what I will refer to as spiritual formation—that many of us found lacking in our religious affiliations. The structure that spiritual formation provides is in teaching, supporting, guiding, and community-building. Spiritual formation was most often geared towards those entering a monastic or clerical religious life, if it was offered at all. My experience as a layperson was of being told what to believe and how to pray without regard for my own ability to discern my moral life and develop my own relationship with God. By the time I found Contemplative Outreach, I was ready for a deeper experience.

Spiritual formation is an individual process or journey that is best experienced within a trusted community. I think the success of the twelve-step programs could be attributed to the structure and spiritual formation they provide within a "fellowship." In the case of Contemplative Outreach, this community is experienced within the context of the Christian Tradition, largely based on the teachings of Thomas Keating.

Through my involvement with Contemplative Outreach of Colorado as coordinator and member of the Advisory Council and Board of Trustees, I developed a longstanding relationship with Thomas Keating. Up to this point in this book, I've referred to him as Thomas Keating, but truth be told, I always called him Father Thomas. Some people choose the more formal way to refer to a priest and call him Father Keating. But out of both respect and affection, I chose to call him Father Thomas. He was a model of humility who never wanted to be thought of as a "master" or "guru." Although he died at the age of 95 in October of 2018, his legacy is very much alive within and beyond Contemplative Outreach.

Many of you may have known Father Thomas as I did. I hope those of you who didn't get to spend time with him will experience communion with him through the warmth I have in my heart for my spiritual teacher and mentor. And so, from here forward, I'm just going to call him Father Thomas as if he's here with me guiding this writing project. In fact, his teaching is so alive within me, it feels as if he really is here. I was giving a Lectio Divina retreat in Florida the year after Father Thomas died and at one point in my presentation I got choked up and said, "I can feel Father Thomas here with us." Many in the audience agreed they too could feel his presence.

Along with two other Trappist monks—William Meninger and Basil Pennington—Father Thomas developed and first taught the method of Centering Prayer in the early 1970s. Father Thomas was then serving as abbot at St. Joseph's Abbey in Spencer, Massachusetts. He attended a meeting in 1971 with other clergy at the request of Pope Paul VI where the Pope asked them to help revive the contemplative dimension of the Gospel amongst both the clergy and the laity. This extremely significant event acknowledged the contemplative dimension of the Gospel as a part of Church history at a time when few lay people had much knowledge of it. This seems obvious to me today because of my experience with the long history of Lectio Divina (praying and meditating with Scripture) in the Christian tradition, but in those days, it was still not the norm for Catholics to even read the Bible outside of the select passages contained in the Roman Missal.

When Father Thomas returned from this meeting, he encouraged his brother monks to develop a method of contemplative prayer that would have the same appeal to young people that the meditation practices from the Eastern traditions seemed to have. Father Thomas noticed that people were stopping at St. Joseph's Abbey to ask for directions to the Buddhist meditation center up the road, and he wondered why these seekers weren't being introduced to the rich contemplative path within the Christian tradition.

William Meninger, while giving a talk on the early development of the method of Centering Prayer, confessed that in his eight years in the seminary and six years as a parish priest he had never learned about contemplative prayer. After a year with the Trappists, he began experiencing contemplative prayer. One of his duties as a monk was to give retreats to parish priests. He wanted to teach them contemplative prayer but, as yet, didn't have the words to explain what it was or how to do it. In 1974 he found a book in the abbey library called *The Cloud of Unknowing*, by an unknown English author. It was basically a manual on contemplative meditation. He found in the book's third chapter a description of his Christian monastic meditative experience in a teachable form. The teaching could be summed up as "being in the presence of God with love." Father William called this prayer "The Prayer of the Cloud." Father Thomas started teaching this prayer to the lay community in the nearby vicinity and Father Basil taught it to priests and nuns at retreats away from the monastery. The name of the prayer was changed to Centering Prayer, inspired by Thomas Merton's description of contemplative prayer.

In celebration of the 10th anniversary of the founding of Contemplative Outreach, a delightful dialogue about the development of Centering Prayer by these three monks was recorded. "Centering Prayer—Origins & Inspirations: Thomas Keating, William Meninger, Basil Pennington" is available on the Contemplative Outreach YouTube channel.[20] Hearing the story directly from the monks gives the real flavor of how and why they developed Centering Prayer.

Father Thomas gave the first intensive Centering Prayer retreat in 1983 where participants practiced Centering Prayer for four to five hours a day. Shortly thereafter, Contemplative Outreach was formed to support parish-based programs in New York City. In 1985, about fifty miles west of New York City, Chrysalis House was formed as an experimental live-in contemplative community where many Centering Prayer workshops and retreats were held. Under Father Thomas's direction, Mary Mrozowski, David Frenette, Bob Bartel, and others experimented with programs to teach and train lay people in Centering Prayer and complementary contemplative practices. These early pioneers created the predecessor to the CLE program, which they called the Nine-Month Course. David Frenette recalls that when they started to develop the course many people were starting to mature in a Centering Prayer practice, and so, the community talked to Father Thomas about developing materials and practices to provide formation in contemplative life.

Father Thomas started another experiment in Denver in 1987 with Sister Bernadette Teasdale. He was living at St. Benedict's Monastery in Snowmass, Colorado at the time and had been working with the Episcopal Diocese in Denver teaching Centering Prayer when the Catholic Archbishop (now Cardinal), Francis J. Stafford, asked him to do something for the Catholic Archdiocese. Sister Bernadette Teasdale, who had been working for the Archdiocese in the Catholic Renew Program, was asked to help Father Thomas with his work in the Colorado Catholic parishes. She had already learned Centering Prayer years earlier from Father Ed Hayes while she was on sabbatical at the Shantivanam House of Prayer, part of the Archdiocese of Kansas. For five years she worked out of the Spirit of Christ parish in the Denver Archdiocese offering introductory workshops in Centering Prayer and

The Spiritual Journey Series video courses all over Colorado, helping people to establish a foundation in Centering Prayer. She eventually moved out of the parish into rented space that became The Center for Contemplative Living, which we just call "the Center." The Archdiocese provided Sister Bernadette with seed money for about five years, with the expectation that revenue earned through the programs offered by the Center and raised through donations would sustain the work. That's when Contemplative Outreach of Colorado became a 501(c)3, so it could accept tax-deductible donations.

With the close proximity of Father Thomas and having Sister Bernadette dedicated to teaching and supporting Centering Prayer, the contemplative community in Denver flourished. Sister Bernadette was always sensitive to the needs of the community and when a significant number had been doing Centering Prayer for ten plus years, she started adding more courses to support this growing community, not just the beginners. In the mid-1990s, Rose Meyler moved to Denver and brought the Nine-Month Course with her. Rose had taken the course in New York with one of the original founders, Mary Mrozowski. Mary died that year, but others carried on her legacy.

Rose approached Sister Bernadette about offering the Nine-Month Course in Denver. And so it began in Denver as it had been taught in New York. Participants committed to meeting at a retreat center one weekend a month, Friday evening through Sunday afternoon, for nine months. I attended one of those early sessions. The course is based on a foundation of Centering Prayer, and each month participants are taught contemplative practices that support their Centering Prayer practice and help them to move into contemplative life "off the cushion" so to speak. Father Thomas would say our practice is daily life, not just the time we spend in prayer.

After offering the Nine-Month Course for about twelve years, interest started to dwindle because so many in the community had already participated in the course. A decision was made to discontinue it, at least for a while. I was disappointed to see it discontinued because I knew the great value it provided for me on my spiritual journey. In 2011 when Sister Bernadette retired and I became the Denver Chapter Coordinator of Contemplative Outreach, I asked Rose if she would consider offering a modified version of the course at the Center. She was very excited at the prospect. We designed a course that we thought would appeal to modern contemplatives. Since the Center doesn't have overnight accommodations, the biggest adjustment to the course was shortening the amount of time

Contemplative Life

the group would spend together. We thought this could have advantages because participants would be required to invest less time and money than when the course involved an overnight stay. They could sleep at home and have Sundays to spend with their families or take care of any other weekend duties. By not staying overnight we were able to substantially lower the cost, which opened up the course to a lot more people. We hired my good friend Diane to prepare home-cooked meals. She understood that spiritual work is hard work and people need healthy sustenance. The challenge was to preserve the integrity of the content of the course to make sure participants were not losing any of the potential for transformation that the course provided.

Because we were making changes to the original course, we felt that we needed to change the name. We decided to call it the Contemplative Living Experience program. It took a while for the new name to catch on, which we shortened to CLE. In order to fill the program each time we offered it, we decided to offer it every other year. I feel blessed that Rose trusted me enough to mentor me as a facilitator and to ultimately turn the program over to me. As I observed the transformation process in the participants each time we offered the program, I couldn't help but think what a shame it is that this program is only offered in Denver and New York. I hope the publication of this book will help bring this teaching to a wider audience, perhaps accompanied by an online course, participants in small groups working together, or for individuals working with a mentor or spiritual director.

Centering Prayer Method

As in the Nine-Month Course, Centering Prayer is the foundation upon which everything else in the CLE program rests. The guidelines for Centering Prayer are quite simple. I am grateful to be commissioned by Contemplative Outreach to teach Centering Prayer because it gives me the opportunity to go back to the basics and come to a deeper understanding of their wisdom. The teaching that follows is derived from the introductory workshops that Contemplative Outreach teaches all over the world.

Guidelines for Centering Prayer

1. Choose a sacred word as the symbol of your intention to consent to God's presence and action within.

2. Sitting comfortably and with eyes closed, settle briefly and silently introduce the sacred word as the symbol of your consent to God's presence and action within.
3. When engaged with your thoughts,* return ever-so-gently to the sacred word.
4. At the end of the prayer period, remain in silence with eyes closed for a couple of minutes.

*Thoughts include body sensation, feelings, images and reflections.

Guideline #1: *Choose a sacred word as the symbol of your intention to consent to God's presence and action within.*

The sacred word is a symbol, a pointer not significant in and of itself, but important in that it signifies our intention to consent to God's presence and action within. One of our teachers at the Center is a healing touch practitioner who often reminds us that "energy follows intention." Indeed, most of the things we do in life that are worthwhile start with intention. Intention speaks of commitment, and it doesn't require us to be perfect. One of the things I see most often in my spiritual direction practice is how hard people are on themselves, much harder than God or anyone who loves us would be. This teaching helps us remember to stop putting so much effort into trying to be perfect and put more attention on intention.

Our intention in Centering Prayer is to consent to God's presence and action within. Consent simply means saying yes to God. Although we may not be aware of it most of the time, God is always present to us and within us. Intentional consent to God's presence during the period of Centering Prayer helps us to become aware of God's presence in all of life. Consenting to God's action within invites the healing process of the divine therapy that enables us to be a conduit of God's love in our everyday life.

Choose a sacred word of one or two syllables that is either a name of God or a reflection of your relationship to God such as God, Jesus, Mary, Mother, Amma, Father, Abba, Spirit, love, peace, be still, mercy, let go. William Meninger says that our sacred word should express the fullness of our love for God. Before you choose your sacred word, take a few minutes, close your eyes, and focus on your heart space. See what word arises in you. It's best not to choose a word that carries any sort of emotional charge for you and that doesn't trigger your thoughts. Once you have chosen a word, don't change it during the period of Centering Prayer.

If you want to change it for the next period that's okay but remember that the inherent meaning of the word is not as important as what it symbolizes. Don't get hung up on having the perfect word, but you're welcome to experiment with a few different words until you settle on one.

Guideline #2: *Sitting comfortably and with eyes closed, settle briefly and silently introduce the sacred word as the symbol of your consent to God's presence and action within.*

Whether you sit in a chair, on the floor, or on a cushion, sit with your back straight, but not so rigid that you are uncomfortable. Choose a posture that you will be comfortable with for at least twenty minutes. If you're not comfortable you will be thinking about your discomfort rather than consenting to God's presence and action within. I would discourage you from lying down because you don't want to be so comfortable that you fall asleep. I will admit, though, that I have learned to sleep sitting perfectly upright! It's best to take a nap before prayer if you're sleepy, but sometimes we just fall asleep. We don't worry about it; we simply return to our intention by saying our sacred word when we wake up.

We close our eyes to minimize distractions from outside ourselves, but also as a symbol to let go of any inward distractions. Settling briefly gives us the opportunity to bring our attention to our intention. Then, as Father Thomas says, as gently as placing a feather on a ball of cotton we silently say our sacred word. The sacred word is not a mantra that we repeat over and over; saying it once is enough to institute our intention to consent.

Guideline #3: *When engaged with your thoughts, return ever-so-gently to the sacred word.*

You are not going to stop your brain from thinking. Did you get that? Let me repeat it one more time. You're not going to stop your brain from thinking! One of my teachers put it this way: our hearts were made to beat, our lungs were made to breathe, and our brains were made to think. Some people get the misconception that during Centering Prayer we are trying to make our minds blank. We couldn't do that even if we tried. Even the practices that are aimed at stilling the mind don't actually stop the brain from thinking.

What are we doing then? We're letting the thoughts come, and we're letting them go. If you can, imagine a river flowing from the headwaters downstream. Our thoughts are like boats floating along the river with the current. We sink below the current of the river into our spiritual level of consciousness and let the boats float by. Occasionally a flashy boat goes by that grabs our attention. Maybe our stomach growls during the prayer period and we start thinking about what we're going to have for lunch. Next thing we know it, a fresh-baked croissant enters our thoughts. That sure looks good. We can almost smell it. We start thinking maybe we could go to our favorite French bakery later and get one! And then memories of that trip to Paris we took a few years back start coming up. Once we start thinking about a thought it's as if we have gotten into that flashy boat and moved downstream in it. Instead of letting the thought go we let our intention go. That's what we mean by "when engaged with your thoughts."

As long as the thoughts come and go, there's no need to repeat the sacred word. But when we find ourselves riding down the river of thoughts in that flashy boat, we ever so gently lay the sacred word onto that soft ball of cotton. We don't worry about it. We don't try to stop it from happening. We simply return to the sacred word when we notice that our attention is no longer on our intention. We don't use the sacred word as a mantra which is said repeatedly, but we may find ourselves returning to the sacred word many times during a period of Centering Prayer. The reason we don't worry about how many times we return to the sacred word is that every return is teaching us to return to God. By doing this repeatedly in Centering Prayer, we will find ourselves returning to God in daily life.

The word "thoughts" in the Centering Prayer Guidelines is an umbrella term to include any thoughts, perceptions, emotions, body sensations, images, memories, commentaries, and spiritual insights. Anything that comes up that draws our attention away from our intention is called a thought. In your early years of practice, expect to return to the sacred word often. Using your sacred word doesn't mean you're doing anything wrong. When you think about how hectic our world is, how bombarded we are with information, and how far away from nature many of us are, it's no wonder our minds race. Most of us don't notice how chaotic our thoughts are until we stop and listen in silence.

Guideline #4: *At the end of the prayer period, remain in silence with eyes closed for a couple of minutes.*

Because of the busy lives we lead, this may be the most difficult guideline. First, we struggle to carve out time in our day for Centering

Prayer. We may be so overwrought with our "to do" list that we have spent our entire prayer period planning our day and returning to our sacred word. We can't wait for the timer to go off to jump up out of the chair and get started with our list. No matter how chaotic our prayer period may have been, we are still filling up our reservoir with peace and silence. It's worth taking a couple of minutes to recognize this with gratitude. The practice of Centering Prayer brings us into a state different from our normal everyday consciousness. Remaining in silence for a few minutes helps us to return to our ordinary level of consciousness bringing the peace and silence we've experienced into the activity of our day.

Some Practical Points

It is recommended that you practice Centering Prayer twice a day for twenty to thirty minutes, once in the morning and once at midday or the end of the day. Why twenty minutes? It usually takes about that much time to calm down the mind and experience the fruits of the practice. Why twice a day? Usually by the middle or end of the day the reservoir of peace and silence that is being filled by our practice is beginning to become depleted and needs to be refilled again. Imagine you've had a really hard day at work and you come home to children who want your attention. It's difficult to meet anyone else's needs if we are depleted. I've known many people who have used their lunch hour to do their second period of Centering Prayer or ask their family for just twenty minutes when they first get home. Or if dinner must come first, then maybe the whole family has quiet time after dinner.

Depending on the demands of your life it may be difficult at first to add in that second period. If it is, don't worry about it. Don't throw out the whole project because of it. Get a solid footing on the first period of Centering Prayer in the morning and set an intention to do it twice a day. Mary Mrozowski said that it took her three years to regularly do Centering Prayer twice a day. During that time, she had an intention to do it twice a day, and sometimes she did. As I said earlier, energy follows intention, even if it takes some time.

Before you begin each period of Centering Prayer set a timer so that you can let go of thinking about the time. Use a timer that is dependable, so you are not tempted to look at the clock and make sure it's working. Use one that has a soft chime, so it doesn't jar you out of your prayer when it goes off. With the advent of smart phones, we now have many meditation timer apps available. Contemplative Outreach even has one.

Find a spot in your house to pray. I find it so helpful to have a chair where I regularly practice Centering Prayer. The chair has become a comfort to me and sometimes when I'm busy and distracted it calls out to me to come and sit. Make an environment, or perhaps an altar, that is conducive to prayer. I light a candle to signify bringing the light of the Spirit into my heart. I like to wrap up in a prayer shawl, especially in the coolness of the morning. Find a prayer or a reading as a "vestibule" into Centering Prayer. Some people use the Psalms. At times I have used the daily Gospel reading from the lectionary. Lately I've been chanting the prayer that the monks at St. Benedict's use when they start mass in the morning: "Oh God, come to my assistance. Oh Lord, make haste to help me. Glory be to the Father, and to the Son, and to the Holy Spirit, as it was in the beginning, is now, and ever shall be, world without end. Amen." Make this time meaningful and prayerful for you and try different things.

Centering Prayer is a discipline. We call it a practice because it's not something you can just think about. You have to actually do it! No one gets very good at soccer or playing the violin or cooking if they don't practice. It's not really that we are trying to get good at Centering Prayer, but it's a little like what I said earlier about programming. People who are good at a sport are so habituated to every possible situation that their reactions are automatic. They don't have to think about it. I never get up in the morning and think about whether I'm going to do Centering Prayer, but it wasn't always that way. In the beginning I treated it like a discipline, and I was committed to it, and I practiced until it became automatic.

Before proceeding into the material on the CLE program in Part Two of this book, start practicing Centering Prayer for at least twenty minutes once a day with the intention of doing it twice a day. Sometimes it helps people to ease into the second period of prayer by committing to do it for five minutes, gradually increasing the time. You will likely find that eventually you want to increase the time!

PART TWO

Contemplative Living Experience

CHAPTER FOUR

Introduction to the Contemplative Living Experience Program

> *"Christ has no body on earth but yours.*
> *Yours are the eyes with which he looks compassionately on this world.*
> *Yours are the feet with which he walks to do good.*
> *Yours are the hands with which he blesses all the world.*
> *Christ has no body now on earth but yours!"*
> Saint Teresa of Ávila (1515-1582)

WE MAY START OUR JOURNEY INTO CONTEMPLATIVE LIFE WITH AN intention to deepen our relationship with God through a practice of Centering Prayer, but we soon discover that consenting to God's presence and action within brings us to a greater awareness of our human condition and an increased willingness to be transformed. Awakening to our human condition opens us to a greater capacity for compassion for others who are navigating life through their own human condition, whether they are aware of it or not. You can start to see how helpful it is to be on this journey with a group of committed contemplatives when we each awaken to our human condition and have a greater capacity for compassion for others. I have a friend whom I have heard say many times "transformation happens in relationship"—relationship with friends, family, spiritual companions, and relationship with God. Transformation is God's work, not ours, but God always gives us the choice to allow the process of transformation to proceed by our consent.

How do you know you are being transformed? Usually, either you or someone else in your life starts to notice that something has changed, something is different in your daily life, how you approach relationships, conflict, work, chores, loss, emotional turmoil. Transformation is about becoming who you are—not your idea of who you are, but God's idea of who you are. Consenting to be transformed does not mean that life is somehow all of a sudden easy, but we start to realize that we are not alone in this project and may even start to experience the peace that comes from interior silence.

As I posed the question "How do you know you are being transformed?" I was reminded of what I have witnessed myself. I have been watching people being transformed for about twenty years now as I've facilitated classes on *The Spiritual Journey Series* at the Center and in churches around Denver. It takes about nine months to go through all the courses in the video series. As people become committed to a regular practice of Centering Prayer and come together to watch the video series, which provides the conceptual background for the practice, in a group with whom they come to bond and trust, something special transpires. I'm convinced there is nothing the facilitator does to make this happen. It's hard for me to even describe what I have witnessed. People seem to reach deep into their hearts, to that place where God lives in us all. I can see it in their eyes, in how they treat each other, in what they share, in the pain they express, the tears, the reflective silence, the settling down of tension and energy, the gratitude, the love. I can see it in them, I can feel it, and I am affected by it. It touches my heart in a deep way and fills me with gratitude for the opportunity to do this work. In 2015 I was starting my third time of facilitating the Contemplative Living Experience (CLE) program. By then I had facilitated the program enough times that I was familiar with the process and the teachings, and I was more comfortable, less nervous about my role. It gave me the opportunity to stand back and observe. As I did that one Saturday afternoon while the group was working on reflecting and writing, I had that same experience as I did when facilitating *The Spiritual Journey Series* video course. Something is happening here, and I am a witness to it. It's almost as if I could feel the Spirit working the room. God takes us where we can't usually go by ourselves. Where that is will be different for each of us but when we do it together, we are all uplifted by the experience. It reminds me of what Jesus says in Matthew 18:20, "For where two or three are gathered in my name, there am I in the midst of them." This is the experience that led me to write this book and help spread the word about this program and the gift of transformation we each are given when we consent to this journey. Let's look at how this program can dispose us to the gift.

The Contemplative Living Experience Program

How do we move from having a contemplative practice to living a contemplative life? Paradoxically, we do this by learning contemplative practices that complement Centering Prayer, our foundation. In Chapter Three, I talked about treating Centering Prayer as a discipline that I had to put some intention behind in order to get to a place where I didn't have to think about or decide whether I was going to do it today. I practiced until it became automatic for me to do it without thinking about it. When we can do the same thing with other contemplative practices, one day we find ourselves living a contemplative life without our knowing exactly how it came about. The CLE program is designed to instill discipline, commitment, and practice into daily life by offering contemplative practices to increase our awareness of the presence of God within us and within all of life. I hope you know it's no accident that you picked up this book. We each come to the decision to explore contemplative life for our own reasons. Often what draws us is a longing for something more from our spiritual practice or for a deeper experience in our relationship with God. Because of that longing, we respond to an invitation from the Spirit.

If you're using this book as part of a group experience, it's important to understand that we're each on a unique journey and the experience will be different for each of us. Some of us may find it difficult to share our experiences in a group, but sharing is the greatest gift we can give each other as we journey together. Not only do we benefit personally from sharing, but we never know when the Spirit will use our words to touch the heart of another. Trust that God will give your group what it needs to make this journey together.

There are many paths to spiritual awakening. The CLE program offers one path, a path that is based on a foundation of Centering Prayer, upon which a variety of other practices are built. We explore these prayer practices in the context of growing in awareness of the presence of God within and opening ourselves more and more to God's transforming action in our lives.

Intention and consent are words we often use when talking about Centering Prayer and other spiritual practices, so it is important to know the difference. Intention is a desire of the will, and consent is the action that manifests the intention. For example, your intention may be to deepen your awareness of God's presence in your life. Your consent is making a commitment to the CLE program and following its suggestions for practice. Intention is only the beginning. We must follow through with our consent. Consent is the action that manifests the intention, but it doesn't end there. We have to keep consenting by being as trusting, as aware, and as open as we can be, and by being faithful to the prayer practices and other suggested activities. Gradually we start to integrate the prayer practices into the ordinary activities of daily life, which is where we truly meet God.

The CLE program is a process of formation that leads to transformation if we consent to it. I invite you to trust the process. This is a journey of the heart that is not over at the end of nine months or at the end of this book. We are opening ourselves to cultivating new habits and new ways of looking at life and living that go far beyond this program. The CLE program is designed to help us live with greater awareness. In fact, awareness is the thread that weaves through this entire experience. Most of us live our lives unaware of what we are experiencing in the present moment. Our thoughts are usually somewhere else, either reliving the past or planning the future. God is present in each moment, but if we're not awake to that reality, we might miss living in the freedom God intends for us. The spiritual practices contained in the CLE program help us to wake up and live in the present moment with greater freedom and increased intentionality, aware of God's presence and action in our lives.

The original CLE program is intended to be experienced over a period of nine months. The metaphor of the human gestation phase may be obvious but is nonetheless powerful. Our purpose is formation in contemplative life, consenting to being transformed by God. It is a birthing process that brings us to new life with greater freedom to live and love as God intends for us. "I will give you a new heart, and a new spirit I will put in you..." (Ezekiel 36:26).

Part One of the CLE program, as you've already read and experienced, contains two foundational teachings. The first is a short explanation of Father Thomas's teaching on the human condition. I say short even though it's many pages long because he spends about seven hours in videotaped conferences expounding on what we all experience but are usually unable to articulate. He takes the teaching that the mystics throughout the ages knew and taught and puts it in modern language with the help of modern science—anthropology, psychology, sociology, and neuroscience. This teaching helps us to understand why we are drawn to contemplative life and what is happening to us as we

Contemplative Life

experience the process of transformation. The second foundational teaching is the Centering Prayer method and purpose. I find that no matter how long I practice Centering Prayer it always helps me to go back to the basics as a reminder of what I'm doing and why.

The flow of the program is towards increased intentionality. The practices in Chapters Five, Six, and Seven—the beginning of what I call "the practice chapters"—help us see how we actively encounter God in our everyday life. We will be invited to recognize that the emptiness and longing we feel is truly God's presence within us urging us to a new and different relationship. We will be invited to wake up to God's presence and action permeating every aspect of our lives, and to notice where our human condition seems to separate us from God. We call these practices external because often what blocks us in our relationship with God is how we react to our environment—to the people, places, things, and events we encounter in daily life.

In these first of the practice chapters (Five, Six, and Seven) we focus on deepening our interior prayer life and growing in our awareness of God's presence within us and among us. The practices taught in these chapters are Logging, Spiritual Reading, Lectio Divina, the Active Prayer, and the Welcoming Prayer. As you learn new practices, we ask you to continue your commitment to a Centering Prayer practice twice a day. You don't have to add all these new practices at once, but eventually, you'll be using them all regularly. Adding new practices gradually over time will help you to integrate them into your life. It's important to remember that the purpose of this program is to practice until the practices become more automatic and you don't have to think about them so much.

We pause after these first few practice chapters to focus on cultivating interior silence. We take the opportunity to reflect on the program and practices we've developed so far, ask ourselves how well we're integrating the practices into daily life, and assess where we are in our understanding of what it means to be a contemplative or live a contemplative life. We learn about Rest and Sabbath-Keeping. Resting is about reflecting on our lives with the inclusion of all these practices and noticing how our awareness of God's presence within us and among us has grown. We also explore what it means to rest in the midst of activity and rest from the activity of the false self. Sabbath-Keeping is a practice that has gone by the wayside for a lot of people, and we ask you to invite this sacred time into your life in whatever way is meaningful for you. For some it is time in solitude, for others it's time with family or friends. It may or may not include public worship. Sabbath-Keeping is a way of being intentional about setting aside time in our lives to rest in God. It is a time of honoring the holy and tending to "higher concerns."

Following this time of integration and rest, our movement turns inward. The practices in Chapters Nine, Ten, and Eleven bring to our consciousness what is blocking our relationship with God, with ourselves, and with others. These practices are internal because we hold things within our body, mind, and spirit that block relationships. It is often not so much what happens to us externally that blocks us as much as it is our perceptions, thoughts, and feelings.

The CLE program helps us move towards increased intentionality not only in our spiritual life but also in the healing of relationships. In the first part of the program, we learn about our human condition with its false-self motivations, and we begin to grow in relationship with God and with others. As the practices we have learned so far start to make a chink in the armor of our emotional defenses, we become more in touch with our true self. We keep in mind what we covered in the chapter on the human condition, what Father Thomas says in *The Mystery of Christ*:

> "Unless we assume responsibility for our emotional programs [false-self motivation] on the unconscious level and take appropriate measures to change them, we will be influenced by them to the end of our lives."[21]

This may be a point where we start to experience a deeper humility and vulnerability. In this program we learn to make choices in keeping with our true self.

Moving into Chapters Nine, Ten, and Eleven, we focus on Contemplative Discernment and Forgiveness. We learn a process of waiting on God and how to discern God's will. Once we have learned the discernment practice, we begin to use it to uncover and start to heal our addictions, attachments, and aversions, which when left unhealed tend to interfere in our relationship with ourselves, God, and others. We all need to forgive certain people in our lives, and intuitively we know that when we don't forgive, we are in a prison of our own making. Most of us don't know how to forgive in a way that truly sets us free. The Forgiveness Prayer is a practice that opens the door to freedom.

The last part of the CLE program is about integrating the external and internal and creating our unique contemplative life plan or what we call a Contemplative Rule of Life, borrowing from the various "Rule of Life" practices in the Christian tradition. We want to remember that this program is about God's work in us. We can't do anything to bring about our own transformation. It is only our willingness to open ourselves to God's work within us that will release us from the shackles of the false self and bring us to the freedom of who God is calling us to be. It's about the freedom to experience ourselves as God sees us, created in God's image and likeness. That freedom comes when we live with greater consciousness and increased intentionality.

As the CLE program comes to an end, we reflect on what we have already integrated and where we might want to focus more of our attention. We start with contemplative service, asking ourselves what the point is of having a Centering Prayer practice and living this contemplative life. It's an important question because the more we consent to God's presence and action within, the more we are changed by this journey. We start to work on creating a Contemplative Rule of Life. By this time, we have learned how important intention is on the spiritual journey and our Contemplative Rule of Life is about how we intend to live our lives going forward. At the close of the CLE program, we make a commitment to contemplative life, however we have set it out in our unique Contemplative Rule of Life, knowing that it will change as we grow and change on our journey.

Contemplative Living Experience Program Formation Guide

Ideally, you'll use this book to go through the CLE program with an experienced facilitator over a period of nine months, learning, practicing, and integrating contemplative practices into your contemplative life. Most people haven't had the opportunity to take the CLE program in person because the two versions of the program are only offered in New York and Denver. This book is designed to offer people the experience of the CLE program wherever you live. You'll benefit most from the experience and teaching of this program by following some simple guidelines:

1. If you're not already practicing Centering Prayer for at least twenty minutes twice a day, set an intention to start doing that.
2. Don't hurry through the material. Read for formation rather than for information (see Chapter Five on Spiritual Reading).

Give yourself time to reflect on the material. And, most importantly, give yourself time to engage deeply in the spiritual practices. The end of each chapter contains a Going Deeper section with recommendations for your practice for that month or however much time you spend with that chapter. Follow the recommendations to the best of your ability.

3. Don't modify the practices. These practices have been taught and practiced this way for many years. Trust that the people who, alongside Father Thomas, created the practices under the guidance of the Holy Spirit have something to offer you that you may not have experienced before. Sometimes the desire to change a practice is a sign of resistance to the transformation it's designed to foster in your life.

4. If possible, go through this book with a small group, perhaps a prayer group or a small group community at your church. If you don't have access to a group, it will still be helpful for you to have a place where you can share your experience with either a spiritual director or a spiritual friend or companion. (If you can do this with a small group, you will find instructions for group spiritual direction, which in the CLE program we call Holy Listening Circles, in Chapter Five.)

5. Trust that if you were attracted to this book the Spirit is calling you to something more. What that is may not be evident at first, but most likely will be revealed with time. Working through this material and following the recommendations for the practices is a big commitment that will bear fruit.

6. Keep a journal or notebook where you can keep track of your experiences, insights, frustrations, and awarenesses. You can use a paper notebook or find a digital way to capture what you're experiencing. You will appreciate having it to look back over. Having your work in one place and being faithful to using your notebook will prove invaluable as you progress. At the end of the program, it's amazing to look back at where you started and how far you've come.

7. Each chapter contains a "spiritual counsel" which you'll find in the Going Deeper section. The spiritual counsel section includes short reflections, quotes, and Scripture readings related to the topic of the month. Bookmark and frequently check in with the spiritual counsel associated with the chapter you're

working through, as it is meant to provide you with wisdom and encouragement along the spiritual journey. You may wish to keep the spiritual counsel close to where you do Centering Prayer so you can use it as a vestibule to prayer or as a prayer itself.
8. Each chapter contains suggested reflection questions in the Going Deeper section to help you deepen your understanding and experience of the material and practices contained in that chapter. You can use your reflections for sharing in your Holy Listening Circle if you are working in a group, or to share with your spiritual director, friend, or companion.
9. Also in the Going Deeper section in each chapter are recommendations for integrating the practices into your life. In the beginning you may need to be intentional about following the recommendations as you adjust to the substantial time commitment these practices require. As you progress in the program you will find that incorporating the practices becomes more automatic.

Going Deeper

Welcome to the first of many Going Deeper sections. Here are some suggestions for practices and exercises that will help you more fully experience the transformation this formation program is designed to foster:

1. Spend a few minutes reflecting and writing about your image of God as it is today.
2. In your notebook write the date at the top of the page and this question:

What are you committing to and what is it you would like to see change in your life as a result of participating in the CLE program? Give yourself some time to reflect on this question and then write your answer. You will be asked to look back at your reflection at the end of the program.

CHAPTER FIVE

Awareness of God's Presence and Action: Logging and Spiritual Reading

"And behold, I am with you always, until the end of the age."
Matthew 28:20

WE BEGIN THE CONTEMPLATIVE LIVING EXPERIENCE (CLE) PROGRAM by cultivating awareness of God's presence and action within us. We may know intellectually, or we may have been taught that God is ever-present in every moment, in everything, in all of life. And yet, most of the angst we experience in life comes from a feeling of separation from God. We may first become aware of this feeling of separation by experiencing a deep longing for something more, often without knowing what that something might be. Perhaps what we're experiencing is God's longing for us, calling us to awareness of the divine union we already have. This chapter introduces two contemplative practices that will assist us in expanding our awareness—Logging and Spiritual Reading.

When the CLE program is offered in person the first gathering usually involves a group of people who don't know each other and yet have the common experience of a Centering Prayer practice, a desire to go deeper in their relationship with God, and a willingness to form community. Much of what we are exploring together is what draws us into this desire to go deeper and to form community. It is in the sharing of this mutual exploration that begins the formation of trust and a bond that endures long after the program is completed. I have watched this happen with many groups who are naturally tentative at first, but soon learn the value of embarking on this journey with others. While this book is structured in such a way that you can work through and learn the contemplative practices on your own, I encourage you, if you haven't already found a group to journey with, to consider forming a group with others who share your desire to discover what it means to live a more deeply contemplative life. This could be a prayer group you already belong to, a group through your church, or a group of friends who are spiritual seekers.

When meeting with a small group we have found it particularly helpful to have "Sharing Guidelines" that all group members can agree to, helping to establish trust within the group. The following are suggested guidelines which you may feel free to modify to meet the needs of your group.

Sharing Guidelines
1. Allow each person to contribute, leaving a few respectful moments of silence between one speaker and the next.
1. Each person's sharing is wholly and unquestionably valid and is offered as a gift of trust to the others.
2. Since this is a journey of the heart, not an exercise of the head, we don't interrupt, discuss, or "correct" anyone's views nor do we offer advice.
3. When we open our heart's experience to each other in trust, we are entering on holy ground, where there is only a response of loving acceptance.
4. On this holy ground, God-in-you is listening to God-in-the-other.
5. All should come away from the sharing with a deepened sense of their own unique value before God and within the group.
6. The person facilitating the sharing will speak for all in acknowledging each person's contribution, usually with a simple "thank you."

Stepping Stones: a Guided Meditation

Whether your experience with the CLE program is self-guided, led by a facilitator, or within a small group, we begin with a guided meditation called "Stepping Stones," which helps us to see how God has been present in the people, events, and circumstances of our life. This guided meditation begins with a relaxation exercise to help us enter a meditative state. At the end of the guided meditation, you will be asked to do some writing from your experience while you maintain this meditative state. You may wish to record the guided meditation by reading it aloud using one of the many free voice recorder apps available for smart phones and then quietly listen and respond. If you're not able to do that, read the guided meditation slowly and quietly and follow the instructions as you read them.

With your notebook (either paper or digital) handy, begin the guided meditation as follows:

Take some slow deep breaths, slowly breathing in and out three or four times. Begin to focus your attention on your body. Take your mind's eye to the top of your head and begin to relax your scalp. You can silently say the word "relax" to let your body know that now is the time to relax. Relax your scalp and the muscles of your face and jaw. Bring your focus, your inner eye, to the muscles of your face and begin to relax the muscles of your face and jaw.

Now bring your attention to your throat area, softly and gently using the word "relax." Take your inner eye and bring your focus to the back of your neck and silently and gently say the word relax.

Now bring your attention to your shoulders. Relax your shoulders and your upper arms. Let them hang loose. Relax. Keep your inner eye focused like a laser beam—powerful, penetrating, a great light. Bring that focus to your lower arms and relax.

Now bring your attention and focus to your back and abdomen. Relax the muscles of your back and abdomen. Bring your focus and attention to your upper legs relaxing your thigh muscles—front and back, gently relaxing the muscles past your knees, into your calves. Relax your ankles.

Now allow any stress and discomfort to leave your body through your toes, becoming very relaxed.

Now take your mind's eye to the area of your heart, entering deep within the recesses of your heart. Picture yourself walking along a passageway that is dimly lit but warm and safe. Proceed along the passageway. At the end of the passageway notice a doorway filled with light. As you approach the doorway filled with light, give yourself permission to cross the threshold and step into the light. Allow yourself to stand for a moment surrounded by this light.

Now continue walking and notice that you have entered a room, a large comfortable room. Look around. Take it all in. You are still surrounded by the light. The light is in the room. You notice a chair in the room which seems to beckon you. Approach the chair and take a seat. Feel yourself seated in the chair. Notice a table beside you and on it is a photo album with your name on it. Look at it for a moment, then pick it up, holding it on your lap. When you open the album, you will see a series of photos containing images of people, events, and places of significance to you from your past. Look at each page carefully and intentionally, asking the Spirit what it is about the picture you need to remember and then briefly jot down in your notebook the image or memory. How was God present to you in that image? How is the Spirit prompting you? You may have ten or twelve pictures to reflect on. Remain in the meditative state as you write, allowing the Spirit to guide your writing. Turn the pages in the photo album slowly, remaining in the meditative state.

When you've finished looking at the photo album, prepare to leave this room, this sacred space. Imagine yourself placing the album back on the table then getting up from the chair slowly and carefully. In your mind's eye, begin to walk towards the doorway through which you originally came. Move slowly and deliberately, the light still surrounding you. Cross the threshold of the doorway and begin to walk back along the passageway that is dim and safe and warm. Move back up through the recesses of your heart, up to today, to the present moment. Pause for a few moments as you reacquaint yourself with your surroundings.

The purpose of this guided meditation is to become aware of times in your life when God's presence was with you whether you knew it at the time or not. Feelings may have surfaced. Images may have come up from your unconscious, perhaps with some unresolved feelings, and you may experience some of those feelings right now. Be with whatever feelings, thoughts, and images you have now, conscious that God is with you. Spend some time looking over what you have written and reflect on God's presence in your life, how the Spirit is speaking to you now about those images or experiences.

Throughout the CLE program, we intentionally deepen our awareness of God's presence in the present moment, connecting to that part of us that has always been one with the divine.

Spiritual Direction

One of our long-time teachers at Contemplative Outreach in Denver, Margaret Johnson, taught a class she called "The Art of Listening." She introduced the following quote in her class: "How hard it is to listen… how healing to be heard."[22] Margaret wasn't sure who the author was, but when she saw this quote in the bulletin of St. John's Episcopal Cathedral in Denver it made an impression on her, probably because it rang true for her. Think about this quote for a few moments now and see if it resonates for you. Have you ever had an experience where

Contemplative Life

you were talking about something from your heart and another person simply listened and you felt heard? How was that experience for you?

When our spiritual life presents challenges it can be helpful to share our experiences with others, whether it be with one other person or with a small group. Spiritual direction is one way of companioning each other on the journey. If you're working through this book with a small group, ideally you'll have an opportunity be part of a Holy Listening Circle which is what we call group spiritual direction in the CLE program. If a small group is not available to you, finding a spiritual director or a spiritual companion to share with will be helpful. If you belong to a church community, check with your pastor or the church office for recommendations. You may be able to find a spiritual director through your local Contemplative Outreach chapter at www.contemplativeoutreach.org. Or you can check the Spiritual Directors International web site at www.sdicompanions.org. Another option would be to ask a friend who is a spiritual seeker.

But what exactly is spiritual direction? At its essence, it's prayer. It starts with the desire to be attentive to our spiritual life. Its purpose is to assist us in becoming more attuned to God's presence in order to respond more fully to that presence in all of life. The focus of spiritual direction is our relationship with God as it is reflected in and challenged by all aspects of life. It's sometimes called spiritual guidance, spiritual friendship, or spiritual companioning. It's different from therapy or counseling, which deal primarily with problem areas of our life in order to bring a healthy resolution to some of life's issues. Spiritual direction is concerned with finding and responding to God, sometimes in the midst of pain or disorder as well as in the context of normal everyday life. Solving problems or issues is not the primary focus of spiritual direction, although sometimes by working with a spiritual director we discover a resolution to a problem or issue. The spiritual director is only the facilitator of the process and may ask questions, offer challenges, suggestions, or support as seems called for by the Spirit. Your prayerful openness to the Spirit, along with that of your spiritual director, determines whatever insights are uncovered or the course of action your discernment takes.

How do we discern the Spirit? By deep listening, sacred listening, or holy listening, or what author and spiritual guide Sister Joyce Rupp calls "generous listening." If we remember what Father Thomas says about God's first language being silence, discerning the Spirit is most often and most assuredly heard in the silence. John Philip Newell, known for his work with Celtic spirituality, suggests that we listen for the heartbeat of God within ourselves, within one another, and within the earth. Pause for a moment and reflect on these depictions of spiritual direction before we move into how to do it.

Listening is a skill we can learn. It requires a decision we make to be present, to pay attention. We put aside our agenda, thoughts, and opinions to focus on the other. We also put aside our desire to shape or control the other, to judge, or to give advice. It calls for the presence of our true self.

Spiritual direction calls for even more in the way of listening—we listen more deeply for who we are in God. We bring not only our attention, but our intention to clear away the inner debris that blocks our awareness of the flow of the Divine Indwelling. We rest in the uncertainty or the "unknowing" of the mystery. We open more fully to the divine energy that is always available in every moment. This deep, sacred, holy listening is prayerful listening.

Generally, in the Holy Listening Circles, the group sits in a circle and one person is designated facilitator and is primarily the timekeeper. The group starts with a short prayer and a few minutes of silence. Then one person shares what's on their heart for the designated amount of time, usually about five minutes. The rest of the group listens in silence. At the end of the sharing the whole group sits in silence for a few minutes, listening for anything that arises from the Spirit in response to the sharing. Then each person responds to the one who shared with an insight, a question, or even a Scripture passage that came to them in the silence. After another few minutes of silence, the next person shares what's on their heart. The process continues until each person has had the opportunity to share.

One of the greatest benefits of engaging in spiritual direction in a group is the variety of perspectives offered both in what is shared and in the responses and questions provided by the group. We learn so much from each other, often by discovering how deeply we're connected even when our personalities, interests, and experiences are so varied. A collective wisdom begins to develop in the group when the members commit to the group process. Relying on the group process and trusting in God promotes a depth of sharing that we may not find in other groups. This type of group is grounded in the shared desire for listening and responding to the Spirit. Our mutual willingness and openness in this desire establishes trust very quickly. The instructions for Holy Listening Circles follow in the section "Holy Listening Circles Method."

My first experience with group spiritual direction was in the year following my two-year spiritual direction program through Benet Hill Monastery. They offered us, as an experiment, a year of peer group supervision facilitated by one of our teachers. We used the model of group spiritual direction. The purpose of peer supervision is not to talk about our clients and their problems, but to talk about and reflect on our personal experience in working with these clients. Using the model of group spiritual direction with the focus on listening and responding to the Spirit in the sharing and the silence helped each of us grow personally as well as in the way we approached spiritual direction. I had what I thought of as a particularly difficult client who was diagnosed with a mental illness. I wasn't sure she was appropriate for spiritual direction and perhaps needed some type of therapy or treatment. I struggled to work with her without judging her and felt inadequate to help her. Bringing this to peer supervision helped me to see my underlying fear of not knowing what to do about her mental illness, when my "job" as a spiritual director was to offer her spiritual companionship. When I could see this, I stopped trying to figure out what to do about her mental illness and started listening to her. The spiritual direction encounter with her changed for both of us after that. What was valuable about this experience for me was getting in touch with my fear, which was getting in the way of being helpful to this client. Initially, I couldn't see this, but the group—with the help of the Spirit in the silence—could.

As we enter into deep listening in the Holy Listening Circles that are part of the CLE program we ask participants to reflect on the words of Father Tom Nelson, a Vincentian priest who regularly celebrated a contemplative mass at the Center in Denver. A homily he gave about listening guides our listening in this sacred circle of trust:

> "In every moment of time listening—especially to God, but also to another person—there is a mysterious moment in which the one who listens steps out from behind a fortress of self-concern and dwells silently in the presence of the one who speaks. This is a moment of great risk and great courage, because it invites us into a different way of being/living in the world; and

over time we may cease being people who listen and become listening people, people whose very being is shaped by the posture of listening. This is the posture of the servant—of a life lived ever more fully in the spirit of love."

Whether you're doing spiritual direction individually or with a group, it will help you to spend time listening first to God in the silence and then listening to others—either a spiritual director, your small group, or a spiritual friend. Giving voice to your reflections and intuitions often leads to discovery of something your inner wisdom is trying to convey.

Holy Listening Circles Method[23]

1. Short prayer followed by two minutes of silence
   Begin with a short prayer welcoming the Spirit into the circle and into our hearts. Allow two minutes of silence while each participant brings their attention to the present moment and lets go of any agenda they may have brought with them. At the end of the two minutes the facilitator invites whoever is ready (the presenter) to begin sharing.
2. Sharing by one person for five minutes
   In each chapter, reflection questions are offered in the Going Deeper section that may be used for sharing during your Holy Listening Circle. The presenter may choose to use those reflections or whatever is on their heart.
3. Silence for two minutes
   At the end of the sharing the group goes into two minutes of silence, making room for and listening for God. With practice, we begin to experience the stirrings of the Spirit, letting go of our own biases or usual ways of responding.
4. Response by group for five minutes
   Our response consists of questions, comments, or even a Scripture passage that came up in the silence prompted by the Spirit. Our questions and comments are not about any desire or agenda we may think will be "helpful" to the presenter. We are simply responding with what stirred in us in the silence.
5. Silence for two minutes

In this final two minutes of silence, the group prays for the presenter. The presenter may want to make some notes of any insights or relevant comments that came up.
6. Facilitator offers a blessing for the presenter
Before transitioning to the next presenter, the facilitator offers a blessing for the presenter.
7. Repeat steps one through six for each participant
No one is required to share, but the experience of listening and being heard helps to promote trust in the group and a willingness to participate.
8. Group reflection on the time together for three minutes
The group spends a few minutes reflecting on the experience, not to analyze or judge, but to notice where God has touched each participant and the group as a whole. The group may also assess the process experienced in this time together for what was most helpful and what may have impeded the flow of the Spirit.

In the first session of your Holy Listening Circle while the group is getting to know each other, spend the time introducing yourself to the group by talking a little bit about your spiritual journey or anything you discovered about yourself in the Stepping Stones Guided Meditation. You also may use any reflection that particularly spoke to you from the spiritual counsel or the reflection questions in the Going Deeper section at the end of the chapter. If you are doing individual spiritual direction or talking with a spiritual friend, you may use the same guidelines.

Logging

The first contemplative practice we learn in the CLE program is Logging. It is a simple tool that helps us develop greater awareness in our lives. Jesuit priest and author Anthony de Mello describes how to cultivate awareness in a very direct way:

> "…Watch yourself. When you talk to someone, are you aware of it or are you simply identifying with it? When you got angry with somebody, were you aware that you were angry or were you simply identifying with your anger? Later, when you had time, did you study your experience and attempt to understand it? Where did

it come from? What brought it on? I don't know of any other way to awareness. You only change what you understand. What you do not understand and are not aware of, you repress. You don't change. But when you understand it, it changes."[24]

Awareness is the first step towards changing or healing from habits and tendencies that no longer serve us. Most of us want to become more aware of how and why we react to life, but wanting to be more aware doesn't make us more aware. We need to develop practices like Logging to help us grow in awareness.

Logging is a form of expressive writing, a practice where we write about an experience from our day for ten to fifteen minutes. It is different from journaling or keeping a diary because it's designed to help us better understand and deal with thoughts, memories, worries, commentaries, emotions—usually afflictive emotions—and the resulting behaviors. Over time, a daily practice of Logging will uncover patterns that we were previously unaware of because our motivation is often hidden in the unconscious.

So often we don't take the time to stop and reflect on what is going on in our lives. When our thoughts, emotions, and behaviors proceed unchecked or unexamined it's as if we have no control over what happens to us and how we respond. But we do have the ability to be responsible and accountable for our emotional life. I first quoted Father Thomas from *The Mystery of Christ* in the section on the human condition in Chapter Two. I'd like to revisit this quote now because I have found it to be invaluable in helping me to understand how important it is for me to wake up to being responsible for my emotional life. In it, Father Thomas says:

> "The Gospel calls us forth to full responsibility for our emotional life. We tend to blame other people or situations for the turmoil we experience. In actual fact, upsetting emotions prove beyond any doubt that the problem is in us. If we do not assume responsibility for our emotional programs on the unconscious level and take measures to change them, we will be influenced by them to the end of our lives."[25]

The purpose of Logging is to bring into awareness how our

Contemplative Life

emotional life is being influenced by the emotional programs related to the human condition on the unconscious level. We often think our emotional programs only relate to what we sometimes think of as negative emotions—anger, sadness, fear, worry, grief. Logging also helps to surface from the unconscious or bring into our awareness how our so-called positive emotions—happiness, joy, pride—can be related to our emotional programs. For example, when we are feeling good, proud, or affirmed we may be reacting to our needs and woundedness from the sensation (esteem and affection) energy center. Logging can help to surface whatever patterns we are experiencing whether we think of our emotional reactions as negative or positive.

The method for Logging is very simple; the challenge is to put it into practice on a daily basis. With our Centering Prayer practice, we often talk about intention and consent. Our intention is to consent to God's presence and action within. Intention is a desire of the will and that desire comes from God. Consent is the action that manifests the intention. We may have a worthwhile intention, but if we don't consent—if we don't take action—nothing happens. The difference is between simply having a desire and actually taking some action to manifest the desire. We may have a desire to become more physically fit, but if we don't consent to exercising and following a healthy eating plan, our intention becomes merely a wish. Contemplative practices like Logging are part of the CLE program because they help us continue to consent—to keep saying yes—in daily life to God's presence and action.

Logging Method

1. Start your Logging practice with prayer, inviting the Spirit to be with you and to inspire you to recall any events from the day where afflictive emotions or commentaries were triggered, or where you regret something you did or said, or sometimes even thought. Also be open to noticing experiences of positive affect and whether they are reactions to esteem and affection needs.
2. Spend a few minutes reflecting, either in the evening about that day, or in the morning about the previous day.
3. This is not a diary or a chronological accounting of your day. You don't need to recount the whole day, just what the Spirit seems to be calling your attention to.
4. Write the date at the top of the page.

5. In just a few sentences, write down any event that surfaces and the impact or emotional response.
6. Write only the facts and leave out any drama.
7. Be honest with yourself. This is only for you to read.
8. Refrain from using pronouns, especially don't give center stage to the self-important "I."
9. Don't worry about grammar, punctuation, spelling, chronological order, or doing it "right."
10. Refrain from analyzing, judging or interpreting. Especially don't judge the writing. Be the observer or witness and be as objective as you can.
11. At the end of the week or month review what you have written and see if you notice any patterns. The false self with its unconscious motivations is often revealed when you review your Logging and start to see patterns.

Be aware of the common tendency to slip into journaling instead of Logging. For example, when journaling you might write something like this:

> *I saw Jane at the grocery store today. She said hello but kept walking and didn't stop to talk to me. That really made me mad. She's been cool towards me ever since we were at a meeting together and I didn't agree with her viewpoint. I don't understand why that would have made her mad. It wasn't personal. I still want to be friends with her but not if she's going to treat me like this...*

When Logging, you might write this:

> *Saw Jane at the grocery store. Said hello but didn't talk. Felt angry, confused, irritated. Worried all day.*

Can you see the difference between just writing the facts versus including other extraneous information that may be feeding the emotional programs or triggering unconscious reactions? Stating the facts helps us stay in the truth. When we engage in a lot of drama around events that we perceive are happening *to* us we tend to create stories and we think the stories are the truth. They often are not reality, but are perceptions, projections and illusions of the false self.

I remember reading a book many years ago called *What to Say When You Talk to Yourself* by Shad Helmstetter. I was intrigued by it because at the time I didn't think of my thoughts as "talking to myself" and I didn't know that with practice I could stop, or at least minimize, my obsessive thinking, or what Father Thomas calls "commentaries" or "old tapes." Logging is a discipline that helps develop new habits of refraining from commenting on and judging everything, or at least helps bring a greater awareness to how prolific our commentaries and judgments are so we can begin to make different choices. What was previously unconscious, by coming into our awareness, now becomes conscious and gives us the ability to let go and be freer. Rather than putting so much energy into keeping the false self intact, we begin to awaken to who God created us to be.

Spiritual Reading

In the next chapter we will be learning how to practice Lectio Divina, an ancient contemplative prayer practice that is often called "praying with Scripture." But first I'd like to introduce the practice of Spiritual Reading, which is similar to Lectio Divina but uses spiritual books other than Scripture. Many significant spiritual books have been written as a result of the author's Lectio Divina practice. For example, much of Father Thomas's teaching in the books he has written refers to Scripture passages as he interprets them. When he talks about the people and events in Scripture it's as if he knew these people, knew what they were thinking and feeling, and may have even actually been there! Of course, his ability to teach and write in this way comes from his lifelong practice of praying with Scripture—reading or listening, reflecting, responding and resting in God.

The same Spirit who inspired the writers of Scripture inspires the writers of other spiritual books. That same Spirit is also alive within us inspiring us as we read and pray with the material. The key to this practice comes from the teaching of M. Robert Mulholland, Jr., in his book *Shaped by the Word*.[26] Mulholland helps us to understand the difference between reading for formation (meaning spiritual development) and for information, which is our normal way of reading anything we might pick up—the newspaper, a book, a set of instructions. When we read for information we read from start to finish, as quickly as we can, and we are trying to master or control the material. We use our intellectual faculties of analyzing, judging, and critical thinking. Spiritual Reading, or reading for formation, is different. We read and respond with our hearts rather than with our rational faculties. We listen for the inspiration of the Spirit in the reading. Just as we talked about listening for God in the silence in spiritual direction, we listen for God in the reading. How is God speaking to me in these words? How do I feel about what I am reading? What am I feeling deep within? How am I being affected by what I am hearing? Why do I feel this way? You don't need to answer these questions, just listen and wait for a response.

In Spiritual Reading, our reading and listening are more in-depth. We allow the passage to open multiple layers of meaning. We're not so concerned with how much we read as with how the Spirit is guiding us in the reading and listening. Our approach to the material and the experience is humble, detached and receptive.

Spiritual Reading Method

1. Choose a spiritual book that attracts you. A great book for Spiritual Reading, which can also be a companion to the experience you go through in this book, is *Into the Silent Land* by Martin Laird. (This is the book we use for Spiritual Reading in the CLE program.)
2. Choose a comfortable, quiet place where you will be without distractions, perhaps the chair you use for Centering Prayer.
3. Bring your awareness to the Spirit who is always with you and in you.
4. Pick a short passage, a few sentences, a paragraph or two.
5. Read slowly and with the intention of being open to whatever attracts you or stands out to you in the reading.
6. Don't hurry. When something seems to stand out to you in the text, stop reading and spend some time reflecting on these or other questions:
   How is God speaking to me in these words?
   How do I feel about what I am reading?
   What am I feeling deep within?
   How am I being affected by what I am hearing?
   Why do I feel this way?

7. You may want to go back and reread from where you started. Take your time.
8. Notice if any prayer rises up in you, anything you want to express to God about what you are reading or your experience.
9. Take a few moments to rest in the experience, in the silence.

Going Deeper

In order to fully integrate the teachings this book offers and experience what contemplative life can be for you, you need to "go deeper" and make a commitment to do the exercises and practices. One of the things I often tell people when I'm teaching these practices is that doing the practice teaches you how to do the practice. We can provide some basic instruction, but the real learning comes when you do the practices with the intention of being guided by the Holy Spirit. When the practices become more automatic, they become prayer because our intention is always to consent to God's presence and action within and in our daily lives. The only way they become automatic is by doing them over and over. You won't like all the practices and you won't want to incorporate all of them into your prayer life, but because it is so natural to be resistant to something new you won't really understand the value of a practice unless you do it over a period of time. No one is perfect and nobody does the practices perfectly or exactly as recommended. Just do your best!

When we do the program in person, the facilitators participate in all the exercises and practices along with the rest of the group. At the beginning of one of the sessions we taught in Denver, I reflected on what my intention for the program would be. I thought to myself, "I always set an intention to do the practices exactly as recommended and never succeed!" But this time I gave myself permission to participate in the program "imperfectly" and not feel guilty about it. When I shared this with the group there was much laughter in the room, but I could also feel a big exhale that no one would be expected to be perfect. I tell you this not to let you off the hook, but to encourage you to do your best and not be hard on yourself if you aren't perfect.

The Going Deeper section of each chapter contains a spiritual counsel comprised of short statements, quotes, or Scripture passages related to the topics contained in the chapters. Most of the material contained in this program has been handed down, almost as an oral tradition, from the creators of the original Nine-Month Course to those of us who came later. And so, the source of some of the statements in the spiritual counsel is unknown. Just know and trust that the spiritual counsels have offered sustenance and encouragement to many people over all the years this program has been offered. I recommend that after you become familiar with the information in each chapter, take some time to read through the spiritual counsel section. And then as you begin to work on the practices for that chapter, remember to peruse the spiritual counsel from time to time. You won't relate to all the statements or quotes, but a few will likely be very meaningful to you, and perhaps different ones on different days. Think of them as inspirational messages to assist you to persevere with the practices and grasp the deeper meaning of the topics.

Spiritual Counsel

1. God is present and revealed to us in many ways: uniquely in Scripture and the sacraments, yet also profoundly through people, creation, events, service, spiritual books, insights, experiences and in other ways. Because of Christ's Incarnation, God is infinitely present to us, yet because of the human condition, we are not always attentive to God's presence. "Speak for your servant is listening" (1 Samuel 3:10).
2. In addition to being attentive to God's presence in us, be aware of and receptive to God's *action* in our lives. God's action is one of healing, purification, and transformation where our life experiences are not isolated events of suffering or joy, failure or accomplishment, sickness or health. Rather, we embrace another dimension of meaning in the divine activity of healing, purification, and transformation and we are changed, moment by ordinary moment.
3. God acts in our lives by inviting us to be aware of aspects of *our* human condition, *our* dark side, *our* brokenness, *our* hidden agenda and motivation, and how this interior state leads to actions that neglect, harm, or affect other people, and even ourselves. As we grow in awareness, we also grow in self-compassion and compassion for the human condition and brokenness of others.

Contemplative Life

4. Jesus said, "Nothing is concealed that will not be revealed, nor secret that will not be known" (Mt 10:26).
5. If we are willing to open our awareness to God's revealing action, allowing the experience of "self-knowledge" into consciousness without getting bogged down in reactions of judgment, fear, guilt, self-analysis, expectations, or low self-esteem, God begins to heal us. Self-knowledge is not abstract, but experiential and personal. Our prayer practices enable us to consent to God's revealing action in our own experience—being aware of it, feeling it, hearing it, welcoming it and seeing God's action in it.
6. "When you turn your attention from the object of your awareness to the awareness itself, there is just silent, vast openness that has never been wounded, harmed, angry, frightened, incomplete. This is who you are"[27] (Martin Laird).
7. With God, we find greater freedom to live in our present human moment, open to grace and our own humanity.

Reflection Questions

Each chapter contains a few reflection questions to help you deepen your understanding and experience of the material and practices. There are no right or wrong answers. Don't feel that you have to write an essay or even write in complete sentences. Spend some time reflecting on the questions and jot down some of what comes to mind. It's helpful to have a record of your experiences and reflections to look back at over time. In addition, your reflections may be some of the content you will choose to share with your small group, spiritual companion or friend, in spiritual direction or in your Holy Listening Circle.

1. Select one statement, quote or Scripture passage from the spiritual counsel that speaks to you and write about your reflection.
2. What in daily life have you become aware of about yourself through Logging or Spiritual Reading?
3. What does it mean to you to be a contemplative or live a contemplative life?

To Practice
Centering Prayer

Centering Prayer is our foundational practice. It is recommended that you do Centering Prayer for twenty minutes twice a day. If you are not yet doing two prayer periods a day, hold an intention to do it twice a day. You also may work towards doing a second twenty-minute period by starting with a second period of five minutes, gradually increasing the time to twenty minutes. Give yourself the gift of this practice as it will bless you with healing and growth on your journey into contemplative life. Father Thomas has often said that one prayer period a day is a maintenance dose. If you are serious about healing and transformation, practice twice a day.

Logging

Logging is a daily practice throughout your engagement with this program. Spend five to fifteen minutes Logging each day. Experiment with finding the right time of day to do this practice. Some people like to do it first thing in the morning with their cup of coffee before they do Centering Prayer. Others will want to do Centering Prayer first. Others will find the end of the day before retiring to be the best time for this kind of reflection. If you are spending more than fifteen minutes per day on your Logging practice you may want to review the method, especially if you are an experienced journaler, as you may have slipped into journaling rather than Logging. At the end of the week or month, review what you've written and make note of any patterns or insights.

Spiritual Reading

Spiritual Reading is a weekly practice throughout your engagement with this program. Spend one hour per week doing Spiritual Reading. You may do it all in one day or spend ten to fifteen minutes a day four to five times a week. Find the rhythm that works for you. Some people will find they need the whole hour in one sitting for the practice to be meaningful. Others will find reading a paragraph or two a day enough to fill them up. You may want to do it before or after your Centering Prayer practice or find another time when sitting with a Spiritual Reading is a refreshing break in the day.

Resources for Further Study

de Mello, A. (1992). *Awareness.* New York, NY: Doubleday.

Dougherty, R. (1995). *Group Spiritual Direction.* Mahwah, NJ: Paulist Press.

Laird, M. (2006). *Into the Silent Land.* New York, NY: Oxford University Press.

CHAPTER SIX

Intention and Consent in Relating to God: Lectio Divina and The Active Prayer

> *"...The word is living and effective, sharper than any two-edged sword, penetrating even between soul and spirit, joints and marrow, and able to discern reflections and thoughts of the heart."*
> Hebrews 4:12

AFTER ESTABLISHING DAILY PRACTICES IN CENTERING PRAYER AND Logging and committing to a weekly practice of Spiritual Reading, we're ready to add two more contemplative practices that will help us develop our intention and consent in relating to God: Lectio Divina and the Active Prayer. Lectio Divina is an ancient Christian practice where we pray with Scripture (also called the Word of God or simply the Word) in a way that teaches us how to be in a dynamic relationship with God. It has been said that Lectio Divina is about having a conversation with God where God is suggesting the topic. We learn through this prayer that the same Spirit who inspired the writers of Scripture is within us inspiring us in the reading, listening, and praying with the text.

The Active Prayer is another practice derived from ancient Christian practices such as the Jesus Prayer or the repetition of a phrase from Scripture. We create an Active Prayer first by using a name for God that most fits how we relate to God. Then we ask for a gift from God. We start with a prayer asking God to help us discern what we need most at this time in our life. The way we use the Active Prayer in daily life helps to supplant our ordinary interior dialogue, which is most often self-critical and judgmental, with our request for this gift we desire to manifest. This is another way to quiet our interior dialogue and listen to the Spirit. Prayer practices such as these help us to establish a slowly growing relationship with God where our intention and consent lead us to something new: resting in God's abiding presence.

Lectio Divina[28]

In the early days of Contemplative Outreach when Father Thomas offered in-person presentations, he often talked about Lectio Divina, more so than he did in his later years. I often wondered why. In the DVD series and book called *God is Love: The Heart of All Creation*, he was asked how his Centering Prayer practice deepened his awareness of the love of God. He began his answer by talking about Lectio Divina:

> "Whatever progress I made was based on pursuing the basic teachings about meditation, especially Lectio Divina, not as separate methods, but as leading to resting in God—that is to say, moving beyond words and thoughts about words and feelings and, from time to time, to rest in God. Such is my understanding of what Lectio Divina is supposed to be. It is not spiritual reading. It is a specific way of reading Scripture that leads into interior silence so that the other acts of the Lectio Divina practice—how much you read, how much you reflect on the text, how much you express your aspirations in words—become briefer and the silence of all thoughts can be more frequent."[29]

When Father Thomas was being formed by the Trappists, Lectio Divina was the doorway into contemplative prayer. It was only after he, William Meninger, and Basil Pennington created and started practicing and teaching the method of Centering Prayer that they realized Centering Prayer was a more direct path into contemplative prayer. Father Thomas explains,

> "Resting in silence emerges directly in Centering Prayer, whereas Lectio Divina is based on the refining of words and phrases from Scripture and slips into this Presence, rather than continuing to reflect and make acts of the will."[30]

Contemplative Life

Perhaps this is why Father Thomas spoke less of Lectio Divina later in his life, but the point remains that both of these practices are methods or doorways that open into contemplative prayer.

Because many of the people I have met have had either negative experiences or very limited experience with Scripture in their formative years, I can see why they probably wouldn't come to contemplative prayer if the only option was through Lectio Divina. But, like Centering Prayer, Lectio Divina is a practice that develops and deepens over time, especially when practiced, as Father Thomas most often suggests, as a private practice. This is called the monastic practice because it was used in monasteries going back to ancient times. If you've had negative or limited experiences with Scripture in the past, it will be helpful for you to put your resistance aside, or at least be aware of it, as you learn this way of praying with Scripture. If you're willing to do that, even experimentally for a time, you may gain access to a treasure you didn't know existed. You may discover that there are deeper levels of meaning in Scripture other than the literal level; that what you are reading is actually about you; that this is the story of a people seeking a relationship with a loving creator; and that these people, as the ancestors of the Judeo-Christian tradition, have much to teach us about life and God.

When I first learned the method of Lectio Divina I wasn't particularly interested in practicing it. In fact, I really didn't like anything about it. Having been raised Catholic, I don't think it's going too far to say we were not allowed to read the Bible. We had a Bible in our house, but I never saw anyone open it. And when we went to mass, we used the Roman Missal, which contained the prayers of the mass along with the Scripture readings for the day. It wasn't that I didn't know many of the Bible stories, I just never spent time praying with Scripture. I only heard the Bible mentioned in mass and in religion classes. In all the years I have been teaching this practice I find that many people had similar experiences in childhood and, as a result, are not drawn to the practice of Lectio Divina. I've spent many years trying to figure out how to teach Lectio Divina so that more people have access to the experience intended in the practice. In the early days of my Centering Prayer practice, I went on Centering Prayer weekend intensive retreats three times a year. We always did Lectio Divina on Saturday evening and I always had to talk myself into going to those prayer sessions. Although practicing Lectio Divina wasn't my natural inclination, I'm grateful I stuck with it. Even though the main practice Contemplative Outreach teaches is Centering Prayer, Father Thomas always encouraged the practice of Lectio Divina, especially its movement into contemplation or resting in God.

We begin Lectio Divina by using our faculties (our inherent mental and physical abilities) to read, reflect, and respond to what we are hearing which leads to resting in God. The way we practice Lectio Divina in a group, the facilitator reads the chosen passage four times and provides verbal instructions of what to do after each reading. Initially, for me, the instruction kept me in my head, wondering if I was doing it right, when this practice is meant to move us into our heart. One Sunday morning while I was on one of these retreats, I decided to try doing Lectio Divina on my own with the Gospel reading for that day's mass and I had a breakthrough of sorts. Somehow, in the quiet of the chapel before others came in, the passage came alive for me, and I experienced the movement into my heart. It was through that experience that I felt called to a regular private practice of Lectio Divina and to teach the practice for Contemplative Outreach in Denver. I remembered hearing Father Thomas's instruction that Lectio Divina is a private practice. He says when we do it in a group it really is more of a liturgy of Lectio. There's nothing wrong with that because we learn from the faith sharing and experiences of others in a group setting. However, most of us will have deeper, more meaningful experiences when we take the time to be alone with God and Scripture and allow this practice to unfold in our hearts.

Interiorizing the Word

One of the things I think most modern-day people struggle with, and even crave, is slowing down. We are all so busy these days we hardly have time to catch a breath. I find it most helpful when learning and practicing Lectio Divina to slow the practice down, slow the process down, slow the prayer down. We don't give ourselves enough time with Scripture. I don't mean that we don't spend time with Scripture. Many people read Scripture regularly or listen to it proclaimed in church services. What I'm referring to—what is most important about the prayer practice of Lectio Divina—is that it doesn't matter how much we read, the theological meaning of the words, or anyone else's interpretation of the meaning. What's important is that we spend time. When we pray with Scripture in the manner of Lectio Divina, we deepen our relationship with God, which I think is what most of us

Contemplative Life

seek in contemplative prayer. We find the message in the words that is relevant to our lives today. We are invited into a conversation with God that leads, if we consent, to communion with the Divine Indwelling.

As in the practice of Spiritual Reading, we turn once again to M. Robert Mulholland, Jr. in his book *Shaped by the Word,* where he offers a method of reading Scripture that helps us slow down the prayer.[31] He describes reading for formation, rather than for information. Reading for information is how we normally read most things in life, how we learned to read. It's how we read the news, most books, and instructions or manuals. We read to cover the material as quickly as possible. We may even be doing this at an accelerated pace in this day and age because we have access to so much information. The reading is usually linear, from beginning to end. We use our intellectual faculties of analysis, critical thinking, and judgment. We're usually reading for comprehension, trying to master the material or at least to understand what the author is trying to say.

It is helpful to read the Bible for information sometimes, but that's not our approach in Lectio Divina. Reading for formation is quite different. Our intention in Lectio Divina is to interiorize the Word, to allow it to penetrate our mind and heart, and most importantly, to have an encounter with God. That intention requires a different manner of reading. We avoid quantifying our reading. Sometimes a paragraph, a sentence, or even a word is enough. We are more concerned with the quality of our reading, which is reflective of the time and attention we give to it, than we are with the quantity. We pause while reading. Reflect. Maybe go back a paragraph or even a chapter. We are moving into a deeper meaning. We allow the passage to open us to its deeper dimension, to probe deeper levels of our being. Sometimes that may feel like an intrusion; there may be some discomfort, but we stay with it and see what it has to say to us. We listen. Instead of trying to master the material, we surrender and allow ourselves to be formed by the Word, and ultimately to be transformed by it. Our approach is humble and receptive, which uses different skills or abilities than the analytical, critical, and judgmental approach of the intellect.

After my experience with Lectio Divina at the retreat where I was called to a daily practice, I wasn't sure how to choose what Scripture I would use for my daily practice. I had always struggled with Saint Paul's letters in the New Testament. I found them dry and difficult to read and understand. Once while on a road trip, I listened to Franciscan priest Richard Rohr's audio series called "Great Themes of Paul: Life as Participation" which I had been introduced to while taking the Nine-Month Course. Just as spiritual books sometimes are written as the result of the author's experience of Lectio Divina, I think this may have been true with this audio series. The way Rohr was able to unpack the great themes he discovered in the writings of Saint Paul helped this teaching to come alive for me in a way reading it on my own never did.

While researching Lectio Divina on the Internet, I stumbled upon this quote by William of St. Thierry, a twelfth-century French Benedictine monk:

> "The Scriptures need to be read in the same spirit in which they were written, and only in that spirit are they to be understood. You will never reach an understanding of Paul until, by close attention to reading him and the application of continual reflection, you imbibe his spirit."

And so, with a little help from Richard Rohr and William of St. Thierry, I decided to use Saint Paul's letter to the Romans for my daily practice. As you might imagine, digging into Romans required me to suspend my critical and judgmental faculties to take a humble and receptive approach. It took me six months, taking a paragraph or sometimes even a sentence at a time. But now, Romans is perhaps my favorite book of the Bible because it taught me how to open myself to be affected by the Word. I experienced being formed by God through Scripture and this practice. What once was a dry and meaningless letter came alive for me because I could hear what it had to say to me in my life today.

A quote from another of the letters in the New Testament, Hebrews, spoke to me deeply when I first heard it while at a conference where Father Thomas was talking about Lectio Divina: "Indeed, the Word of God is living and effective, sharper than any two-edged sword, penetrating even between soul and spirit, joints and marrow, and able to discern reflections and thoughts of the heart" (Hebrews 4:12). It made such an impression on me; the words seemed to penetrate me as described "between soul and spirit, joints and marrow." This passage became a visceral example to me of where this practice could lead me—out of my head and into my heart.

The Word is living, but this is something we may miss in Bible study or in church sermons. Even though the Christian Scripture was

Contemplative Life

written some 2,000 years ago, praying with Scripture using the method of Lectio Divina makes it come alive for us in our lives today. The Word has the ability to penetrate our mind and heart, if we consent. Just as with any prayer practice, and any relationship, we can stay at the surface level, which is what usually happens when we don't take the time and give it our attention. Or we can move to a deeper level of relating to God, as Lectio Divina moves us out of our heads and into our hearts.

In 2021 I participated in a Contemplative Outreach United in Prayer Day where, normally, Contemplative Outreach communities all over the world host a day of prayer within their community. During the COVID-19 pandemic so many groups were already meeting on Zoom, an opportunity opened up for people to come together in prayer no matter where they lived or what language they spoke. We prayed together for twenty-eight continuous hours. I attended many of these sessions and was especially attracted to non-English speaking groups. One of the sessions was a group of Armenian-speaking Canadians. After Centering Prayer, they led the group in Lectio Divina in Armenian using one of the Psalms. Even though I didn't understand what was being read, I felt as if God was whispering into my ear. I was being penetrated not so much by the words, but by the Word.

Lectio Divina is a prayer rooted both in the Word of God in Scripture and in the life and example of Jesus. If you have any experience in gardening, you know that when you plant a seed or even a tree, what you hope is that the seedling or sapling "takes root" in the earth. That's when it becomes established and begins to thrive. The gardener knows that all he or she can do is provide good soil and adequate water and sunshine. The rest is the work of nature, outside of the control of the gardener. So it is with us when we imbibe the Word and let it take root within us. We are slowly transformed as we interiorize the Word and allow the Spirit to pray in us as Saint Paul describes in Romans 8:26, "The Spirit…comes to the aid of our weakness; for we do not know how to pray as we ought, but the Spirit itself intercedes with inexpressible groanings." When the Word takes root in us in the silence of our hearts, below our ordinary level of consciousness, what in the beginning of our practice was a conversation with God moves to communion with God.

Storytelling

The first time I taught Lectio Divina in the Contemplative Living Experience (CLE) program, I was graced to have in the group a Native

American participant named Nellie. I wanted to make the point that while there is a historical basis to much of what comprises today's Scripture, it is largely made up of stories. In Western culture many of us have not experienced the art of the oral tradition of storytelling, but Nellie shared with us the purpose of storytelling in her Native American culture. She said the storytellers were the ones entrusted with transmitting the historical, mythological, and spiritual traditions of their people. They were the teachers. The stories are meant to document the history, customs, rituals and legends of the culture, and to teach, give meaning, and preserve tradition. The same is true of Scripture. Our beloved Nellie died in May of 2013, but her wisdom lives on in her story.

I once gave a retreat on Lectio Divina in Hawaii and wasn't sure how to convey the same message about storytelling, since people who live in Hawaii might not have had the same experience with Native American culture that we have in the Southwest United States. While touring before the retreat I went to the Polynesian Cultural Center. When I went to the section about the Hawaiian Islands, the moderator asked if the audience knew what was most important about hula. I thought it would be related to the arm and hand movements. Others had many guesses. The moderator told us that what was most important is that the dance and chant known as hula conveyed the stories about the history, culture, and tradition of the Hawaiian peoples. And so, I discovered how to convey the importance of stories to the group in Hawaii, using the culture they were most familiar with in the example of the hula.

The Christian Scriptures, comprised of what Christians call the Old and New Testaments, are the stories of the ancestors of our faith that relay to us the history, customs, rituals, and culture of the Christian tradition. The storyteller always has the option of changing or embellishing a story to fit the audience. Most of the stories in Scripture were handed down orally before they were ever written. They were likely changed over time before they were written, so they were not static. And they continue to change as we engage in this conversation with God who is the storyteller, telling us stories about our lives. Yes, there is historical significance to the stories, but in Lectio Divina, we are going deeper into the meaning of the stories in our lives today and how God is drawing us into the intimacy of communion.

Jesus is perhaps our greatest example of a storyteller with his use of parables, which for me are some of the most engaging stories in Scripture. Engaging with the story helps us to remember its meaning.

Think of some of the stories you remember from Scripture—the Prodigal Son, the Good Samaritan, the wedding feast at Cana (where Jesus turned water into wine), the multiplication of loaves and fishes, the Last Supper, Jesus's baptism in the Jordan River by John the Baptist, the Transfiguration, the agony in the Garden of Gethsemane. And from the Old Testament—the Creation story, the parting of the Red Sea, Moses and the burning bush, manna in the desert, Noah's ark, Jacob's well, Abraham and Isaac. As you recall some of these stories you may have learned as a child, reflect on the meaning of the stories. Has the meaning changed for you over the years? Do you remember enough about the story that you could tell it? Have you ever used the story to teach someone else? It's important to remember that the Word is living and that the practice of Lectio Divina keeps it alive in our lives today.

Even though some Bible stories have a commonly held meaning or significance, when we encounter God in conversation, we allow God to suggest the topic—and God may have something entirely different in mind for us than the customary meaning. For example, in the story of the Good Samaritan (Luke 10:25-37), most of us would probably agree that the meaning has to do with helping someone in need. But in the beginning of the story someone asks Jesus what he must do to inherit eternal life. Jesus's first response is, "Love the Lord your God with all your heart and with all your soul and with all your strength and with all your mind." He goes on to say, "Love your neighbor as yourself," and then tells the story of the Good Samaritan. When doing Lectio with this passage, after hearing this story so many times and thinking there was nothing new for me in listening to it again, what struck me was not the story of the Good Samaritan, but Jesus's first response. I pondered and ruminated about his admonition to love God with all my heart, soul, strength, and mind. I started asking myself if I was doing that, and what does that look like, and what does it mean to love with all my heart, soul, strength and mind and did I have that much faith? I ended up spending many days pondering and praying with that one sentence and finally, resting in the knowledge that I was doing the best I could and that was enough for God. This was not what I expected. God was reaching out to me with a lesson about love and intimacy. I will not likely read or hear the story of the Good Samaritan in quite the same way again. This is how Scripture comes alive for us even though we are listening to stories that are thousands of years old that we may have heard many times. The same Spirit that inspired the writers of Scripture is alive in us inspiring us as we listen.

Julie Saad

Overview of the Scholastic and Monastic Methods

There are two methods of Lectio Divina: scholastic and monastic. Contemplative Outreach uses the scholastic method to teach the practice. It's also usually the method that is used when doing Lectio Divina in groups. It divides the practice into stages or steps, like rungs on a ladder. The monastic method is the more ancient method that was practiced by the Desert Mothers and Fathers and later in monasteries in both the Eastern and Western Christian traditions. It is a more natural, almost organic movement of the Spirit in the prayer that develops as we learn and practice. Rather than rungs on a ladder, we start to realize the movement is like moments along the circumference of a circle, all interrelated and guided by the Spirit. Father Thomas encouraged using the monastic method once you learn how to do the practice via the scholastic method. He often called Lectio Divina a method-less method because once you learn it well enough to allow the Spirit to take over, you let go of the words of instruction and of any residual "trying" to do it right. Most of us learned to ride a bike by first using training wheels or balance bikes. Once we get the hang of balancing on two wheels, we no longer need the training tools. You will find the same to be true of the practice of Lectio Divina once you "get the hang of" the movement of the Spirit.

Table 1.

Stages of Relationship	The Four Moments	The Four Senses
Acquaintanceship Getting to know you	Lectio Reading (Listening)	Literal Historical message, example, text
Friendliness Finding common ground	Meditatio Reflecting (Pondering, Ruminating)	Allegorical Stories, metaphor, myth
Friendship Commitment	Oratio Responding (Prayer of the Heart)	Moral How we are called to live
Intimacy Relating being to being	Contemplatio Resting (Being)	Unitive Oneness of Being

Table 1 summarizes the movement of Lectio Divina into deeper levels of relating, interacting, and understanding through the Stages of Relationship, the Four Moments, and the Four Senses. Our intention in this prayer is to have an encounter with God. Prayer is how we relate to God. We experience the development of our relationship with God in much the same way as our human relationships. We start with acquaintanceship where we are getting to know each other. Once we find we have some things in common and are interested in continuing the relationship we move into friendliness. With time and attention friendship develops where we become more committed to the relationship. This commitment ultimately leads, if we consent, to intimacy where we are relating being to being, most often in the silence of our hearts.

In both the scholastic and monastic methods, we refer to our interaction with God as the Four Moments. The Latin terminology for these Four Moments is lectio, meditatio, oratio, and contemplatio. The English translation, which we more commonly use in teaching, is reading, reflecting, responding, and resting. What we're really doing during those four moments is

1. listening with the ear of our heart
2. pondering, ruminating, wondering, opening ourselves to inspiration
3. allowing a prayer to rise up from our hearts, and
4. being with the one who loves us unconditionally.

The Four Senses lead us into deeper levels of meaning and understanding. The practice contains a mysterious dynamic that as we move to deeper levels of understanding we begin to encounter the living God in and through the experience. The first sense is the literal level of meaning, which is the historical message, the example and specific teaching of Jesus, the text and the words, the language that is used. When we experience the allegorical sense, we interiorize the stories and slowly begin to realize the gospel is about us, that our lives are mirrored in its pages. This sense is the voice that speaks to us in symbol, metaphor, and story. The moral sense is not moralistic but rather opens us to listen and hear how the Spirit calls us to live. The unitive sense is the experience of oneness of being.

The difference between the scholastic and monastic methods is that in the scholastic method we follow the four moments in order, starting with reading, moving to reflecting, then responding, and finally, resting. It's helpful in the beginning days of practice to use the scholastic method to become familiar with the four moments, what they mean, and how we experience each one. While we're learning, we usually experience having to put more effort into the prayer. Most people will naturally move into the monastic method after becoming comfortable with the practice, so it's best not to worry about which method you are using.

In the monastic method we don't follow any particular order but allow the Spirit to guide the prayer. While resting we may experience ourselves being drawn back to one of the other moments. We may find we want to reflect more deeply on what we hear being said to us, or respond, or read the passage again. Then we may be drawn back into resting in the silence. This happens naturally when we allow the Spirit to orchestrate the experience. We are also more likely to naturally experience the Four Senses as we let go of any effort in the prayer and allow the Spirit to reveal the deeper levels of meaning. You might think of the Four Moments as the mechanics of the practice while the Four Senses are what is being awakened in us—the movement into the depths of our being and our relationship with God.

Lectio—Literal Sense

The senses are how we perceive—how we take in information and experiences. Just as we use our senses of sight, sound, touch, taste and smell to take in our environment, we use the spiritual senses to take in and experience the Word of God.

With the literal sense we pay attention to the words, their meaning, the historical meaning and the example of Jesus—what he taught and how he lived. We listen to the stories, where they take place, the characters, and what is being said. As we listen, we move into being receptive to the One who speaks in us, so that what we hear may be more than the words convey. We allow the words to penetrate every level of our being, even between soul and spirit, joints and marrow, as we read in Hebrews 4:12. We notice when a word or phrase resonates with us and we sit with it, listening with the ear of our heart, allowing it to repeat itself over and over in our consciousness and welcoming it in faith, until that word or phrase awakens the Word within.

Modern scholars focus primarily on the literal sense, seeking the historical message, the meaning of the words, and the cultural background. This is important work, but it is not the purpose of our prayer. We are not seeking information, but insight and encounter, the essence of what is being communicated. It's not necessary to glean the precise meaning of the text, but simply to be with the Word in a disposition of love and trust. We are coming to this encounter with God anticipating an exchange that will be a deepening of our growing relationship.

Lectio literally means reading, but what we are really doing is listening—but not just listening with our ears. We are listening with the ear of our heart. In *Shaped by the Word*, M. Robert Mulholland says,

> "Listen for God to speak to you in and through, around and within, over and behind and out front of everything that you read."[32]

He calls this a posture that begins the process of reversing the learning mode where we are unconsciously trying to master the information. This way of listening starts to shift us into an intention of reading for formation.

Lectio Divina requires a little more effort than Centering Prayer. In order to listen deeply we apply some skills that we call "active listening." Whether or not we think of ourselves as good listeners, listening is a skill we can learn as we develop the ability to listen more deeply than we normally do in everyday life. Active listening is a decision we make to be present and to pay attention. We put aside our agenda, thoughts, and opinions in order to focus on the other (in this case, God). We put aside our desire to shape or control the other. Active listening requires a commitment and calls for the presence of our true self.

As in Centering Prayer, it helps to prepare ourselves for our time of prayer. Father Thomas is very clear that Centering Prayer and Lectio Divina are two separate and distinct practices and suggests that if we are doing the two practices in the same prayer period, we do Centering Prayer first. When we're not starting with Centering Prayer, we start our Lectio Divina practice by entering into the silence, quieting the body and mind. We become fully attentive and alert and bring our awareness to the intimate presence of God. We take time to just be with God who is always present to us whether or not we are aware of it.

We choose a short text and read it slowly. You may want to experiment with reading it out loud so that you are hearing it as well as reading it. We listen with our full attention and begin to personalize the words. We don't think about it, but rather we allow the Word to awaken in us. Remember, we're not trying to master the material or read a certain amount, which is why it's helpful to use something short.

In reading the passage, or listening, we have an attitude of receptivity. There is a subtle difference between listening and reflecting. So often we do not listen as deeply as we might. We tend to rush right into reflective thoughts and miss the real point of the conversation. Try to stay with the word or phrase that catches your attention, reflecting on what is being said, not what it means. Begin to repeat the word or phrase. The repeating of the word or phrase is what gradually moves us into meditatio or reflecting.

Meditatio—Allegorical Sense

The allegorical sense is a voice that speaks to us in symbol, metaphor, and story. As we repeat the word or phrase that resonates with us in Lectio Divina, it engages us in a deepening of our dialogue with the Word. Through our spiritual senses, we move into deeper levels of meaning and understanding so that what we might call "hidden meanings" begin to emerge. We say hidden because they may not have the same meaning to each person who reads the same passage, but also because when we consent to God's presence and action within, the Spirit is at work below our level of consciousness.

A movement is occurring of interiorizing the stories in Scripture and we slowly realize the Gospel is about us, and that our lives are mirrored in its pages. Scripture is not only the stories of our ancestors but the story of our own life journey. Father Thomas tells a story in *Intimacy with God* about when he first joined the novitiate in the Trappist order and his novice master told him to read the Old Testament.[33] He was more interested in reading the mystics like John of the Cross, but with a heavy heart did as he was told. He says that as he proceeded through Genesis and Exodus, all of a sudden a light appeared on the other side of the page and he realized that this was the story of his life, almost as if his psychiatrist had written the stories. It became for him the most exciting book he had ever read.

When we move into the level of understanding brought about by the allegorical sense, we begin to move toward a deeper commitment, which in turn, means a greater vulnerability and openness to God and to ourselves. The Spirit reaches so much deeper into our wounds, our psyche, and our spirit—our inmost being. An interior dialogue may happen as we are awakened to a more subtle and intuitive awareness of God's presence within.

One of the great obstacles to hearing the Word of God is our identification with the false self and its habitual expectations, demands, or "shoulds." When we move into the allegorical sense and start to identify with the stories, our level of trust deepens, and we are able and willing to confront the darker side of our personality so that purification or what Father Thomas calls "the unloading of the unconscious" begins to occur. We may start to recognize our attachment to our own ideas, programs, and plans. Our growing awareness allows our true self to begin to motivate us, rather than the false self with its excessive demands and hidden agendas.

When we move into meditatio, we continue to let the Word speak to us, and we continue to repeat the word or phrase that attracted us. We may notice a subtle shift from reading to reflecting, perhaps reflecting on what the word or phrase has to say to us in our life today. Pondering the text brings us to the essence, the truth of the Scripture that is often hidden beneath the words. Sometimes we just need to hold the words in our heart and let them speak to us. Ruminating with a passage in Scripture is a similar experience. We sit with what emerges from the text, allowing the Spirit to expand our listening capacity and open us to its deeper meaning. We ask the Spirit to teach us how to open our minds and hearts and understand what the Word is saying to us. In John 14:26 Jesus says, "The Holy Spirit...will teach you everything."

One time when I was on a retreat at St. Benedict's Monastery in Snowmass, Colorado, one of the monks came to the retreat house to lead us in Lectio Divina. He told us a story about his experience with Lectio using this phrase from Psalm 42:2 "...Behold the face of God." He spent a year pondering what the face of God might be. At the time it was difficult for me to imagine spending a year on one phrase, but since then many times I have spent days and weeks with one short passage that resonated deeply with me to listen to what else it had to say to me… and what else… and what else…

We each have our own unique perceptive faculties that we bring to prayer. We start to use more of our faculties—imagination, intuition, emotions, and senses. Some of us have active imaginations and may be able to enter the scene, be present, observe, and listen to the people in the story. Father Thomas always used Scripture to teach. Whenever I listened to him or read any of his books, as he talked about Peter or Mary and Martha, I would have the feeling that he knew them personally. This for me was an example of imbibing the Scripture and allowing it to penetrate our faculties. Others of us might interiorize the words and allow them to repeat and resonate. The Word is becoming a part of us and changing our experience of God. This may make us feel uneasy, or it may make us feel loved. Whatever you're feeling or experiencing, trust that it is unique to you and being guided by the Spirit.

Meditatio doesn't really mean meditation in the true sense of the word. Meditation is an activity of our intellect and imagination and falls short of our purpose in this prayer. By using our capacity to reflect, ponder, ruminate, and wonder we move into the deeper levels of our being where we experience an encounter with God.

In *Shaped by the Word*, Mulholland suggests asking yourself some questions that may help facilitate this movement: "How do I feel about what is being said? How do I react? How do I respond deep within? What is stirring in the depths of my spirit? Why do I feel that way? Why am I responding in that manner? Why do I have these feelings within? What is going on down inside me? How is the Spirit of God touching my spirit?"[34]

Are you beginning to learn something about yourself by getting in touch with some of these deeper realities of your being?

Oratio—Moral Sense

The word oratio means response, and our response in Lectio Divina is a prayer that rises up from our heart. This relates to the moral sense because once we have been praying in this manner for a while, we start to become familiar with the way God is speaking to us through the Word. The moral sense is not moralistic; it's not about what we think or someone else thinks we "should" do. It awakens in us a desire to put into practice what we have heard, what the Gospel is inviting us to, and it replaces the desires of the false self. It is more about responding to what we hear when we're no longer blocked from the movement of the Spirit. If you think about some of Jesus's teaching, especially the parables, they are not moralistic but are designed to shake up the value system of his hearers. His teaching sometimes upsets our ordinary expectation of what the point or the end of the story is going to be so that we are shocked into a new way of seeing reality.

As new realizations emerge, we begin to understand how Jesus is calling us to live. We open ourselves to the light and energy of the Word and respond in faith. Instead of moving away from someone in need like the priest and Levite did, we start to respond like the Good Samaritan and do something to help. We want to do something about what we are learning and experiencing, to become an instrument of God's love in the world and allow God's action to supersede our own. We hear the Word of God and are inspired to put it into practice. In this way we begin to transmit the Word of God to all whom we encounter in our daily lives.

Oratio, also called the prayer of the heart, is the beginning of the path that leads to contemplation. It's the prayer that comes from our own heart, from our very personal experience of encountering God in the Word. This prayer will be unique, personal, and honest. It may be a sigh, an expression of gratitude, a cry for help, a song of joy, a poem, a tear, an image. It might come out of our joy or out of despair. It really may just be a feeling that doesn't need to be named. Sometimes we may create an Active Prayer out of the word or phrase that attracted us.

The only active effort we exert in this prayer is to keep our hearts open. With an open heart, our hearts become full of love and desire and our response comes less and less out of our intellect. We begin to experience the love and desire God has for us. Once we experience this encounter with God, we realize that love is not really a feeling but a state we enter into when we have an open heart. Love *feels* the same whether we are the giver or receiver of love. We also begin to realize that the longing we experience in our hearts is really God longing for us. As Jesus says in John 15:16, "It was not you who chose me, but I who chose you."

Contemplatio—Unitive Sense

The unitive sense is resting in God, resting in the union of life with no separation, where you and God are united and where you can turn at any moment to find God, always accessible. This sense corresponds to the level of union in a relationship characterized by intimacy. When we move into this deep rest, this oneness with the divine, we are in a place that is deep, intimate, and intense, beyond thoughts and words, in fact, too deep for words. With the open heart that we may have prayed for or experienced in oratio, we discover the unity that is only possible with an open heart.

Sometimes when we experience this oneness in prayer, we're able to carry it into every part of our life. We experience Christ's energy, the energy of Incarnation, divine energy, in and through our lives and we become the same light and truth that Jesus exemplified. We limit ourselves if we think of light and truth as concepts to be mastered rather than experiences to be lived that each one of us is capable of and meant to transmit in daily life.

When we start a period of Lectio Divina we quiet ourselves down, but when we move into contemplation, we become silent through no action or effort on our part—simply resting in God. While resting, we may experience ourselves being drawn back to one of the other moments of Lectio Divina. We may find we want to reflect more deeply on what we hear being said to us, or respond, or read the passage again. Then we may be drawn back into resting in the silence. This is where the resting in Lectio Divina is different from the resting in Centering Prayer. In Centering Prayer, when we have a thought, we return to the sacred word. In Lectio, a thought or feeling may draw us back into one of the other moments of the prayer.

Lectio Divina is a prayer rooted in the Word of God. When we have a regular practice of Lectio Divina, the Word takes root in us. In contemplatio, we start to experience a sense of rootedness that comes through being one with the Divine Presence. The transforming power of the Word is in its interiority. This is where we experience the therapeutic touch of the divine, working below our level of consciousness. We begin to see reality as it really is, not as we would like it to be, and we become aware of God's divine life in the deepest center of our being.

Contemplation is a gift from God, and we prepare ourselves to receive it by resting in God's presence. This is where the human/divine conversation moves to communion. When we rest in God's embrace, we let go of words and thoughts and just allow ourselves to be aware of God. We are more concerned with being than we are with doing. There may be a word that arises from Scripture that expresses the message we gleaned from the reading that will help us stay in the silence like our sacred word does in Centering Prayer. Our intention here is to surrender to God's presence.

Contemplation may be thought of as the experience of the presence of God. All we can do is simply respond with a loving and peaceful attentiveness. The presence of God can only be received. It is not something we can hold onto or seize. Our efforts are of no avail and will become an obstacle to the interior peace and love that is God.

Becoming a Word of God

Lectio Divina opens us and awakens us through Scripture to God's abiding presence within us. We awaken to this presence within us that already exists. So when we talk about becoming a Word of God, we are talking about becoming who we are at the deepest level of our being—we might say, at the ground of our being.

Very few people experience a sudden, dramatic "burning bush" spiritual awakening. For most of us it takes time and practice to become who we are at the deepest level. We go through many layers of growth and understanding, often through painful memories and emotions. Depending on how deeply we may have been wounded in our early development, we may feel that we are not making any progress, that the same issues surface over and over and over again. Father Thomas often used what he called the spiral model to teach both Centering Prayer and Lectio Divina. Over time both practices move us to deeper levels of our being, but it is not a straight linear path. What we often don't realize is that while a recurring issue may be the same, we are not the same as we were last time around. Father Thomas illustrates this point in *Intimacy with God*:

> "Notice the spiral movement of the four senses of Scripture. You are not just going around in circles. As you return to the same passage in Lectio Divina, it begins to take on new meaning. As you gradually interiorize the four senses of Scripture in your life, you come back to the same texts but at a higher (or deeper) level of understanding. The spiral motion is the way all aspects of contemplative life develop. It is not a rocket that goes straight up. You keep coming back constantly to the same old routines, but they are not really the same because *you* change, even though nothing may change outwardly in your life. This is the invitation that Christ seems to be offering when he says, 'He who has ears to hear, let him hear,' implying that we could listen better if we could only listen deeper."[35]

Julie Saad

In the scholastic method of Lectio Divina, we focus more on reading or listening than the other moments. Listening is our starting point and where we go from there depends on how well we listen. Recall the teaching on active listening where we make a decision to be present and pay attention, put aside our agenda, opinions and expectations, and listen with the ear of the heart from our true self.

In *The Spiritual Journey Series* video course, in what's called "The Basic Course," Father Thomas teaches the practice of Lectio Divina as a way of introducing us to contemplative prayer and life. He says:

> "...You've really heard the Word of God when it has reached the inmost level of one's being. Then you become the Word of God. Now the Gospel is being expressed and manifested in your life, to your friends, and to the people you're serving. And it's inspiring you."[36]

What we are experiencing and will continue to experience is a process of taking in the bread of life, assimilating it and being assimilated by it. "I am the bread of life. Whoever comes to me will never go hungry," Jesus says in John 6:35. What are we taking in when we take in the bread of life? This Scripture passage is a part of the story where the disciples are asking Jesus to give them a sign so they might believe in him. They remind him that their ancestors ate manna in the desert, and he reminds them that it wasn't Moses that gave them the bread, it was the Father who gave them the true bread from heaven that gives life to the world. They say, "Sir, give us this bread." In a similar story of the Samaritan woman (also known as the woman at the well) Jesus tells her that he will give her living water and she says, "Sir, give me this water." Father Thomas says that there are two ways of praying. The first is to ask, as the disciples did in both of these stories. The second is to hunger and thirst with our entire being for what we most need and desire. This is what we are doing in contemplative prayer—hungering and thirsting with our entire being. We are no longer motivated by the desires of the false self coming out of our energy centers (the programs for happiness Father Thomas discusses in "The Human Condition"). This is what awakens our spiritual senses. Just as the external senses perceive our material reality, our spiritual senses perceive the divine reality.

Here's an analogy that captures the process pretty well: In lectio or reading, we put the food in our mouth. With our literal sense we listen to the message and begin the process of dismantling our illusion that God is absent, or that we are separate from God. In meditatio or reflecting, we chew and begin to break up the food. With our allegorical sense we realize that the same graces we are hearing about in the Gospel are taking place in our personal lives. In oratio or responding, the flavor is extracted, and we begin the digestive process and savor the taste. With our moral sense we are moved by the example of Jesus's life and take courage that it might be possible to overcome our emotional programs for happiness that prevent us from accessing the full light of God's presence and action within us. In contemplatio or resting, we experience the sweetness, which gladdens and refreshes and becomes a part of us—what it means to assimilate. With our unitive sense, we experience the abiding presence of God, a presence that is not undermined by what we feel or think, by what others do, or even by tremendous tragedy. We have found our Source. We become the Word of God and express the Divine Presence, just as Jesus expressed it in his daily life.[37]

In *Shaped by the Word*, Mulholland uses this passage from Ephesians 1:4 to help us understand how God is calling us to become a Word of God: "God chose us in Christ before the foundation of the world that we might be holy and blameless before God in Love." He says the word "chose" comes from two Greek words that mean "to speak" and "out of" or "forth from." With this understanding, he would translate this passage to mean God spoke us forth in love. Our most basic and essential call, what we might say is the will of God, is to become fully who we were created to be with our particular gifts and limitations. How do we do this? It's helpful to remember that our work is to sit down in our contemplative practice, whether Centering Prayer or Lectio Divina and open ourselves to God's presence and consent to God's activity. When we do this, God reveals to us what we are to do. In *Fruits and Gifts of the Spirit*, Father Thomas says, "God's activity is the work of the Holy Spirit in your particular embodiment in this world."[38]

Mulholland reminds us that each one of us is the incarnated Word of God:

> "Our physical life, our psychological, mental, emotional life—our whole created being—is the vehicle for the expression of that 'word' God speaks us forth to be in the lives of others. We are created to be incarnate 'words' of God. In all that we are and in all that we do

with one another in the world, God is seeking to bring to full expression that 'word' God is speaking us forth to be."[39]

I like to think of each of us as a perfectly tuned musical instrument, made even more beautiful when we are playing in the symphony of life with each other, with God as our conductor. I can't be the symphony or the instrument you were created to be or the conductor. I can only be the word God speaks me forth to be.

Our word, the word God speaks us forth to be, can be shaped by the Word of God in Scripture and it can transform us if we are willing and if we surrender in faith and trust, if we are willing to be vulnerable. Often our word becomes garbled and distorted by the values of our culture and our ingrained attitudes (once again, our programs for happiness that just don't work). Contemplative practice transforms the flawed words we may have become into the word God wants to speak us forth to be in the world. Being faithful to our practice leads us into listening with the ear of our heart to the ground of our being so that the Word we hear in Scripture resonates within us and draws forth who we are called to be. When Scripture becomes an encounter with God, God begins to shape the word God speaks us forth to be in the world. We are invited into a new way of being with God. We start to live out of the unitive sense where God's Spirit and our spirit are one. Coming to this oneness is the intention of Lectio Divina.

The heart of our journey is to receive what God is transmitting to us, that is, God's light, life, and love. As we grow in our relationship with God, we realize more and more that what's most important about us is not us, but the Divine Presence in us. God in us is relating to God in everything else. In *The Spiritual Journey Series* Father Thomas says,

> "...You have the destiny to be transformed and the capacity to transmit your personal transformation, that is, your absorption of the divine mystery, your assimilation into the Word of God, into daily life among the people you know and with whom you live. And it's the very failure of your efforts to serve that teaches you little by little how to serve, which is with complete dependency on the divine inspiration—mercy—so that

Contemplative Life

you serve without demanding success. And this is what changes the world…"[40]

In our humility we may find it hard to believe that how we live our lives can change the world. Father Thomas often tries to get that reality across to us. In *Intimacy with God* he says,

> "Bonding with others takes place as the love of the Spirit is poured forth in our hearts. We feel that we belong to our community, to the human family, to the cosmos. We feel at home in the universe. We feel that our prayer is not just a privatized journey but is having a significant effect in the world. We can pour into the world the love that the Spirit gives us in prayer."[41]

This is what it means to become a Word of God. This is not just our individual project for personal gratification.

An interior development is occurring, usually unknown to us. We are gifted with compassion, humility, charity and purity of heart that permeates all we say and do. Others may notice this in us before we do. We are moved not only into silence, but from silence to expression. Because it may be unknown to us, the expression may be energetically rather than in words. We are becoming something different, and words often can't explain it. In *Reflections on the Unknowable*, Father Thomas says,

> "Silence is the greatest teacher there is. God's creative Word is uttered in sheer silence, and it is our ability to resonate with it that furthers our transformation. We can't get there by ourselves. So, we consent to God's doing it in us."[42]

It's not something we do, but that God does. It's something we consent to.

This movement from silence to expression affirms that on this spiritual journey our experience of contemplation always leads to service—service to those we live with, to the stranger, to our friends and neighbors, perhaps even to the world. Sister Maria Tasto, one of the animators of the Lectio Divina teaching for Contemplative Outreach, says our journey is from fear to inner freedom. Probably the strongest feeling that underlies our emotional programs for happiness is fear, but silence and our encounter with God in prayer develops an inner freedom where we become aware of the presence of God in the events of daily life. Every event of daily life becomes a revelation of God. Father Thomas says in Lectio Divina we become more accustomed to how God is speaking to us. Sister Maria says that we become more attentive and able to listen with the ear of our heart. We discover all is in God and God is in all.

Some years ago, Contemplative Outreach created a video series called "The Lectio Divina Institute."[43] Father Thomas offers a beautiful teaching of the monastic practice of Lectio Divina in this series, called "Centering Prayer & Lectio Divina" which is now available on YouTube. At the end of the video, he talks about the "fifth stage" of Lectio Divina, what we're calling "Becoming a Word of God." Here is an excerpt from that video's transcript:

> "So the fifth stage of Lectio is when you no longer have to listen to the Word because you are the Word… what I would call unity with the Word, or unity listening or consciousness, so that you no longer listen to the Word, but are the Word, and are manifesting the Word of God in daily life and transmitting it, insofar as it has taken possession of you in daily life. This is when other people are drawn to you… The real communication is to be or become the Word of God in your very being and that is the triumph of grace and we might call that the fifth stage of Lectio when you are or have become God's Word in your particular human situation, with all its circumstances, suffering, or joy, or whatever, and in all the people you know or love or work for or are professionally attached to, so that when you are walking around the world or going anywhere or doing anything you are constantly pouring into the world the divine energy of who you are and whoever is on that wavelength will begin to receive it or be touched by it. This is the crowning fruit of transformation into the Word of God and the joy of being no self."

Lectio Divina Method

Now that we've covered the teachings, variations, and fruits of Lectio Divina, let's begin to pray with Scripture in the manner of Lectio Divina.

1. Quiet your body and mind either by starting with Centering Prayer or some vestibule practice of your choosing. Say a prayer to the Spirit asking for guidance or the ability to be open to what might be revealed to you in your life today. You might bring your awareness to your breathing, or any intentional movement toward being fully attentive to the presence of God.
2. Choose a short Scripture passage and read it slowly. Listen carefully. Use the ear of your heart. Allow the Word to speak to you.
3. With a disposition of love and trust, notice if a word or phrase attracts you, strikes you, stands out for you, confuses you, stirs you. Use your intuition and notice what attracts you or stirs you in some way. Don't worry about why, just notice. Receive the word or phrase into your heart without any further purpose.
4. Pause. You may want to go back and read the passage again. Start to repeat the word or phrase silently in your heart. Don't think about the meaning of the words. Simply allow the text to awaken.
5. Begin to reflect on the word or phrase that attracted you. Allow it to penetrate between your soul and spirit, joints and marrow. Ponder the word, ruminate, and wonder what this word or phrase might mean for you in your life today. Continue to silently repeat the word or phrase that attracted you.
6. As you listen and reflect notice if you feel called to respond in some way, perhaps a feeling of gratitude, humility, joy, sadness, even anger. Or perhaps your response is a sigh, a tear, a longing, or abandonment to the will of God. This is the prayer of the heart, the prayer of your heart from your unique experience in this conversation with the Divine.
7. Allow yourself to become silent. Once you have spent some time in conversation with God you may feel drawn to relax into the present moment, into resting. Let go of any thoughts, words or feelings. Allow yourself to just be without doing as you move into resting in God.

8. Allow the Spirit to draw you into what comes next. You may be led into reflecting, pondering, ruminating, wondering; or into a prayer arising from your heart; or into simply resting in the presence of God; or back into reading.
9. Go slow. Take time. Pause. Return to any moment as the Spirit leads.
10. When you feel complete, remain with eyes closed for a couple of minutes before returning to the ordinary activities of your day.

Some Ways to Choose Scripture Passages for Lectio Divina

1. Use the Gospel readings from the daily lectionary.
2. Pick a book of the Bible to go through over a period of time.
3. Use the suggested "Scripture Themes for Prayer" in Part Two of *Too Deep for Words* by Thelma Hall.
4. Open the Bible at random and pick something on that page. You may want to page through the Bible and notice if any passage attracts you to begin reading.

The Active Prayer

As you may remember from Bible study or any reading you've done about Scripture, the Epistles are letters that the apostles wrote to encourage communities of faith. The early Christian communities who received these letters would read them repeatedly to sustain each other in times of uncertainty.

An often-quoted admonition from Saint Paul to the Thessalonians is to "pray without ceasing" (1 Thessalonians 5:17). In the early days of Christianity (during the third through fifth centuries) the desert monastics put Saint Paul's admonition into practice in their daily lives. They prayed all 150 Psalms every day. The many who were unable to read took to repeating words or phrases from Scripture as they went about their day and work. In the fourth century, Saint Anthony the Great created what is called a prayer rope, typically with 100 knots, to aid in the repetition of prayer. The Jesus Prayer was developed around the same time. One of its earliest forms was "Lord, Jesus Christ, son of God, have mercy on me." It was said that the repetition of this prayer, often with the aid of a prayer rope, could open one's heart, and so, it became known as the prayer of the heart. It continues to be a method of contemplative prayer in the Eastern Orthodox tradition and in recent times has made its way into the Western tradition as well. Some other prayers that were commonly used as repetitive prayer are:

> *Come Lord Jesus.*
> *Lord have mercy on my soul, or simply, Lord have mercy.*
> *Jesus, open my heart to your love.*
> *Lord, do with me what you will.*
> *Lord save me.*
> *Oh God come to my assistance.*
> *Oh Lord make haste to help me.*

What would "praying without ceasing" look like to you as a modern-day contemplative?

Our purpose in taking up contemplative practices is to be conscious of God in all of life. We start out by raising our awareness of God's presence in our Centering Prayer practice. We soon discover that we are experiencing the fruits of Centering Prayer in daily life, outside of our prayer time! This is encouraging, but when we start to experience the negative feedback of afflictive emotions, commentaries (coming from our imagination), and interior dialogue, our human condition can interfere with our developing relationship with God. We may lose track of our intention to consent to God's presence and action within us. If we're not yet habituated to relying on God's grace to persevere in life, we may feel that we don't have any control over our afflictive emotions or the thoughts and commentaries that can be so disturbing to us. But thankfully, by the grace of God, we can choose to put these unwelcome intruders in their proper place. As we continue on this journey and become more aware of our afflictive emotions, commentaries, and interior dialogue, we begin to see that they are nothing more than long-held patterns. These patterns are clues to us that we're acting or reacting out of our emotional programming—out of our unconscious, and not out of the reality of the present moment. That's why Father Thomas calls these patterns "old tapes" that we run over and over again, only to make us feel worse. The Active Prayer is a practice that helps us to hit the pause button on these patterns and, eventually, erase the old tapes.

The Active Prayer is used in much the same way our Christian ancestors used lines from Scripture, the Jesus Prayer, or other short prayers. We will create an Active Prayer that becomes an aspiration for us. We aspire to no longer be controlled by our afflictive emotions, commentaries and interior dialogue, but to move more deeply into our heart and into the heart of God. We do this by repeatedly saying the Active Prayer in the silence of the heart in the midst of our daily activities, when our mind is not otherwise occupied with conversation, work, or something requiring our concentration. Over time, and with faithful practice, the Active Prayer starts to supplant the commentaries, interrupting their usual flow, eventually erasing them.

The first Active Prayer I created for myself is "Faithful One, heal my loneliness." I've always been someone who liked to spend a lot of time alone and didn't often feel lonely, but I began this practice at a time in my life when I had a lot of pressure and stress in my work life and didn't have much of a social or family life. It felt like all I was doing was working, eating, and sleeping, with no time for relaxing and being with friends and loved ones. It felt that there was no end in sight. And so, I was experiencing a painful loneliness. I used this Active Prayer for several years until I realized that I rarely felt lonely anymore. I decided it was time to change my Active Prayer, but I had a hard time defining what gift I wanted to ask from God. At about the same time, I was in spiritual direction and kept bringing to my sessions a strong desire to take a trip to the Grand Canyon. I had been there many years earlier and remembered how it gave me the sense that the earth is split wide open. I wasn't keen on traveling alone and finally my spiritual director asked me what significance my desire to go on this trip had for me. As I pondered his question a new Active Prayer came to me one day: "Faithful lover, open my heart." I realized that because of the past pain of lost love, I was struggling with being open to love and was living with a closed heart. The gift I was asking from God was to split my heart wide open. Once I started using this new Active Prayer my desire to go to the Grand Canyon went away. What an interesting way God has of speaking to us sometimes!

Active Prayer Method

1. Close your eyes and bring your awareness to the presence of God. Be open to the Spirit and listen with the ear of your heart.
2. What is your endearing name for God, or a quality of God? (Examples: Spirit, Beloved, Father or Abba, Mother or Amma, Faithful One, Merciful Spirit, Lord, Agape, Yahweh, Divine Spirit).

Contemplative Life

3. Are you aware of a need you have in your life right now? Ask for it as a gift. Articulate it. God already knows what you need but articulating it can help you to manifest it. When we call on God to help, being open to the promptings of the Spirit, often something unexpected is brought forth. Don't limit God. God is capable of so much more than we can imagine. Sit for a few minutes listening with an open heart. Then write down the words that come to you. Use positive words. In other words, don't use the word "not" and don't state what you "don't" want. Instead, focus on your aspiration. Don't judge, analyze, or interpret. Allow the Spirit to create your prayer.
(Examples: Open my heart. I place my trust in you. Heal my loneliness. Teach me to love like you do. Grace me with kindness. Lighten my heart. Help me to know you.)
4. Your Active Prayer—including the name of God and your request—should be between six and twelve syllables.
5. In the first days and weeks of using the Active Prayer you may find that it changes. Your original Active Prayer may feel awkward, or you may be inspired to find different words. After that initial adjustment period, settle on an Active Prayer and don't change it. Father Thomas taught that it is easier to work the Active Prayer into your heart if you stay with a single aspiration over a long period of time.

How to Use the Active Prayer

1. Repeat it often without effort, but with intentionality.
2. Use it when your mind is not occupied in conversation, work or some other activity requiring concentration. For example, when you are taking a shower, doing the dishes, walking the dog, exercising at the gym, standing in line at the grocery store, or driving.
3. Don't worry if you forget to use your Active Prayer on some days. Bring yourself back to your intention and begin again.
4. By repeating the Active Prayer often, you are working it into your heart so that eventually, instead of you saying the Active Prayer it starts to rise up within you and say itself. At some point you may find that without your knowing when or how it happened the gift you requested is given.

Julie Saad

Some Helpful Nuances

1. Some find it helpful to synchronize the Active Prayer with your breath, with the beat of your heart, or with the pace of your walking.
2. Some find it helpful to put the Active Prayer to a chant, finding a rhythm to the syllables. You can use the method of Gregorian chant, or the melody of a favorite hymn, or just see if a chant comes to you.

Going Deeper

Spiritual Counsel

In Chapter 5 we introduced the spiritual counsels—short statements, quotes or Scripture passages related to the topics contained in the chapters. These are bits of wisdom meant to be your companion as you work with the material in each chapter. You won't relate to all of the statements, but a few may encourage you in grasping the teaching and deepening the practices. I recommend that you first become familiar with the teaching in the chapter and then spend some time with the spiritual counsel as a whole, noticing which statements attract you or stand out for you. You can then spend more time reflecting on what attracted you and what it might be saying to you or revealing to you. From time to time, you may want to go back over all the statements to see if something new attracts you.

1. Awareness of God's presence and action in showing us our human condition and need for grace is an invitation to a deeper relationship with God. "Love the Lord your God with all your heart, with all your soul, with all your mind, and with all your strength" (Mark 12:30).
2. Lectio Divina is about having a conversation with God where God is suggesting the topic. "Listen for God to speak to you in and through, around and within, over and behind and out front of everything that you read"[44] (M. Robert Mulholland).
3. By using our capacity to reflect, ponder, ruminate, and wonder we move into the deeper levels of our being where we experience an encounter with God.

Contemplative Life

4. "Indeed the word of God is living and effective, sharper than an two-edged sword, penetrating even between soul and spirit, joints and marrow, and able to discern reflections and thoughts of the heart" (Hebrews 4:12).
5. "…You've really heard the Word of God when it has reached the inmost level of one's being. Then you become the Word of God. Now the Gospel is being expressed and manifested in your life, to your friends, and to the people you're serving. And it's inspiring you"[45] (Thomas Keating).
6. "God chose us in Christ before the foundation of the world that we might be holy and blameless before God in Love" (Ephesians 1:4). God speaks us forth in love.
7. The Active Prayer becomes for us an aspiration. We aspire to no longer be controlled by our afflictive emotions, commentaries, and interior dialogue, but to move more deeply into our hearts and into the heart of God.

Reflection Questions

Like the spiritual counsels, the reflection questions are meant to help you deepen your understanding and experience of the material and practices. I encourage you to spend some time writing your reflections, rather than just thinking about them. There's something about putting pen to paper (or fingers to keyboard) that helps the reflection move outside yourself so that you can look at it. You will likely be surprised at times by what you write. And you will appreciate having a record of your reflections to look back over. It's a way of looking back at your process of transformation. In addition, this may be some of the content you will choose to share with your small group, spiritual companion or friend, in spiritual direction or in your Holy Listening Circle.

1. How are you aware of God acting personally in your daily life, especially through your Lectio Divina and Active Prayer practices? What gifts have you received from being consistent with your Lectio Divina and Active Prayer practices? What struggles?
2. What are the (sometimes subtle) ways you resist relating to God, doing your contemplative practices, receiving new life and freedom?

3. In what simple way have you been changed, healed, brought new life and greater compassion on your spiritual journey?
4. What does it mean to you to be a contemplative or to live a contemplative life?

To Practice
Centering Prayer

Centering Prayer is our doorway into contemplation. Don't underestimate the value of committing to practice for twenty minutes twice a day. Listen to what Father Thomas says in *Open Mind, Open Heart* about why twice a day is recommended:

> "Twice a day keeps you closer to the reservoir of silence. If you get too far away from the reservoir, it is like being on the end of the water line after everybody has taken what they want from the reservoir... You need to keep filling your reservoir until you eventually strike an artesian well. Then the water is always flowing."[46]

Logging

Spend five to fifteen minutes Logging each day. Continue to experiment with finding the right time of day to do this practice. What works better for you so that you remember to Log every day? Is it easier for you to recall the day's activities and your reactions if you Log at the end of the day? Or are you fresher and more able to tune into what the Spirit brings forth in you in the morning? Is there another time of day when you need a break and have more time for reflection? Remember that if you are spending more than fifteen minutes Logging, look back over the method, especially if you are an experienced journaler. You may have slipped into journaling rather than Logging. Did you review your Logging entries at the end of the week or month? Have you started to notice any patterns? What insights are you receiving?

Spiritual Reading

Spend one hour per week doing Spiritual Reading. You may do it all in one day or spend ten to fifteen minutes a day four to five times a week. Find the rhythm to do this kind of reading that works for you. You may want to review the method for Spiritual Reading to make sure you haven't slipped into reading for information.

Lectio Divina

Practice Lectio Divina three times per week using Scripture passages of your choosing, either from the daily lectionary, from a book of the Bible you've decided to work through, using suggested topical readings in a book such as *Too Deep For Words*, or by simply opening the Bible and reading what is in front of you, noticing if a particular passage attracts you. At first you will use the scholastic method until you learn the rhythm of the four moments—reading, reflecting, responding and resting. Once you become more familiar with the four moments you will find that you naturally start to move into using the monastic method and awaken your spiritual senses. Some people find it helpful to alternate Lectio Divina with Spiritual Reading so that you are spending about the same amount of time each day either with Scripture or a spiritual book.

Active Prayer

Use your Active Prayer daily when your mind is not occupied in conversation, work or some other activity requiring concentration. Remember that the Active Prayer becomes an aspiration. We aspire to no longer be controlled by our afflictive emotions, commentaries and interior dialogue, but to move more deeply into our hearts and into the heart of God. We start to experience the fruits of our aspiration when we have repeated our Active Prayer enough that it starts to come to us automatically. Find a time to do it intentionally at first. For example, as part of your morning routine when you are brushing your teeth and showering, or when you are out for a walk or exercising at the rec center, or when you are preparing dinner and cleaning up. You will have days when you forget to do it altogether, so just find a time the next day and you'll soon discover it becoming more automatic.

Julie Saad

Resources for Further Study

Lectio Divina:

Hall, T. (1985). *Too Deep for Words*. Mahwah, NJ: Paulist Press.

Mulholland, M. (2000). *Shaped by the Word*. Nashville, TN: Upper Room Books.

Keating, T. (2017). *Intimacy with God* (Chapter 7). New York, NY: The Crossroad Publishing Company.

Tasto, Maria. (2013). *The Transforming Power of Lectio Divina*. New London, CT: Twenty-Third Publications.

Funk, M., OSB. (2010). *Lectio Matters*. New York, NY: Continuum.

Keating, T. Lectio Divina Series: Centering Prayer & Lectio Divina (available on YouTube). Contemplative Outreach, Ltd.

Keating, T. (Winter 1998). The Classical Monastic Practice of Lectio Divina. Contemplative Outreach News, Volume 12, Number 2 (www.contemplativeoutreach.org)

The Active Prayer:

Keating, T. (2006). *Open Mind, Open Heart* (pp. 171-172). New York, NY: The Continuum International Publishing Group Inc.

Koock, T. (2005). *Active Prayer: The Contemplative Life Program 40 Day Practice*. Contemplative Outreach, Ltd.

CHAPTER SEVEN

Letting Go and Receiving True Life: The Welcoming Prayer

> *"So whoever is in Christ is a new creation;*
> *the old things have passed away;*
> *behold, new things have come."*
> 2 Corinthians 5:17

WE OFTEN HEAR ABOUT THE IMPORTANCE OF "LETTING GO" IN spiritual and religious circles and in the twelve-step programs. But what does letting go really mean and how do we do it? Maybe even more important, what are we letting go of and why would we want to? In this chapter we will be exploring the Welcoming Prayer, a practice for daily life that helps us uncover what it is we need to let go of in order to receive the true life God intends for us.

I have a vivid memory of watching Father Thomas teach about letting go. He holds up clenched fists in front of his chest and then lowers them out in front of his body as he opens his hands. He is demonstrating that as we unclench—let go—we open ourselves to receive. So often we think that our lives would be better or happier if only people would behave the way we think they should, or if we could control the outcome of events and circumstances. As you read these words you may recognize the reality that you have very little control over other people, places, things, and events, and yet emotionally you resist, you cling, and you remain captive to your desires that people be different than they are, that life be different than it is. As long as we are held captive by and cling to our desires—as long as our fists are clenched—what are we open to receive? Would we even recognize a gift of grace if it was presented to us? Take a few moments to reflect on a time in your life when you received the gift of grace. Was it something you could have predicted would happen? Was it within your power to make it happen? In my experience, even with all I've learned about contemplative life and practice, it usually isn't until I've exhausted everything I think is within my power to think, feel, or do that I am finally willing to let go of my effort and consent to God's action in my life. When I am so busy trying to do and fix everything on my own, I don't leave room for God's action.

Daily life frequently presents us with obstacles that prevent us from living life in the present moment and block our awareness of the presence of the Divine Indwelling. These obstacles are really just our attachments to what we think will make us happy or fulfill our needs and desires. When these attachments cause us to want life, people, circumstances, and events to be other than what they are, we end up spending a tremendous amount of time and energy trying to change them. The Welcoming Prayer helps us to address them in real time by identifying and letting go of both the emotional attachments and our desire to change what is not within our power to change. It gives us a tool right at our fingertips to be at peace with what is, even as we're experiencing something other than peace.

Life is a balancing act of doing and being, of action and contemplation. One is not better than the other; both are essential to how we live our lives. When our doing and being come out of our consent to God's presence and action within, we experience interior freedom and peace, what we might call "true life." The practice of Centering Prayer is sometimes called the prayer of consent. It is our foundational practice that starts us down the path to experiencing interior silence and building up a reservoir of peace. As we emerge from that deep place of peace into the challenges inherent to daily life, our emotional programs are often triggered by our unconscious attachments and desires, quickly draining the reservoir, disrupting our interior silence. The Welcoming Prayer can help us restore the reservoir we filled during our time of Centering Prayer. That's why we call the Welcoming Prayer "consent on the go." It's an active practice that brings our awareness to our reactions so we can make choices that are life-giving rather than emotionally draining.

The Welcoming Prayer[47]

The Welcoming Prayer is a complementary practice to Centering Prayer. One time I heard Father Thomas say it was the second most important practice, after Centering Prayer of course, because it helps us to further the transformation process started in our Centering Prayer practice. It is a practice for daily life where we come face to face with our human condition.

Father Thomas's teaching on the human condition, particularly the energy centers—security and survival, esteem and affection, and power and control, and how they develop early in life before we are capable of rational thinking—are relevant to our need for the Welcoming Prayer. These energy centers develop when our instinctual needs are not being met or we perceive they're not being met, and they develop into what Father Thomas calls emotional programs for happiness. They are our mechanism for attempting to get our needs met. We call them programs because they're programmed into our unconscious and can easily be triggered by afflictive emotions, thoughts or commentaries, memories, or even body sensations.

In addition to these emotional programs, we often become over-identified with what Father Thomas calls cultural conditioning—our loyalty to groups we may belong to or grew up with, which is another factor that can be triggered from our unconscious. The energy centers in combination with our cultural conditioning will develop in our unconscious into hidden values, values we may unknowingly be attached to. This is what Father Thomas refers to as the false-self system. We think we're acting out of what is important to us, but if we discern these values using our rational and intuitive faculties, we will likely find we don't really hold these values. Because these energy centers and our cultural conditioning have developed over time and come out of our unconscious, they co-opt rational thinking and intuitive knowing.

It usually unfolds like this: we have a reaction to a triggering event—a person, event, or even a thought—that is not in proportion to what happened, in other words, an overreaction. Then we may find ourselves wondering why we reacted so strongly, but we are unable to come up with a rational explanation. Because these energy centers come out of our early childhood value system, we are operating in our adult world with unconscious childhood motivation. We might say that our buttons have been pushed and we think because we have buttons that can be pushed there isn't much we can do about it.

The Welcoming Prayer is a practice that not only helps us when our buttons are pushed but can potentially deactivate the buttons. It gives us a choice when we experience a triggering event to either react as usual out of our unconscious or false-self motivation, or to respond from a place of interior freedom, from a place of love. When we respond out of choice rather than react automatically, we take responsibility for our emotional life. Until we experience and bring into awareness what it's like when we don't take responsibility, we don't fully understand the consequences.

One Friday afternoon, about five minutes before the end of the workday, my phone rang. All my coworkers had left for the weekend. Being a responsible employee, I answered the phone. A man who was not one of our customers was calling on behalf of his friend and proceeded to hold me captive for twenty minutes, yelling at me and speaking in a condescending manner. Even though I was experienced at working with unhappy customers, there was something about the way this man treated me that started a slow burn of anger in me. The anger continued to build after the call ended and followed me all the way home. I tossed and turned all night long, unable to shake what I was experiencing. Saturday morning was always my favorite time of the week when I could get up without an alarm, do Centering Prayer, drink coffee, and spend some time journal writing. Even Centering Prayer and journal writing did nothing to dissipate my anger. Now I was becoming angry that I was unable to enjoy my Saturday morning because I was so angry. Finally, I said in a loud, angry voice, "I don't want to feel this way." At the time I didn't have a regular practice of using the Welcoming Prayer. Not only were my buttons pushed, but my emotional programs were off to the races, unbridled. When I finally came to the realization that I was resisting what I was experiencing, I immediately remembered the Welcoming Prayer and what I had been taught about resisting unwanted and uncomfortable feelings. I was able to stop resisting feeling the anger, and whatever other constellation of emotions was triggered, and instead allow myself to feel it and sink into it; to let the energy of the emotion move through me. I remembered to welcome God into what I was experiencing and stop trying to change it. It's not important to try to figure out what caused the reaction or even to name the emotion. The man who started this cascade of emotions was not the cause of it. As Father Thomas says, the fact that I was experiencing these upsetting emotions was a sign that the problem was in me. When I was able to stop resisting feeling the emotions and welcome God into them, I was really welcoming my way into the present moment, into the presence of God. The past and whatever was triggered was released.

Contemplative Life

A regular practice of Centering Prayer builds within us a reservoir of interior silence or peace, but Father Thomas has always said that our real practice is daily life. He also says that what is destructive about the energy centers is that they block the free flow of grace. They are like blocks in the nervous system, the musculature of the body, and the psyche. They prevent us from living in the here and now. How do we maintain this reservoir when we are confronted with people and events that trigger something in us? Inevitably, whatever reservoir we built up during our times of Centering Prayer is soon depleted by triggering events and our emotional reactions or over-reactions. The Welcoming Prayer offers us a practice for daily life that gives us a greater opportunity to maintain our reservoir of peace and respond rather than react to any turmoil we experience. We experience a greater freedom in how we live our lives because we're making choices rather than reacting out of our unconscious.

Mary Mrozowski, who I introduced earlier as one of the co-founders of Contemplative Outreach, was the creator and spiritual mother of the Welcoming Prayer. [48] Mary was a spiritual teacher long before she attended the first Centering Prayer retreat Father Thomas held at the Lama Foundation in New Mexico in 1983. As a lay contemplative and spiritual teacher, she understood the importance of helping people live a contemplative life outside the monastery, which meant dealing with daily life in a world that had values that were often incongruent with the contemplative life. She had a gift for creating spiritual practices for daily life. Before the Welcoming Prayer came into being, she was teaching what she called "the letting go practice." She felt it was important to let go of emotions, feelings, commentaries and thoughts that control us. When we let go or surrender, God steps in to change our perception of what is happening so that we can see what is really happening with clarity. We may believe that the Divine Indwelling is the ground of our being, but the thoughts and feelings coming from our unconscious block our experience of oneness with God and keep us trapped in the illusion of separation.

In "The Human Condition" course in *The Spiritual Journey Series*, Father Thomas presents a teaching he calls "Dismantling the Emotional Programs." Sometimes we have our own work to do in order to get out of the way of God being able to work in us. In this series, he offers a method developed by Ken Keyes, Jr. called "mind freedom." When frustrated, the energy centers set off a cycle that we get caught up in, almost like a cycle of addiction. Thoughts and commentaries are triggered, reinforced by our imagination, which may set off defensive or aggressive behavior. The feelings, emotions, thoughts and behaviors in turn reinforce the energy centers and keep the cycle moving unless something interrupts it. The mind freedom method suggests that when we notice the same emotional turmoil recurring, we name it right away without analyzing it, then pinpoint the triggering event and our emotional response. Then we can ask ourselves if we are willing to let go of our desire to control the other person or event and let go of our desire for approval, esteem, or affection. It's our choice. With practice we begin to see that this hidden, unconscious value system is the root of our frustration, blocking our relationship with God and others. Father Thomas tells us:

> "These energy centers were developed by repeated acts. They can be taken down by repeated acts. There's nothing absolute or mysterious about them. They're just a habit. Since they have deep emotional overtones, it takes a little repetition, determination, and patience to keep letting go of the value system by a deliberate act every time it presents itself."[49]

Mary Mrozowski's gift for creating spiritual practices, in this case particularly her experience with a letting go practice, along with Father Thomas's teaching on dismantling the emotional programs came together to give us what we now know as the Welcoming Prayer. In Centering Prayer our intention is to consent to God's presence and action within. The Welcoming Prayer helps us to extend our consent to God's presence and action in the midst of life's many challenging moments.

In practicing the Welcoming Prayer, we work with our energy centers or emotional programs by recognizing how they are affecting our responses. These programs related to the need for security and survival, esteem and affection, and power and control are largely unconscious, and since our bodies are the storehouse of the unconscious, this practice focuses primarily on paying attention to our bodies. We often don't remember most of what happens to us in life, especially early life, but our bodies are faithful recorders of it all. The body primarily records what gets stuck in our bodies or triggered in our bodies in the form

Contemplative Life

of energy. We experience this energy through our feelings, emotions, thoughts, body sensations, and commentaries. When we practice the Welcoming Prayer, we start by scanning and paying attention to our bodies. The Welcoming Prayer has three movements: the first is to feel and sink into whatever we're experiencing in our bodies, then to welcome the experience as an opportunity to consent to the Divine Indwelling, and finally, let the experience go, consenting to what is.

First Movement—Feel and Sink Into:
Feel and sink into what you are experiencing this moment in your body—the feelings, emotions, thoughts, body sensations, or commentaries.

Spend a few minutes observing your body, becoming aware of what is going on in your body. Often our bodies are trying to tell us something before we even have a thought about it. Pay attention to your body and scan it from head to toe. Notice if you are feeling any pain, tension, tight or tense muscles. Notice your pulse. Can you feel your heartbeat? Any fluttering, cold or warm, feelings of heaviness or lightness? When you're angry, afraid, grieving, joyful, or happy, how do you know this is the feeling you are experiencing? What do you experience in your body with each of these feelings? Your body expresses your feelings, even unconscious feelings. Think of some of the expressions we use when we are experiencing strong feelings—gut wrenching, eating me up inside, tied up in knots, butterflies in my stomach, burning with anger, all choked up.

The first movement of the Welcoming Prayer is to feel and sink into whatever you are experiencing in your body. Begin by bringing your attention to your body, scanning your body head to toe, becoming aware of any feeling, emotion, body sensation, thought or commentary. This is what we call a body scan. Just check in with every part of your body with curious inquiry. Whatever you experience, you don't need to name it. It's best not to resist it, judge it, fear it, condemn it or try to modify it in any way. Simply allow the sensation to be. Don't rush this part. We have a tendency, especially if we are experiencing uncomfortable feelings, to try to make them go away. This is often the reason feelings can be troublesome for us, because we either repress or suppress them. When we stop resisting feelings they tend to change to a lighter sensation or disappear altogether as we allow the energy to dissipate. But first we must sink into them by acknowledging them and letting them be. The Welcoming Prayer helps us to recognize that our feelings are simply energy moving through our bodies. We start to lose our attachment to them. If we allow the free flow of energy, we are well along the road to releasing and letting go.

We use the word "feeling" as an umbrella term for any emotions, thoughts, commentaries, and body sensations we may have. We may not be experienced or skilled in the language of feelings or in paying attention to our bodies. Many of us were taught at an early age to suppress our feelings. We might not be aware of it, but when we're having thoughts or commentaries, especially if they seem to come out of nowhere, they are often triggered by emotion. Noticing the thought or commentary can lead us back to the emotion which we can then feel and sink into. We don't want to spend too much time thinking about what we're experiencing. We may have a defense mechanism against feeling our feelings by staying in our minds rather than focusing on our bodies. The point of this movement in the practice is to experience our bodies. Whatever we experience when we do a body scan, we stop and feel it, sink into it, stay with it. If something changes, we notice that, and then continue the process of feeling it and sinking into it.

After many years of practicing and teaching the Welcoming Prayer, I discovered that when I consent in Centering Prayer and in daily life, God reveals where my feelings, attitudes, and behavior need attention and healing. I became aware of a pattern in my process when I experienced afflictive emotions. This didn't just happen once but happened with many people and circumstances over the course of a couple of years. I was doing everything I knew to do to let go of the pain—using the Welcoming Prayer, talking to close friends and my spiritual director, journaling, praying for relief. I was not experiencing the peace of release. My inability to get to a place of peace with what I was experiencing was causing me to suffer. I began a discernment exercise about whether I needed to accept my process as it was or change my process. What I realized was that I was rushing this first movement of the Welcoming Prayer—*feel and sink into*. I thought I was feeling and sinking into these emotions, and they just weren't moving through me. You can even tell by my language where I was missing the boat— "*I thought* I was feeling…" I was in my head instead of in my body. When I stopped trying to put words (thoughts) to what I was experiencing and focused on the body sensations, my process changed without my having to decide to change it. I let the feeling come up and put my attention on what I was experiencing in my body. I would do my best not to think about what I was experiencing but just notice it and follow it with my attention. It was often very painful to keep my attention on what I was experiencing in my body, but I became more willing to do it once I started experiencing the fruits of the practice. I became more adept at feeling the energy of the emotion and letting it run its course. It would either dissipate or change. If it changed, I would let the new feeling run its course. It was as if a pressure valve was released. I realized that this was what was preparing me to move into the second movement of the prayer. But the prayer was ineffective for me until I learned to spend adequate time in the first movement.

Second Movement—Welcome:

Welcome what you're experiencing this moment in your body as an opportunity to consent to the Divine Indwelling. Welcome the Divine Indwelling into the feelings, emotions, thoughts, body sensations or commentaries in your body by silently saying the word "Welcome."

Welcome becomes for us a sacred symbol of our intention to consent to the presence and action of the Indwelling Spirit in whatever we are experiencing. This is what makes this practice a prayer. Welcome does not simply mean acceptance; it is more of an embrace, much as you would welcome a beloved into your home or heart. You are welcoming the Indwelling Spirit, the God who is already present within you, into the feeling, emotion, thought, body sensation, or commentary you are experiencing in this moment. God is present to us in every moment and every event. When we use the Welcoming Prayer, we become more conscious of this presence.

Sometimes people get the impression that we are welcoming the feelings—the fear, anger, sadness, grief—the pain. Mary Mrozowski says that we are welcoming the feeling because God is in it. God is in everything. If we are experiencing pain, God is saying "pay attention." When we surrender the pain to God, God changes it. What we are welcoming is God in the pain. There's a subtle difference between welcoming the feeling and welcoming God in the feeling. If we're experiencing pain, we're not likely to be motivated to welcome the pain and will continue to resist it even as we go through the motions of the prayer. Welcoming God in the pain helps us to stop resisting what we are experiencing. When we stop resisting, we're coming closer to surrendering.

Mary Mrozowski says that we need to surrender the feelings and emotions to the Indwelling Spirit so that the Spirit can change them, can change us. Then we can respond in relationships and events in daily life instead of reacting from our unconscious motivation. Surrender is not something we are readily willing to do when we are uncertain to whom we are surrendering. By welcoming or embracing God into what we are experiencing, something changes. We awaken and surrender to the presence of God in this moment, not the moment when the event or circumstance occurred, but now—the present moment. This is a process of trust and faith that only comes through experience, not by thinking about it. Welcoming and surrendering to the presence of God in the moment prepares us for the third movement—letting go.

Third Movement—Letting Go:
Let go by saying the following sentence: "I let go of my desire for security, affection, control and embrace this moment as it is."

When we let go of our desire what we're really letting go of is our attachments, those hidden values in our unconscious kept alive by the energy centers. It's normal in our formative years to need love, to feel safe, and to have some element of control in our lives, but as adults these desires become obsessive demands that no longer meet our needs and keep us trapped in the false-self system.

In the Welcoming Prayer we're letting go of our neediness, of our unconscious woundedness, and of our unresolved hurts that are coloring every interaction and relationship and causing us to suffer. We may think that our suffering is being caused by the other person or the event. But it's not about the other person. It's about us. The other person did not create our anger, hurt, loneliness, or whatever it is that upsets us. He or she may be the stimulus, but it is we who have the unconscious hurt or woundedness that needs healing. Understanding this accomplishes what Father Thomas means when he says we need to take responsibility for our emotional life.

In *Open Mind, Open Heart* Father Thomas says, "Letting go means passing *through* the experience, not around it, not running away from it, or stuffing it back into the unconscious."[50] The Welcoming Prayer is not about getting rid of whatever pain we're experiencing. It changes our relationship to the pain so that we no longer have a need to suffer. When we let go of our desire to change what is, paradoxically, change often happens on some level. The person, situation or event may not have changed, but when we let go it allows us to move on and to be free from the desire to change something over which we have no control. We will experience a peace that comes when we stop resisting and instead accept and embrace what is.

Using the Welcoming Prayer does not mean that we take no action. Rather, it means that we can choose our response without the encumbrances of past woundedness. We have the clarity to respond appropriately instead of reacting out of our unconscious motivation. We start to develop the ability to witness our behavior when our emotional programs are triggered and to stop identifying with them. The reactions that come out of the energy centers are not who we are. When we know who we are we are freer in our life and relationships.

When the Mind is an Obstacle
Many of us overidentify with our mind. We think our mind and the feelings and emotions attached to it are who we are. We may even become obsessed with the thoughts and commentaries that our minds create. The Welcoming Prayer is about getting free from our attachments and obsessions, about letting go and letting God change whatever is going on. We don't have the power by an act of our own will to change the unconscious. Mary Mrozowski said about the only thing the will is good for is to surrender to God. The Indwelling Spirit is right here, deep within us, waiting for us to surrender.

Expectations can get in the way of getting free from these emotional programs. We may think that because we're doing this practice our feelings, thoughts, commentaries—all our problems—should magically disappear. What is happening with this prayer, just as with Centering Prayer, is that what was stuck in the unconscious begins to surface. Sometimes we may experience the situation getting worse before it gets better. What we think is the same feeling keeps coming back as we continue to work with it because the feeling doesn't have anything to do with the people or events in our lives today. It has to do with an emotional program from early childhood that is being triggered. Father Thomas has a teaching that he calls the spiral model where he says we may come around again and again in life to what we think is the same issue, but we are in a different place, perhaps at a higher or deeper level of consciousness. By working with these same feelings or issues whenever they arise moves us closer to their roots. Over time we may notice that they have less of a grip on us until one day we find we are detached from them, free from them.

We may not realize that our thoughts and commentaries are illusions. Because they have feelings and emotions attached to them, they seem real. I'm not talking about thinking, which is a natural human faculty, but when our mind hi-jacks our thinking ability causing us to obsessively think about our thoughts. When you are in the present moment you are thinking about what you are doing, not the past or future. Once thinking about our thoughts gets triggered it becomes an obsessive process that we feel we have no control over. The obsessive thoughts stir up feelings and emotions and we get trapped in our minds. When we are in this state, we may not be able to do the Welcoming Prayer. Mary Mrozowski offers a practice to help with what she calls "unjamming the mind." When you are aware that you are trapped in this program of obsessive thinking about your thoughts, say to yourself "no thought is worth thinking about." That may be enough to stop the program. If it starts up again, say "no thought is worth thinking about." These obsessive thoughts about the past or future are usually not true and can even be destructive, like "I'm not worthy," or "I didn't do it right," or "I could have done better," "or "I'm so stupid," or "If only this were different." These thoughts carry a destructive energy that we can end up manifesting in our life and then overidentifying with. When you say the words "no thought is worth thinking about" to the mind it can be an opening or expansion of awareness into the present moment, freeing you to be with whatever it is you're doing. It also frees you to feel and sink into what you are experiencing in the moment in order to welcome God into the moment and let go.

Just as in Centering Prayer, we're not trying to stop our minds from thinking. Our human faculty that allows us to think is a gift from God. What we are doing is putting some space between thoughts; the more space we create between thoughts, the more we quiet our minds so that we can hear God.

Fruits of the Welcoming Prayer

> "...The energy centers (are) just like weeds in the desert. If you can keep them dried out by not reinforcing them or watering them with your imagination or by giving into them, very quickly they wither up and die. There's

no substance to them. They're just childhood habits that we never got around to change when we became an adult"[51] (Thomas Keating).

When we take responsibility for our emotional life, we finally get around to changing our childhood habits. Our attitudes and behaviors start to change when we become aware of the patterns we've been trapped in since early childhood. We begin to welcome our feelings because we see them as gifts offering us the opportunity to see our patterns. Relationships change, not because the other person has changed, but because we have made peace with what is. Our awareness of God's presence within increases. As we become more aware of God who is always present to us, we become more willing to let go of our attachments or desires and surrender to the present moment. By having an intention to let go of our emotional programs, we begin to see how much power they've had in our lives and how often they're subtly influencing our reactions. As we become more skilled at letting go by regular practice, we are able to let go of emotions as they arise. The unconscious energy we hold onto by resisting is more readily and easily released and, as Father Thomas says, divine energy rushes into the void.

Depending on the circumstances, you may not be able to do all three movements of the Welcoming Prayer while in the middle of an uncomfortable situation. However, I have had times when I became aware that afflictive emotions were being triggered in a situation and was able to simply say to myself "welcome," bringing my awareness to God in the moment, which helped to settle me down. I could go back later and check in with my body for any residue of emotion from the experience. In the early days of learning this practice it takes a commitment to remember to do the practice. Once you start to experience the fruits of the practice, doing it will become more automatic and you will be living your true life more authentically.

Welcoming Prayer Method

1. Think of an experience you had today or this week, something that was upsetting to you in some way or pushed your buttons.
2. What feeling do you have now about this situation? Start your body scan and notice any feelings, emotions, thoughts, body sensations or commentaries. It's important to notice what you

are feeling now, and not try to recreate how you felt when you had the experience.
3. First Movement—Feel and sink into what you are experiencing this moment in your body. Don't think about it. Don't resist it. Feel it. Stay with it. Don't rush through this part.
4. Second Movement—Welcome what you are experiencing this moment in your body as an opportunity to consent to the Divine Indwelling. Welcome the Divine Indwelling into the feelings, emotions, thoughts, body sensations or commentaries you are experiencing in your body by saying "welcome." The word "welcome" becomes for us a sacred symbol of our consent to the presence and action of the Indwelling Spirit. Traditionally the word "welcome" is said three times. Welcome, welcome, welcome.
5. Third Movement—Let go by saying the following sentence: "I let go of my desire for security, affection, control and embrace this moment as it is."
6. Go through all three movements even if you experience a change after the first or second.
7. Repeat the three movements as often as necessary until you experience a change or release.

When to Use the Welcoming Prayer

1. Use for the little upsets to prepare you for using it with bigger things. For example, if you practice when you are driving in traffic or in a long line at the grocery store, you will be more likely to remember to use it when you become angry with your spouse or your boss, or have a financial or medical crisis, or worry over a child's behavior.
2. Do a body scan morning and night to help uncover experiences that may be out of your awareness.
3. Use when you are provoked by events or persons in your daily life. With a regular practice you will be able to do the Welcoming Prayer while you're in the midst of an experience. You will still benefit when you use the prayer later and reflect on the experience. Be sure to practice with what you are feeling now, in the present moment, not trying to recreate what you experienced during the situation.

Contemplative Life

4. Use when you become aware of afflictive emotions, commentaries or interior dialogue taking your attention away from the present moment. You are not trying to suppress emotions or change your thoughts as much as using the occurrence of these emotions and thoughts as an opportunity to bring your attention back to the present moment and the presence of God.
5. You may use the Welcoming Prayer in anticipation of a tense or anxiety-producing event when you are already experiencing feelings.
6. The Welcoming Prayer may be helpful for long-held feelings that you have been unable to let go of. However, another practice covered in this program in a later chapter—the Forgiveness Prayer—may be more appropriate in this situation.
7. Some have come to think of the Welcoming Prayer as a "presence practice." Father Thomas was often heard saying "Centering Prayer for one hour a day, the Welcoming Prayer for the other twenty-three." Get in the habit of using the Welcoming Prayer throughout the day to bring your attention to the presence of God in the moment.

Going Deeper

Spiritual Counsel

Remember that the spiritual counsel section is comprised of short statements, quotes or Scripture passages that are related to this chapter's topic. After you become familiar with the information in the chapter, read through the spiritual counsel section. Notice if one or two seem to attract you and spend some time reflecting on them. And then peruse the spiritual counsel from time to time as you begin to work on the practices. You won't relate to all the statements or quotes, but a few will likely be very meaningful to you, and perhaps different ones on different days. Think of them as inspirational messages to assist you in persevering with the practices and grasping the deeper meaning of the topics.

1. Practicing awareness and consent brings us to a deeper letting go of the hidden attachments that bind us to the identity of the false self.
2. Because of the wounds of the past, we are unconsciously attached to seeking fulfillment of valid human needs in ways

that cannot bring true life, meaning and satisfaction. Finding them fulfilled in relationship with God brings true life, meaning and satisfaction.
3. It is interior attachment to seeking these compensatory needs that attaches us to things in our life. Letting go of these attachments brings freedom. Interior freedom allows us to let go of exterior attachments, have our true needs met in daily life, and respond actively to situations under the inspiration of the Spirit.
4. A deepening movement of the Welcoming Prayer is when we become totally one with the energy of the feeling while letting go.
5. Because the spiritual journey can feel empty, lonely, and difficult, we sometimes need to affirm the ways we have been changed, healed, brought to new life and greater compassion, and offer thanks to God.
6. In intimacy we respond in our relationship with God by becoming more human, more deeply ourselves before God. "... That he may grant you in accord with the riches of his glory to be strengthened with power through his Spirit in the inner self, and that Christ may dwell in your hearts through faith; that you, rooted and grounded in love, may have strength to comprehend with all the holy ones what is the breadth and length and height and depth, and to know the love of Christ that surpasses knowledge, so that you may be filled with all the fullness of God" (Ephesians 3:16-19).
7. "I let go of trying to change myself and let you, God, change my heart" (David Frenette).

Reflection Questions

The reflection questions are meant to help you deepen your understanding and experience of the material and practices. Spend some time reflecting on the questions and jot down what comes to mind. It's helpful to have a record of your experiences and reflections to look back at over time. In addition, this may be some of the content you will choose to share with your group, spiritual companion or friend, in spiritual direction or in your Holy Listening Circle.

1. Select one thought from the spiritual counsel that really spoke to you and briefly explain why.

2. What in daily life have you become aware of about yourself through the contemplative practices of Logging, Spiritual Reading, Lectio Divina, the Active Prayer and the Welcoming Prayer?
3. Have you been resistant to any of the practices so far? Which ones and how have you been resistant?
4. How has practicing the Welcoming Prayer affected your temperament? What gifts have you been receiving from using the practice?
5. What does it mean to you to be a contemplative or to live a contemplative life?

To Practice
Centering Prayer

Without a regular practice of Centering Prayer, the rest of the contemplative practices don't make as much sense. Centering Prayer is our foundation upon which our transformation is built. Listen to what Father Thomas says in *Open Mind, Open Heart* about our daily practice:

> "As your sensitivity to the spiritual dimension of your being develops through the daily practice of this prayer, you may begin to find the awareness of God's presence arising at times in ordinary activity. You may feel called to turn interiorly to God without knowing why. The quality of your spiritual sensitivity is developing and enabling you to pick up vibrations from a world you did not previously perceive. Without deliberately thinking of God, you may find that God is often present in the midst of your daily occupations."[52]

Logging

Continue to spend five to fifteen minutes Logging each day. Have you found the time of day that works best for you yet? If not, continue to experiment. Don't forget to review your Logging at the end of the week or month to notice if any patterns are emerging. If you're spending more than fifteen minutes per day on your Logging practice you may want to review the method, especially if you are an experienced journaler. You may have slipped into journaling rather than Logging.

Spiritual Reading

One hour of Spiritual Reading per week is recommended, either all at one time or ten to fifteen minutes four to five times a week. You may want to alternate Spiritual Reading with your Lectio Divina practice.

Lectio Divina

Practice Lectio Divina three times per week using Scripture passages of your choosing, either from the daily lectionary, from a book of the Bible you've decided to work through, using suggested topical readings in a book such as *Too Deep for Words*, or by simply opening the Bible and reading what is in front of you. At first you will use the scholastic method until you learn the rhythm of the four moments—reading, reflecting, responding and resting. Once you become more familiar with the four moments you will find that you naturally start to move into using the monastic method and awaken your spiritual senses. Consider alternating Lectio Divina and Spiritual Reading so that you are spending roughly the same amount of time each day with one practice or the other.

Active Prayer

Use your Active Prayer daily when your mind is not occupied in conversation, work or some other activity requiring concentration. Remember that the active prayer becomes an aspiration to no longer be controlled by our afflictive emotions, commentaries and interior dialogue, but to move more deeply into our hearts and into the heart of God. We practice using the Active Prayer until it starts to arise in us automatically.

Welcoming Prayer

Use the Welcoming Prayer daily. Begin when you wake up in the morning by doing a body scan and welcoming and letting go of what you discover. If you uncover in your Logging any lingering, unresolved emotions triggered during the day, take a few minutes to use the Welcoming Prayer. Remember to work with the feelings you are experiencing in the moment rather than trying to recreate what you were feeling when you had the experience. If you practice with some of the smaller upsets during the day you will be more likely to remember to use the Welcoming Prayer with the bigger upsets. It takes practice to remember to use the Welcoming Prayer in the moment of a triggering event, but you will still benefit from using the prayer later. You may also want to get in the habit of using the Welcoming Prayer throughout the day to bring your attention to the presence of God in the moment.

Resources for Further Study

Begeman, P., Dwyer, M., Haisten, C., Fitzpatrick-Hopler, G., Saulnier, T. (2016). *Welcoming Prayer, Consent on the Go: The Contemplative Life Program 40 Day Practice.* Contemplative Outreach, Ltd.

Bourgeault, C. (2004). *Centering Prayer and Inner Awakening*, (Chapter 13 – The Welcoming Prayer). Cambridge, MA: Cowley Publications.

Haisten, C. (2005). *The Practice of Welcoming Prayer*, www.contemplativeoutreach.org.

Hawkins, D., M.D., Ph.D. (2018). *Letting Go: The Pathway of Surrender.* Carlsbad, CA: Hay House, Inc.

CHAPTER EIGHT
Rest and Sabbath-Keeping

> *"Come to me, all you who labor and are burdened,*
> *and I will give you rest.*
> *Take my yoke upon you and learn from me,*
> *for I am meek and humble of heart;*
> *and you will find rest for yourselves."*
> Matthew 11:28-29

IN THE CONTEMPLATIVE LIVING EXPERIENCE (CLE) PROGRAM AS IT has been offered in Denver, the teaching on rest occurs in early December during the holiday season, which for many is a very hectic and busy time of year. Whether or not you are in the middle of the holiday season, after a few months of learning practices and figuring out how to integrate them into our lives, we need some time to rest.

The theme of this chapter is rest—resting in God and resting in the midst of activity, which includes resting from the activity of the false self. Resting in activity may seem contradictory until we start to see resting as an inner state we *receive* in Centering Prayer. It's not something we can seek to attain but is more a gift we receive when we have a consistent Centering Prayer practice. As this rest or what we might also think of as interior silence is instilled in us, we start to notice that we are different in our daily lives. The other practices we are learning in this program help us to maintain this state of rest or interior silence in our activity in the world.

Take some time now to rest—to pause from any effort to learn and practice—and notice what you have received, how you have changed. You might also ask others who are close to you in your life what they are noticing. So often our loved ones notice changes in us before we do.

A few years ago when I was teaching the CLE program, I had the experience during this teaching on rest of hearing something that I don't recall hearing before. (I'm sure you have had the experience of hearing something only when you're ready to hear it.) I had heard the teaching about rest and even about resting in the midst of activity. But I did not previously hear the part about resting from the activity of the false self. The CLE facilitators make a point of participating in the program alongside the participants so that we experience what the rest of the group is experiencing, but also so that we model our own continued transformation. This idea of resting from the activity of the false self not only resonated with me that year but has stayed with me ever since. In *The Spiritual Journey Series* Father Thomas presents a teaching he calls "Dismantling the False-Self System." While he makes it clear to us that healing and transformation are a gift of the grace of God, we do have a part to play. It's our life, after all, and while grace is a totally gratuitous gift, we are called to consent to God's activity in our lives.

What is God's activity? And how do we consent to it? Because I was intentionally pondering this new realization and how it applied to my life, I started to become more aware of the activity of the false self mostly by using the practices outlined in this program. Pondering is something we learn to do in both Lectio Divina and Spiritual Reading by slowing down and spending more time reflecting and pondering as part of the second moment. Even as I pondered, my awareness about the activity of the false self remained a bit fuzzy until I remembered one of the purposes of Logging. When we have a daily practice like Logging, of briefly writing down an event from the day and its impact or our emotional response, we have a gold mine of information about the activity of the false self. The recommendation for this practice is to review our Logging weekly or monthly. (Don't forget to do this part of the practice because this is where we start to notice patterns of behaviors and reactions.) When we start our practices with a prayer to the Holy Spirit and let go of trying to control the process, we're more capable of being able to see the reality of a situation rather than our perception, which may not be true or real. My Logging practice started to reveal to me a pattern of reacting with anger and indignation when I perceived myself to be right and the other person to be wrong. My emotional reaction propelled me into self-righteous action that I would almost always feel bad about later and regret my response. Email was a particularly dangerous communication form for me, because I could carefully craft my words in such a way that I could put the person down without sounding mean. But once I sent the email I would begin to feel remorseful and could not let go of what I had done. It

Contemplative Life

would often keep me awake in the middle of the night. This was a longtime pattern of behavior that I had not previously been able to see so clearly. As I became more aware of the pattern, I was able to start using the Welcoming Prayer when I felt anger and indignation before taking any action, which helped me get to a place of accepting "what is" and deciding what to do about it using my rational faculties rather than reacting emotionally. I still have a tendency to repeat this pattern, but today I am more likely to either call the person to clear things up (rather than shooting off an email) or I recognize that an energy center has been triggered and just let it go—the grace of the Welcoming Prayer.

As we become more accustomed to the experience of rest—resting in God during our time of prayer and as we move from prayer into the activity of daily life—we become more sensitive to the activity of the false self. When we experience afflictive emotions, or our mind is bombarded with commentaries, or we feel the pressure of our cultural conditioning, we start to notice how much energy we expend running our programs for happiness. Rest is a more natural state that occurs when we are present to the presence of God within. Take heart that none of us is able to maintain this state all the time. When we experience the activity of the false self or even when we simply feel drained or experience a low ebb in our energy level, these are clues that the activity of the false self is operating. Now, in addition to Centering Prayer, we have other practices for daily life in our toolkit to help us move back into this state of rest.

Rest

It was in the sixth century that Gregory the Great described contemplation as *resting* in God. In *Open Mind, Open Heart* Father Thomas says,

> "In this resting or stillness the mind and heart are not actively seeking [God] but are beginning to experience, to taste, what they have been seeking. This places them in a state of tranquility and profound interior peace. This state is not the suspension of all action, but the mingling of a few simple acts to sustain one's attention to God with the loving experience of God's presence."[53]

Julie Saad

The contemplative practices we're learning in this program, along with our Centering Prayer practice, are a few of these simple acts we can do to keep our attention on God. Throughout this program we ask what it means to be a contemplative or live a contemplative life. The answer will be different for each of us as we explore and discover the depths of our being. The more we keep our attention on God in daily life, the closer we come to that state of tranquility and interior peace where we are resting in God rather than seeking God. We have found what we have been seeking.

As the thirteenth-century Persian poet Rumi wrote, "What I most want is to spring out of this personality, then to sit apart from leaping. I've lived too long where I can be reached."[54] How many of us feel this way and long for quiet and solitude? We live in a time of instant and constant communication through our smart phones, texts, emails, social media, news streaming, etc. We're over-stretched with too much to do and come to the end of our day tired, but conscious of what we've left undone. This kind of stress leaves us anxious, worried, angry, unable to sleep restfully. When we feel this way it's a sign that we've lost our sense of a reasonable use of time and that our lives are no longer in balance. Ask yourself: is your natural attitude or disposition one of restfulness or restlessness? When you have free time what do you do? Do you schedule something just to get busy? Life is meant to be full, but it's also meant to be enjoyed. We need to be intentional about including into our busy lives times of rest, celebration, and enjoyment without the stress and pressure of everyday concerns.

Often when we think of what it means to rest, we assume we're talking about resting our bodies. Father Thomas talks about resting in God as the harmony of body, mind and spirit that can rest in God in the ordinary activities of our day. Our practices are a way of reducing the obstacles to resting. Our intention in Centering Prayer and our other practices is to be open, receptive, and surrender to the presence of God in the present moment. Centering Prayer invites us to just be with God; there is nothing for us to do, nothing needs to be fixed or changed, everything is perfect as it is. When we accept this, and are grounded in it, we can bring this state of "beingness in God" into everyday life.

It's important to be aware that deep rest will often start the process of unloading of the unconscious, what the Christian tradition has historically referred to as purification. The pain of the emotional programs for happiness is brought to consciousness so that it can be healed. It is in this deep rest that the Spirit works and where we become aware of the activity of the false self—the strong emotions, restlessness, attachments and aversions—that reinforces our need for power and control, esteem and affection, security and survival, and causes us to want to change everyone and everything else. The unloading we experience in deep rest results in what Father Thomas calls evacuation, where the primitive emotions and thoughts are released. While this can be uncomfortable, it is necessary for our healing, and it brings freedom from the grip of the false self. This is an opportunity to use the Welcoming Prayer to help us accept what is, not what we would like it to be. We're not trying to get rid of the activity of the false self but to rest in God in it, to let go of the desire to change things or be in control. Whenever we experience deep rest, the work of the Spirit through unloading and evacuation follows. Our faithfulness to our practice begins to calm the false self, lessen its impact.

We are invited in daily life to rest in God by simply being with whatever is in the present moment, seeing each person and event as a gift, offering the opportunity to heal the needs of the false self. As we "do" our practices, what we are really doing is turning to God in the moment. The more we turn to God, the more we rest, and the more integrated rest becomes in all aspects of our lives. This is the transformation of consciousness to which we are committed. Father Thomas has said that contemplative life is Christ in you leading your life in complete solidarity with your life just as it is. This is the mystery of the Incarnation, that Christ lives your life for you, with you, and in you. Gradually we become less and less involved in the drama of life, the over-identification with the accomplishments of the false self. We are growing in awareness of God's life in us.

Sabbath-Keeping

Because of the busyness of life in our modern world, especially with the pressures of our culture, it will likely be difficult to even imagine how to incorporate rest into daily life. Where to begin? As with all our practices, we begin with intention. Sabbath-Keeping is a practice that can help us to be intentional about incorporating rest into our lives. The suggestion is to find a particular time of the week to set aside as sabbath. As time goes on, with faithful adherence to sabbath time, we learn to incorporate rest more and more into our daily life.

In his book *Sabbath*, Abraham Heschel talks about sabbath not as a day off, but a day made holy by the grace of God. We may have grown up thinking that the sabbath required something of us—that we go to church, refrain from work, or take a day off from shopping. The commandment is "Remember the sabbath day—keep it holy" (Exodus 20:8). God is not so much requiring something from us as asking us to remember sabbath. You might recall that the Pharisees were always giving Jesus a hard time about how his disciples were not following the letter of the law. During one of those times Jesus said to them, "The sabbath was made for [people], not [people] for the sabbath" (Mark 2:27). The sabbath is a gift to us from God, a day of rest.

You can expect it to be challenging to set aside sabbath time. It may be helpful to think of it as a process we grow into with time and intention. The Jesuit theologian John Haughey says,

> "The sabbath is a paradox. It is a day that requires great discipline to do nothing. Our efforts are focused on letting our guard down so God can get to us. The reason we aren't given dominion over the seventh day is so that we can learn to let God achieve dominion over us."[55]

The paradox for us is that we may have to work at setting aside time to rest, to let God meet us where we are. We may be further challenged by our false self's desire to be in control. We may think in our rational mind that we are willing to allow God to "get to us" or have "dominion over us," but the unconscious motivation of the false self may sabotage our efforts to establish sabbath time in our lives. Notice if you are resistant to setting aside time in your week to just be with God and think about what might be causing that resistance.

What is sabbath time? It's a time when we cease work and other everyday pressures in order to make the time holy. It frees us up for higher concerns and reminds us that we don't live to work but work in order to live and love. Sabbath time is time for enjoyment and celebration. We may choose to be in solitude with God, but we may also choose to enjoy time with family and friends, eat a wonderful meal, and dress in our "Sunday best." It may be a time of reflection and reconciliation. It is a way of sanctifying time rather than just passing time and can therefore be any time in our week—an afternoon, an hour, a walk in nature, a

Contemplative Life

dinner with a beloved. It is meant to be a time of spiritual enrichment and should be prepared for and anticipated with great joy. The time won't come into being on its own. We must be intentional about setting aside time and preparing for it. If you were going to set aside sabbath time for spiritual enrichment, what might you need to do in order to prepare for it and not be distracted by other concerns?

Sabbath-Keeping Method

1. Set an intention to create time and space in your life for sabbath.
2. Decide on a time during the week that you can dedicate to sabbath, whether it be a day, a half of a day, or even a few hours.
3. Prepare for your sabbath time by doing anything that needs to be done ahead of time to allow this time to be free.
4. Intend to let your guard down so God can get to you.
5. Decide how you want to spend your sabbath time—in solitude, being rather than doing, with friends or family, in nature, in prayer and reflection, or some other spiritually enriching activity.

Going Deeper

Spiritual Counsel

The spiritual counsel is offered to encourage you in deepening your understanding by reflecting on the teaching in this chapter on Rest and Sabbath-Keeping. First become familiar with the teaching in the chapter and then review the spiritual counsel to see what statement, quote, or Scripture passage stands out for you or attracts you. Go back and review the spiritual counsel throughout the time you are working on the material in this chapter to see if anything new surfaces. These passages are meant to be inspirational messages to assist you in persevering in the practices and grasping the deeper meaning of the topics.

1. Resting in God is the natural evolution of the Lectio Divina process. It can be accelerated by a method. Centering Prayer prepares us for the fourth movement of Lectio Divina, resting in God—being—an attitude of loving acceptance (welcoming) of who we are. There are no bad moments in it; it's God's

particular love for us. Centering Prayer reduces the noise and makes it possible for us to hear the message from the Divine Reality. "Whoever has ears to hear ought to hear" (Mark 4:9).
2. The whole movement of Centering Prayer is to heal the unconscious and to infuse into us Divine Life which is beamed into us all the time. Centering Prayer quietly calms the false-self system, and begins to insinuate itself into our life. Everything will work better—body, mind, spirit—it's the way it's supposed to be. We are resting from the activity of the false-self system.
3. We can enjoy deep rest in extraordinary activity. Resting in activity is in being—not doing—and letting go of the needs of the false self for control, approval, security, or needing to change. Resting from the energy of the false self in Centering Prayer and in activity opens us to resting in God. This deep rest is the fruit of our intention to consent to God's presence and action (dismantling of the false self) in our lives. God's activity goes on with or without our knowledge or felt experience at the time. Transformation is God's work. "By waiting and by calm you shall be saved, in quiet and in trust shall be your strength" (Isaiah 30:15).
4. The deeper the rest, the more certain it is to reduce the defense mechanisms that we are using to repress material from early childhood. So the deeper the rest, the more certain is the unloading of the unconscious. If you enjoy deep rest, it is inevitable to have unloading and evacuation.
5. Every time you evacuate something in the body, you move closer to the Center; there is space and into that space rushes the Holy Spirit with various gifts. When it no longer matters what comes up, you are close to Divine Union.
6. The Sabbath is not only about refraining from work, but about creating a restfulness that is also a celebration. It is a day for the body as well as the soul. "The Sabbath was made for [people], not [people] for the Sabbath" (Mark 2:27).
7. The Sabbath comes with its own holiness. We enter not simply a day, but an atmosphere. It does not simply come into being; the depth of the experience is created by how we behave on the other six days of the week—they are the pilgrimage to the Sabbath.

Reflection Questions

Spend some time reflecting on these questions and jot down some of what comes to mind. Don't feel you have to write anything at length or even write in complete sentences. You will appreciate having your reflections over the time you are working with this book to look back over. In addition, you may choose to use some of the content to share with your group, spiritual companion or friend, in spiritual direction or in your Holy Listening Circle.

1. Select one thought from the spiritual counsel that spoke to you and briefly explain why.
2. What in daily life have you become aware of about yourself through the contemplative practices of Logging, Spiritual Reading, Lectio Divina, the Active Prayer, the Welcoming Prayer and Sabbath-Keeping? Give concrete, personal examples.
3. What gifts have you received from the practices you have been learning? What struggles? How have you been resistant to the practices so far?
4. How have you incorporated Rest into your daily life?
5. What does it mean to you to be a contemplative or to live a contemplative life?

To Practice
Centering Prayer

Spend some time reflecting on where you are with your Centering Prayer practice. Remember that Centering Prayer is the foundation upon which we build our contemplative life. Are you practicing for twenty minutes twice a day? Have you been called to increase the amount of time you practice during at least one of your prayer periods? Are you still struggling to get in your second period of prayer? Listen to what Father Thomas says about the amount of time we spend in Centering Prayer from *Open Mind, Open Heart*:

> "Twenty to thirty minutes is the minimum amount of time necessary for most people to establish interior silence and to get beyond their superficial thoughts. You may be inclined to remain longer. Experience will teach you what the right amount of time is… As your sensitivity to the spiritual dimension of your being

develops through the daily practice of this prayer, you may begin to find the awareness of God's presence arising at times in ordinary activity."[56]

Logging

Continue to practice Logging daily for five to fifteen minutes. Are you remembering to Log every day? Are you aware of the difference between Logging and journaling? Remember to review your Logging at the end of the week or month to notice if any patterns are emerging. The patterns we tend to see show us the activity of the false self. Increased awareness of the activity of the false self helps us to change or let go of any behaviors, emotions, thoughts or commentaries that no longer serve us.

Spiritual Reading

Continue to practice Spiritual Reading weekly. Spend one hour per week doing Spiritual Reading, either all in one day or ten to fifteen minutes four to five times a week. Have you tried alternating your Spiritual Reading with Lectio Divina? What other ways have you found to incorporate these practices?

Lectio Divina

Practice Lectio Divina three times per week using Scripture passages of your choosing, either from the daily lectionary, from a book of the Bible you've decided to work through, using suggested topical readings in a book such as *Too Deep for Words*, or by simply opening the Bible and reading what is in front of you. Consider alternating your Lectio Divina practice with Spiritual Reading. Remember that doing the practices teaches us how to do the practices. If it's not working for you to alternate Lectio Divina and Spiritual Reading, try something different. For example, try doing Lectio Divina three days in a row with the same Scripture passage and reflect on how that experience is different from doing it once with one passage.

Active Prayer

The Active Prayer is a daily practice to use when your mind is not occupied in conversation, work or some other activity requiring concentration. Are you remembering to use your Active Prayer every day? If not, set an intention to use it every day or make yourself some sort of reminder. After some time of using it intentionally it will start to come to you automatically.

Welcoming Prayer

Continue to use the Welcoming Prayer daily, either by starting and ending your day with a body scan, welcoming, and letting go or by noticing when you are bothered by afflictive emotions or commentaries. Sometimes your Logging practice will help you to remember an event, thought, or emotion that the Welcoming Prayer would help with. It takes practice to remember to use the Welcoming Prayer in the moment of a triggering event, but you will still benefit from using the practice later.

Sabbath-Keeping

Find a time that fits into your life each week to set aside for sabbath, whether it be a day, an afternoon, or a few hours. Be intentional and prepare ahead of time so that you can devote the time to spiritual concerns, rather than the concerns of daily life. Consider how you can spend the time *being* rather than *doing*.

Resources for Further Study

Heschel, A. (2005). *The Sabbath*. New York, NY: Farrar, Straus, and Giroux.

CHAPTER NINE
Contemplative Discernment

> *"The purpose of discernment is to know God's will, that is, to find, accept, and affirm the unique way in which God's love is manifest in our life."*[57]
> Henri Nouwen

IN THE FIRST PART OF THE CONTEMPLATIVE LIVING EXPERIENCE (CLE) program, we focus on deepening our interior prayer life, leading to the awareness of God's presence in all that is—even in our brokenness, conflicts, and failed relationships. By the time we reach the latter part of the program, if we have been practicing what we've learned the best we can, we're starting to have a better understanding of what in us blocks not only our relationship with God, but our relationship with ourselves and others. We're learning what gets in the way of being and becoming the person God created us to be. The teaching in the previous chapter on Rest and Sabbath-Keeping gives us a chance to pause and start to integrate what we're discovering about ourselves. It also provides the opportunity to look at what interior silence and resting in God means, to notice how we are already experiencing it, and to commit to daily practices that help cultivate spiritual growth. We're now at a place where we can start to ask ourselves: What is it like to have a prayer life? What is God calling me to? What does it mean to live a contemplative life? What in me needs to be healed? What relationships in my life need healing?

Our focus shifts towards increased intentionality in how we are living our life. The interior life we're experiencing brings us to greater humility and vulnerability and lowers our defenses. We are now more capable of looking at our part in relationships and taking responsibility for the emotional programs for happiness our false selves have constructed. And we're better able to assess where we are in our life as we begin to make choices more in keeping with our true self.

Contemplative Discernment

As we ask ourselves what it means to be a contemplative, we find that living a contemplative life is a process of discovery more than a prescribed series of lessons to be learned. We don't look to others for "the answer," although inquiring and listening to others can certainly inform our answers. Though we haven't formally talked about or learned a discernment process thus far, living with questions is a big part of living in discernment. When discernment starts with going to God with our questions and desires, the answers will find us.

In his book *Addiction & Grace*, Gerald May describes discernment as:

> "...living life prayerfully—bringing oneself to God as honestly and completely as possible, seeking God's guidance as openly as possible, and then, in faith, responding as fully as possible... trying to bring all one's faculties into harmony with God's transforming grace..."[58]

With this definition in mind, our discernment process becomes prayer with God at the center.

Many of us may not have learned a method for making decisions based on our interior spiritual life because we were raised in a religious tradition that told us what to believe and informed us what was right or wrong for us. We were not allowed to trust our own inner compass, but instead were taught to rely on exterior instruction for moral guidance and even basic decision-making. The intention in contemplative discernment is not to throw out what we may have learned from religious tradition, but to open ourselves to the voice of the Spirit speaking to us within and in all of life. Discernment can then become for us a way of life, a habit of living from our heart—a discerning heart. As we will learn, at times we actively and consciously "work" on discernment and then we take it to prayer or give it to God and rest in knowing that the decision will be revealed.

Or perhaps we were not raised in a religious tradition, but our cultural conditioning had the same effect of discounting the value of personal discernment. Either way, many of us were not given the tools we need to access our conscience and intuition in making the types of decisions that require inner guidance. Most ordinary decisions in daily life are straightforward and can be made by simply using our good intentions, judgment, and common sense to decide which action meets our goals most effectively. But for decisions that are more important or have greater consequences and require more of our energy and attention, we may need to use a discernment process. Discernment helps us to uncover whether the desires driving a given decision are inspired by love or by our attachment to a particular outcome. The discernment process can also help us to become aware of hidden motivations coming from the emotional programs for happiness or the influence of our cultural conditioning that affect our decisions and keep us from making free choices from our true self. When we are experiencing confusion or conflict around an issue, when we have a significant, potentially life-changing decision or choice, or if we are uneasy about a decision or commitment we have already made, we may find it is better to discern than to decide too quickly.

The first step is to recognize when we need to discern. It may be during times of crisis or change, perhaps in a job or relationship or move. It may be when circumstances of life seem to press in on us, like difficult parenting issues, illness, or end of life decisions. Or we may be faced with interior turmoil due to bringing to consciousness the effects of the false self on our lives, leaving us feeling alone and confused, in need of forgiveness. The discernment process helps us to approach these situations knowing that we are not alone. It eases the pressure and gives us the space and time we need to feel at peace. This process sometimes may feel like inaction but is actually very active. As we wait on God in faith to reveal the course of action most consistent with who we are or want to become in communion with God, we're not determining what is right or wrong or trying to achieve a decision. Rather, we embrace an opportunity to deepen our relationship with God and receive the gift of grace. As we sort through the options we are presented with, we have the opportunity to encounter God in the present moment and let go of our limiting hidden motivations. Our choice becomes consenting to God, remembering that whatever we decide God is with us guiding us to what's next if we are open, listening, and paying attention.

As we become accustomed to living a contemplative life, we start to realize that God is always speaking to us. Our practices—Centering Prayer, Lectio Divina, the Welcoming Prayer, and others—make us more sensitive to God's language and more open to signs from God that we all encounter in everyday life but often don't pay attention to. Father Thomas has often said that God's first language is silence. When we're practicing silence and experiencing interior silence, we're more attuned to hearing what Scripture calls the still, small voice within (1 Kings 19:12). We learn to read the signs of God's guidance in Scripture, Spiritual Reading, in what the people in our lives are saying to us, nature with its seasonal patterns and cycles, events and life circumstances and how we respond to them. We may also see signs in dreams, fears and resistances, and synchronicities. We use all our faculties and our whole network of intelligence—feelings, attractions, impulses, inclinations, intuition, judgment, body sensations. We start a sorting and sifting process, staying open, receptive, and listening.

What may be the most important ingredient in discernment is waiting with an open heart. We live in a fast-paced world focused on being productive, accomplishing something, creating a five-year plan—full of noise and doing. In the discernment process we will be tempted to give in to this aspect of our cultural conditioning and try to enter into making decisions before we're fully ready. Waiting takes time and, if you're at all like me, it seems as if we never have enough time. Rather than being a matter of doing or not doing, waiting is an act of being, a summons from a deeper place within. In her book *When the Heart Waits*, Sue Monk Kidd says,

> "Waiting...means descending into self, into God, into the deeper labyrinths of prayer. It involves listening to disinherited voices within, facing the wounded holes in the soul, the denied and undiscovered, the places one lives falsely. It means struggling with the vision of who we really are in God and molding the courage to live that vision."[59]

Waiting is not passive. It requires our full attention as we allow what comes from within to arise. It is a rich opportunity to observe our inner process, see where our emotional programs for happiness interfere with our ability to make choices free from the encumbrances of the false self.

Contemplative Discernment will usually result in making a choice, but even more than simple choice-making, it is consenting to God's presence and action in our lives. Our consent in discernment may be to *do* something (change jobs, go back to school, leave a relationship, move) or to *be* something (kinder, more loving, less judgmental, more creative). Whether our consent concerns doing or being, we commit to making free choices in harmony with God's loving presence in our lives—with God's will for us. We are more willing to take responsibility for the choices we make. As we become more intentional about our relationship with God, the discernment practice brings our lives more consciously under the influence of God. Any motivation that is still coming out of our cultural conditioning and emotional programs for happiness is likely to interfere, causing conflict and confusion in the discernment process. These may be clues that what is needed is more prayer, more consent, more waiting on God. Discernment is a matter of the heart, not the ego. When we turn to our heart, our true self surrenders our will to the will of God. This usually leads to an experience of peaceful knowing.

What does the will of God mean to you? We may have somehow gotten the notion that God has some prepackaged plan for us. Over the years I have heard so many people agonize over trying to figure out what God wants them to do as if God's will is some secret message to be decoded. They suffer as if they have one chance to get it right or wrong. I've been there. But as I become more attuned to Contemplative Discernment, I find that God is with us, loving us and guiding us no matter what we do. When our will is aligned with God's will we know that God is always present to us, always calling us into a deeper love, and we in turn allow God's love to flow through us to others and to all of creation. This conviction allows us to be the presence in the world that God created us to be, and from that place, we know what we are to do. We're no longer compelled to follow what we think we "should" do. We know what the desire of our heart is, and we are in harmony with who God is calling us to be. God's will is not so much about what we do, but how we live our lives out of our conviction. In his book *Discernment: Reading the Signs of Daily Life*, Henri Nouwen says, "The purpose of discernment is to know God's will, that is, to find, *accept*, and *affirm* the unique way in which God's love is manifest in our life."[60] Aligning our will with God's will is the fruit of the discernment process.

I have been a part of Contemplative Outreach since 1994, mostly through the Center for Contemplative Living in Denver. I retired from my full-time work with a public pension plan at the end of 2008 and had just started devoting more time to volunteering at the Center when, in 2009, the Center's founder, Sister Bernadette Teasdale, decided to retire. I was asked to be a part of a transition team to help carry out the way forward for the Center, but first we had to decide what that way would be. We went through a two-year process to learn all the tasks involved with Sister Bernadette's position. We developed a dual leadership model for the future, but it didn't appear as if any clear candidates were coming forward to apply for either position. Throughout the process of participating on the transition team, I had been discerning whether I wanted to step into one of these leadership positions. Even though I was enjoying being retired, I felt God was calling me to apply for the position of coordinator. And so I did. But after being in the position for about a year, I began to experience unrest, unease, discontent. I was no longer at peace with my decision. At the same time, I was distraught because I was so sure in my discernment process that I was meant to take the position. I felt I had somehow failed myself, the Center, Sister Bernadette, Father Thomas, and even God, because in my heart I knew I couldn't stay in the position. What I didn't realize at the time was that when discernment becomes a way of life and we have an intention to align our will with God's will, we continue to receive signs from God. I soon saw that I had not failed. I had served the Center through the transition phase and then God called me to something else. I didn't know to what yet, but the signs were clear. I served as the coordinator for the rest of the second year and then I went on to become the coordinator of the CLE program, to become a writer in the online courses offered by Contemplative Outreach, and to join the board of the Contemplative Outreach international organization, all of which I would not have had time to do in addition to my responsibilities as coordinator. I continue to serve in ways that give me peace, contentment, and joy and I trust that God will continue to guide me.

I'm grateful I had begun to develop a greater capacity to hear and heed my inner guidance when I was going through all the decisions involved with my work and volunteer service. In the CLE program we start the discernment process with a practice or method. At first it may seem to be a list of pros and cons like we may have used in the past to make decisions. What's different about the discernment process is that as we list the pros and cons, what we call advantages and disadvantages, we ponder our responses and look for hidden motivations; we notice any feelings that arise, especially afflictive emotions, and use the Welcoming Prayer to let go if they are getting in the way of the process; we notice and record insights that arise from our intuition; and we end with a consent to God, either to continue to discern, or perhaps a decision. The practices we teach in this program are meant to be experiential and by practicing them according to the prescribed method, we discover how they become not only prayer but are integrated into contemplative life. As described by Henri Nouwen,

> "Discernment is rooted in spiritual practice, yet it is not a step-by-step process. It requires learning to listen for and recognize over time the voice and character of God in our hearts and daily lives."[61]

Those who engage in discernment practices over time, along with other contemplative practices, find discernment to be a way of life. We no longer seek to understand how God is speaking to us; we have developed the apparatus to recognize the signs and to trust what arises in the silence.

Contemplative Discernment Method

1. Start with a prayer, inviting the Holy Spirit into your discernment process. Ask the Holy Spirit "What is before me?" "What is God asking of me?" Pause, observe, watch, see what arises. Ask for guidance, detachment from the outcome, and freedom with respect to any preference.
2. What is going on in your life right now? What is pressing, unresolved, unclear, or causing concern, pain, or conflict? Make a list without judging, analyzing, or eliminating anything. Each time you enter into the discernment process choose one issue. Add to the list as needed.
3. Clearly state the issue you've chosen to yourself and to God. Write it succinctly using nonjudgmental language. Use a blank sheet of paper or blank screen and write the date at the top. You will likely be doing the discernment process with the same question several times over the course of a few weeks or months. Use this format for your question to state the issue "What are the Advantages and Disadvantages of my or me…?" Be specific, include only one issue per discernment question, and include a time frame so it's not too open-ended.
Examples:
A. *What are the advantages and disadvantages of me searching for another job this year?* or

B. *What are the advantages and disadvantages of my staying in a hotel when I visit my brother in June?* or

C. *What are the advantages and disadvantages of me talking to Claudia about her behavior at John's party?*

You can see from these examples that it's not necessary to get into a lot of detail about the issue when crafting the question. You know what the issue is and all that's behind it and many of the details will come out when you write about the advantages and disadvantages. Ask yourself if the question resonates within your heart. If it doesn't, you may need to go back into prayer to reformulate the question.

4. Ponder the issue, allowing the unconscious or hidden issues to emerge into consciousness. Repeat the question a few times, even saying it out loud.
5. Make two columns, one for advantages and one for disadvantages. Leave room at the bottom of the page to record any insights that arise as you are writing advantages and disadvantages and any consent you reach once you finish the process.
6. Start with the advantages column. Say to yourself "What are the advantages of my or me …?" Write whatever comes to mind—thoughts, feelings, emotions, or commentaries. Be succinct. Use one or two words or a phrase per line. No need for full sentences. Don't judge or eliminate what comes to mind. Just write it down.
7. Ponder. Repeat the question several times as you write down your responses.
8. Use the Welcoming Prayer if anything comes up that stimulates a reaction, emotional response, or resistance. Pay attention to any body sensations you become aware of.
9. Write down any insight or new information that surfaces as you go through this process.
10. When you think you have written all your responses to the question, ponder the question one more time. Don't just think with your head. Be open to the Spirit touching your heart.
11. Then let go of any attachment you may have to anything written in the advantages column. At the bottom of your list write the words "I let go of any attachment to these advantages."
12. Now go to the disadvantages column. Ask the question "What are the disadvantages of my or me…?"

13. Go through the same process. Ponder the question, write your responses, use the Welcoming Prayer if some emotional response is triggered, jot down any insight or new information. When your list of disadvantages feels complete write the words "I let go of any attachment to these disadvantages."
14. The same comment could surface in both the advantages and disadvantages columns.
15. Go through the discernment process several times before you come to making a choice or a decision. It's helpful to leave some time, a week or so, in between doing the written discernment process as the Spirit will continue to work in you and reveal more to you. Continue with the process until you have no new self-knowledge or insights. Have you reached a consent? (Your consent may be to continue to discern.) Write down your consent.
16. If after going through the process several times you are unable to come to consent other than continuing the process, check to see if the issue is clearly stated or if the question needs to be restated.
17. When you come to make a choice of action, this becomes your consent to God. A decision is an action of the will manifesting intention.
18. The goal is not 100% assurance, but the peaceful confirmation of your choice, a sense of things falling into place, a sense of harmony within yourself, a sense of clarity about this issue.

Going Deeper

Spiritual Counsel
Pause for a few minutes here and reflect on how you have been engaging with the spiritual counsel so far. Have you been engaging regularly? Have you forgotten about them? Don't worry if you haven't fully engaged with this area of the program yet. Keeping up with the practices and continuing to learn new material is a lot. I think it's helpful to remember that sometimes when we forget about a practice or suggested use of material it can be a sign of resistance. Please don't think of resistance as something that is "bad" or "wrong." It is normal for all of us to resist what may be interfering with our status quo in life and if you have a regular Centering Prayer practice and are working with the material in this book you are disrupting the status quo in a big way! That's called transformation.

Julie Saad

In this chapter the spiritual counsel contains short statements, quotes or Scripture passages about Contemplative Discernment, and are meant to be inspirational wisdom statements to encourage you and assist you in going deeper in your reflection about the topic. If you haven't been using them, try setting an intention now to spend some time with one or two of them after you have become familiar with the material in this chapter.

1. Discernment means "living life prayerfully—bringing oneself to God as honestly and completely as possible, seeking God's guidance as openly as possible, and then, in faith, responding as fully as possible... trying to bring all one's faculties into harmony with God's transforming grace..."[62] (Gerald May).
2. Some characteristics of discernment are *honesty* (acceptance—risks that God is good); *dignity* (risks that we ourselves are good); *community* (journey, not a private thing between ourselves and God—our own eyes see only what they want); *responsibility* (requires taking action—we need to seek grace, reach out for it, and act in accord with it); *simplicity* (living with love).
3. In Contemplative Discernment we allow the choices and decisions of our life to become both a means to encounter God in the present moment and a way to let go of the hidden motivations that limit our spiritual journey with God. Then our choice of action can also become consent to God. "I cannot do anything on my own... because I do not seek my own will but the will of the one who sent me" (John 5:30).
4. The most painful times of life are those that encompass periods of transition—mourning the death of a loved one, grief after a divorce, the loss of a job, relocation, and separation from friends. In a time of transition, the purpose of prayer and discernment is not to anesthetize oneself to remove the pain. We pray (discern) to lift the problem and its pain up to a higher level where it ceases to be destructive.
5. If we become aware of feeling disappointment or excitement around the issue, it is an invitation to return to the Discernment Process. "...He is not the God of disorder but of peace" (1 Corinthians 14:33).
6. When our enthusiasms fail, and our painfully made decisions amount to nothing, it is not a time for useless depression. The

Contemplative Life

challenge now is to discover what can be learned from the experience so that the spiritual journey may continue. God has not offered us a job to do in life; he has offered us a covenant of love to fulfill. That covenant can be fulfilled even when all jobs fail.
7. God's purpose for each of us is that we reach the fullness of our personal potential. If we accept this, discernment is not trying to sniff out a hidden preplan of God, but to make the best creative choice we can make in any given set of circumstances. "...We do not cease praying for...his will through all spiritual wisdom and understanding...bearing fruit and growing in the knowledge of God, strengthened with every power, in accord with his glorious might, for all endurance and patience, with joy..." (Colossians 1:9-14).

Reflection Questions
The reflection questions will help you deepen your understanding and experience of the teaching on Contemplative Discernment. They give you the opportunity to pause and take the time to see where you are with your engagement with the practices. We tend to get busy and think we don't have time for reflection, but reflection is part of what helps us integrate what we're learning and experiencing. Your reflections may contain the content you will choose to share with your group, spiritual companion or friend, in spiritual direction or in your Holy Listening Circle.

1. Select one thought from the spiritual counsel that spoke to you and briefly explain why.
2. Are you fully committed to doing the practices taught in this program? Are you forgetting to do any of the practices? Do you find yourself resisting doing any of the practices or following the method as outlined?
3. What have you struggled with in using the Contemplative Discernment Practice? What gift have you received?
4. What does it mean to you to be a contemplative or to live a contemplative life?

To Practice
Centering Prayer
Why do we say Centering Prayer is the foundation upon which we

build a contemplative life? Even when people make a commitment to this program wholeheartedly, they will still struggle with daily life and with their motivation to continue. I tell you this as a way of encouraging you because this is to be expected. You are not alone if this is your experience. For so long we have lived the life of the false self, the self that experiences being separate from God, the self that does not want to change and keeps throwing roadblocks into our path. The chief roadblock, feeling separate from God, is described by Father Thomas in *Open Mind, Open Heart*:

> "The chief thing that separates us from God is the thought that we are separated from [God]. If we get rid of that thought, our troubles will be greatly reduced. We fail to believe that we are always with God and that [God] is part of every reality. The present moment, every object we see, our inmost nature are all rooted in [God]. But we hesitate to believe this until personal experience gives us the confidence to believe in it. This involves the gradual development of intimacy with God... Centering Prayer is a way of awakening to the reality in which we are immersed."[63]

We are already immersed in the reality of the presence of God within and in all of life. My hope for you is that you to have the confidence to believe in it. That confidence comes with a committed practice of Centering Prayer.

Logging

Continue to practice Logging for five to fifteen minutes each day. Hopefully, you have found a rhythm to incorporating this practice into your daily life by now. Remember to review your Logging at the end of the week or month and make note of any patterns you see emerging.

Spiritual Reading

Continue to practice Spiritual Reading for one hour per week, either doing it all in one day or spending ten to fifteen minutes a day four to five times a week. If you haven't yet, you may want to experiment with alternating your Spiritual Reading practice with Lectio Divina.

Lectio Divina

Practice Lectio Divina three times per week using Scripture passages of your choosing. Have you noticed that you are moving into using the monastic method, allowing the Spirit to move you from moment to moment—reading, reflecting, responding and resting?

Active Prayer

Use your Active Prayer daily when your mind is not occupied in conversation, work or some other activity requiring concentration. Is your active prayer coming to you automatically yet? Are you noticing any reduction in obsessive thoughts and commentaries or afflictive emotions? I encouraged you to create an active prayer by asking for a gift from God. Pause and reflect on whether that gift is manifesting for you. If you are not yet using the Active Prayer regularly, set an intention to remind yourself to practice.

Welcoming Prayer

Use the Welcoming Prayer daily. Are you using the Welcoming Prayer to do regular body scans to become more aware of anything unresolved you may be holding onto? Are you remembering to use the Welcoming Prayer when you experience being triggered by an afflictive emotion, thought or commentary? If you are using the Welcoming Prayer at a time later in the day while reflecting on an experience, are you remembering to work with the feelings you experience in the moment rather than trying to recreate the feelings you had while you were going through the experience? If you experience afflictive emotions or a sense of unease while doing the Contemplative Discernment practice, remember to use the Welcoming Prayer to help you continue the process of discernment.

Sabbath-Keeping

Find a time that fits into your life each week to set aside for Sabbath, whether it be a day, an afternoon, or a few hours. Be intentional and prepare ahead of time so you can devote the time to spiritual concerns, rather than the concerns of daily life. Consider how you can spend the time being rather than doing. How are you incorporating Sabbath-Keeping into your week? If you find it difficult to find the time, set aside an hour or two to begin with and see how it can grow from there.

Contemplative Discernment

Repeat the discernment practice at least two or three times. It is recommended that you practice once a week for several weeks. Pay special attention to any insights you have and whether you have reached consent. Always start with a clean sheet of paper (or blank screen) and put the date at the top. If you are struggling to reach consent, check to see if the issue is clearly stated or if the question needs to be restated. If you reach consent early and want more experience with the practice pick another issue from the list you created.

Resources for Further Study

Begeman, P., Best, M. (2020). *Discernment: Practicing the Holy Spirit, The Contemplative Life Program 40 Day Practice.* Contemplative Outreach, Ltd.

Dougherty, R. (2009). *Discernment: A Path to Spiritual Awakening.* Mahwah, NJ: Paulist Press.

Funk, M. (2013). *Discernment Matters.* Collegeville, MN: Liturgical Press.

Kidd, S. (1990). *When the Heart Waits.* New York, NY: HarperCollins Publishers.

Levoy, G. (1997). *Callings: Finding and Following an Authentic Life.* New York, NY: Three Rivers Press.

Nouwen, H. (2013). *Discernment: Reading the Signs of Daily Life.* New York, NY: Harper Collins Publishers.

CHAPTER TEN
Addictions, Attachments, and Aversions

*"The power of grace flows most fully when human will
chooses to act in harmony with divine will."*[64]
Gerald May, M.D.

THE SPIRITUAL JOURNEY IS ABOUT DISCOVERY, OFTEN INVOLVING something we are moving towards and yet we know not what. If we commit to spiritual discipline and the practices offered in the Contemplative Living Experience (CLE) program, we are in effect committed to being transformed. How we change is different for each of us. Yet, each in our own way, we are following a path that mystics throughout the Christian tradition have described and experienced and offered to us.

It is not an easy path. In the beginning, what often draws us to contemplative life is the peace and consolation we experience when we come into relationship with the God of love. Whatever we thought of God in our past, which for a lot of us was a punishing God we feared, the direct experience of love and grace is like coming home. But home can sometimes be a mixed bag. It can be a place of comfort and nourishment and it can be a place of confrontation and challenge. By engaging in the CLE program through this book—independently or with a group—we've been deepening our commitment to a life of prayer through contemplative practice. This program and whatever elements in our life have brought us to it have been preparing us to face all of what it means to surrender to this God of love, a God we are learning to trust by consenting to the presence and action of the Divine Indwelling.

You might remember this quote from The Human Condition chapter where Father Thomas challenges us to live the Gospel values:

> "The Gospel calls us forth to full responsibility for
> our emotional life. We tend to blame other people or

situations for the turmoil we experience. In actual fact, upsetting emotions prove beyond any doubt that the problem is in us. If we do not assume responsibility for our emotional programs on the unconscious level and take measures to change them, we will be influenced by them to the end of our lives."[65]

We likely think we've already taken responsibility for our emotional life because we have a closer relationship with God, we have committed to a life of prayer, and we and those we love are noticing changes in us. And yet when our emotional programs for happiness—the energy centers and our cultural conditioning—become frustrated, more often than not, we still have an automatic emotional response that usually leads to suffering (our own, those with whom we've interacted, or both!) Father Thomas suggests we have work to do to dismantle the emotional programs for happiness:

"...The real work of the spiritual journey consists of patiently, calmly, and humbly acknowledging that the values are still thoroughly alive in the unconscious... An emotional upset is the infallible sign that we are attached—addicted—to one of these centers."[66]

The values he refers to are alive in the energy centers clamoring for power and control, esteem and affection, security and survival within our unconscious mind. What is most troublesome about these emotional programs is that they block the free flow of grace, affecting our well-being along with our relationships with others and with God.

In early childhood, the energy centers begin to form in us due to genuine and valid needs. When our needs are not met, or we perceive they are not being met, or for any reason we feel the need to protect ourselves, we learn to lean on energy centers custom made by our emerging false self. These go-to psychological defenses are formed by repeated acts and thus become habit patterns of behavior that include thoughts, feelings, and actions. By the time we become adults, these habit patterns no longer serve us, but because they are entrenched unconscious emotional responses, we suppose this is "how we are" and sometimes even *who* we are. Our identification with these habit patterns will cause us pain and suffering until we take responsibility for our emotional life. This moment of truth starts with awareness—the patient, calm and humble acknowledgement that the energy centers are running our lives. When we think we are our thoughts, feelings, behaviors, and the labels we or others put on us, we lose sight of who we really are.

Because our emotional programs for happiness are created by repeated acts resulting in these habit patterns, Father Thomas suggests they can also be dismantled by repeated acts. This is where our spiritual practices come in, starting with Centering Prayer. With a committed practice, over time we start to experience interior silence and build trust in our relationship with the God of love. Our consent to the presence of God within gives us a new sense of self, the self that God created us to be, our true self.

At the same time, we begin consenting to God's action within. Sometimes God's action simply heals what needs to be healed in our woundedness, and sometimes God reveals to us what needs attention in what Father Thomas calls "the unloading of the unconscious." As we mature in our Centering Prayer practice, we begin to become aware of the automatic reactions that get triggered by the emotional programs for happiness. We also become more aware of our woundedness and what needs to be healed. Our Logging practice starts to shine the light on some of the patterns we may have been caught up in for years. Such awareness is the first step in seeing that we are free to choose something different. We gain knowledge, insight, wisdom, and encouragement from others on the spiritual path through Spiritual Reading, Lectio Divina, and spiritual companionship. We begin to see that we are not alone on this journey. Even Saint Paul experienced some of what we are going through. "What I do, I do not understand. For I do not do what I want, but I do what I hate" (Romans 7:15). Thankfully, when we're feeling what Saint Paul expressed in his letter to Romans, we have several established practices we can turn to. The Active Prayer gives our mind something to do besides obsess on our thoughts and commentaries and shows us a way to pray without ceasing (1 Thessalonians 5:17). The Welcoming Prayer provides a way to experience and release our afflictive emotions instead of continuing to suppress them, showing us that God is with us in whatever we are experiencing in daily life. Rest and Sabbath-Keeping give us the opportunity to pause and integrate what we're experiencing with this new life in God. And, as we explored in the previous chapter, Contemplative Discernment teaches us to align our will with God's will and to desire the peace that comes with surrender.

All of this brings us to the point on the spiritual journey where we are open and willing to face the dark side of our personality, sometimes called our shadow side. As the founder of analytical psychology Carl Jung wrote:

> "Everyone carries a shadow, and the less it is embodied in the individual's conscious life, the blacker and denser it is. At all counts, it forms an unconscious snag, thwarting our most well-meant intentions."[67]

Our shadow is that part of us that we don't want others to see, that we are ashamed of, that we fear or attribute to harm others have done to us. We work hard in life to keep this part of us hidden deep in the unconscious by repressing thoughts and feelings. But just when we think things are safely stowed away and under control, something will trigger a reaction. That's when what we have relegated to the unconscious makes itself seen and heard, often reinforcing our fear and shame, strengthening the hold the energy centers have over us. Because this is all happening in our unconscious, we often don't know what hit us and we feel it's all outside of our control. Until we awaken to some level of self-awareness, we generally don't have control. Sometimes even after we become aware, we still don't have control. This is one of the hallmarks of addiction.

Even with the advent of twelve-step programs beginning with Alcoholics Anonymous in 1935, we still have considerable stigma in our culture around addiction. When we hear addiction, we usually think of alcoholism or drug addiction. If our personal addiction doesn't look like we imagine those addictions look, we deduce it's not a big deal. Certainly, addictions to substances can be some of the most destructive of addictions, but they are not the only forms of addiction. Habitual patterns that we no longer freely choose become compulsions and can be very destructive. They become addictions because they have control over us. And no one is immune from addiction. We don't usually think of things like work, responsibility, being right, food, self-improvement, relationships, sex, television, reading fiction, exercise, gambling, depression, shopping, sleeping, money, success, or technology as being addictions. There is nothing intrinsically wrong with any of these things, but when they take over our lives, they can wreak havoc like any drug.

In his book *Addiction and Grace*, Gerald May says that all of us are born with an innate desire for God, a longing for love. As we grow up and start to experience life, because of our human condition, we feel separate from God. We may spend the rest of our life trying to fill the emptiness we feel from this unfulfilled desire—from the feeling of separation—with things, behaviors, people, and substances, that in a way become like gods for us. Our desire for God which is an innately good and human desire, becomes attached to these things outside ourselves. These things steal the time and attention we would be better off devoting to love. It's as if our life energy is enslaved by these attachments and gets used up, leaving little left over for relationships and other pursuits. The attachment of our desire leads to addiction, robbing us of a happy and free life.

One of the things Father Thomas says over and over again in his teaching is "Repent!" And by that he means "change the direction in which you are looking for happiness."[68] When we hear the word repent, we may think it means we should do some sort of penance or feel guilty about some way we behaved, or some thought we had. This is not at all what Father Thomas means. His admonition to repent has more to do with understanding our need for detachment. We are not actually detaching *from* our desire, because our desire and longing for God is a natural inclination. It is more of a detachment *of* desire, freeing up our desire for God from what cannot possibly bring us to the fulfillment of this desire. Detachment frees us from anxious grasping and clinging, expanding our capacity to love.

As anyone who has struggled with addiction knows, the grip we are in with any addiction is not something we can simply decide to stop on our own. We do, however, have the ability to choose to awaken to what continues to cause us suffering, to seek help, turn to God, and be open to receive grace. Many of us may have had addictions for years without awareness of them. It is when the addiction is frustrated or causes conflict that we notice something needs our attention. Most addictions start with attachment to a specific object, person, behavior, or substance. It usually starts off innocently enough with a habit where we notice some relief of what's troubling us or causing stress, but then the object of our addiction turns into something we can't live without. We also may experience an addiction that starts with an aversion, perhaps to public speaking, anger, or other afflictive emotions, intimacy, conflict, large crowds, being overweight, responsibility. The same pattern can develop from feeling relief by avoiding these things. Whether our addiction comes from something we are attached to or have an aversion to, the key is that our energy is bound up in seeking the substance or behavior we can't seem to do without.

Contemplative Discernment with Addictions

As a facilitator and also a participant in the CLE program, when the topic of addictions comes up in the program, I'm never sure what I'm going to work on. I would always try my best to follow the teaching and pray for the Spirit to reveal to me what needs to be healed today. Over the years I have worked on my addiction to coffee and compulsive eating. A few years ago, I had an awakening to how much of my life I spent trying to fix myself. It's one thing to do the inner work that the spiritual journey invites, but it's yet another thing to be on this endless pursuit of self-help. I would think I had finally found the answer when Amazon would suggest a new book based on my previous searches and purchases. I was always looking for the next diet, spiritual practice, exercise program… that was going to be "it"—the solution to my discontent and seeking. I was obsessed, never satisfied. As I worked with the discernment practice around my addiction to trying to fix myself, and it took many months of discerning and letting go, I discovered that I don't need to be fixed. I am exactly as God created me to be and every person, event, circumstance, feeling, and "issue" contributed to forming this me that is perfect just as I am. Do I still work on myself? Of course. Do I still uncover emotions and behaviors that are troublesome? Yes. The difference is in my motivation and how I feel about myself as I work these things through. It is no longer about fixing something that is flawed. It is about noticing what remains that keeps me from being free and at peace. And it's about continuing to use my spiritual practices to return me to a state of equanimity. I admit I can still get hooked by the latest, greatest diet, but even with that I have learned to pay more attention to my body and the type of food and amount of food that helps me to feel good and have good health. It was a painful process for me to admit how flawed I felt and how much time and money I invested over so many years trying to fix something that wasn't broken. Uncovering this lesson and experiencing this pain has helped me to be more at peace with who I am, just as I am today.

Some characteristics of addiction that help us determine the extent of the impairment caused by addiction are: 1. tolerance, where we need more and more of the substance or behavior to have the same level of relief; 2. withdrawal, where we experience mild to extreme discomfort, irritability, and stress when we stop the substance or behavior; 3. denial, where we are unable to see the adverse effects of the addiction on our life and those with whom we interact; 4. loss of willpower, where we are unable to stop on our own. Have you already started to identify something in your life that needs attention, either from the examples given above or from being able to identify an attachment or aversion in your life that is affecting your freedom? You may need to take some time to pray about this and let the Spirit surface something for you. The book by Gerald May I've been referencing, *Addiction and Grace*, contains some helpful charts that suggest many attachments or aversions you might identify with.[69]

Once we have identified some behavior that is causing repeated frustration and conflict and needs attention, we can turn to our Contemplative Discernment practice. Gerald May says,

> "Addiction cannot be defeated by the human will acting on its own, nor by the human will opting out and turning everything over to divine will. Instead, the power of grace flows most fully when human will chooses to act in harmony with divine will."[70]

As we learned in the last chapter, the discernment process uncovers hidden motivations, which often leads to new insight and, ultimately, to consent. By now, if we're being honest with ourselves, we see more clearly how addiction has impacted our lives as we discover ways we've been unable to change or stop certain behaviors by our own will. If we're not there yet, this may be the opportunity to try one more time to stop a given behavior and see where that leads. If that's where you are, don't think of it as a bad thing; the process just gives us more information and experience to bring into discernment. And we must remember to use the Welcoming Prayer whenever any afflictive emotions arise in the process of discernment. We may also notice things coming up in our daily Logging practice, because we may find ourselves in a more vulnerable place as attitudes shift.

We use the Contemplative Discernment practice to bring awareness to how addiction is affecting our lives and to consent to God's action, which may simply be the bestowing on us of the grace that is the active expression of God's love in our lives. Our consent may be no more than opening ourselves to the willingness to receive grace. Facing our addictions is difficult. It shows us where we are not free, where we are acting in ways that are counter to our desire for God, and if we are really honest, it shows us where we are not taking responsibility for our emotional life. It's not only difficult, but painful as we may start to grieve what might have been and what we are leaving behind—the only self we have ever known. Part of the process is to experience the pain we have long been avoiding.

Father Thomas calls God's healing action in our lives "divine therapy." But he always understands sometimes divine therapy alone isn't enough and uncovers issues that require professional help. I was with him at the closing of a ten-day retreat I attended where I shared about suffering for many years with depression. While he encouraged me in my Centering Prayer practice by telling me that depression doesn't interfere with the prayer, he also encouraged me to continue with the treatment I was receiving. A friend of mine told me about relaying to him how she had recurring nightmares due to childhood abuse, and he suggested to her she might try dream therapy. He also was a very strong supporter of twelve-step programs and thought Contemplative Outreach could learn from their model of recovery. It's difficult sometimes in the process of self-discovery and self-knowledge to do it alone, so please don't try. And don't get caught in the trap of thinking that God will magically heal all our wounds. Sometimes what God is doing for us is showing us where we need help. This reminds me of that "joke" you probably have heard where the preacher is caught on the roof of his church during a flood. Two boats and a helicopter come to rescue him, and he turns them down saying he has faith that God is going to save him. After he drowns and goes to heaven, he asks God why he didn't come to save him. God replies, "I sent two boats and a helicopter. What more did you want?"

It will help us if we can approach this work with hope. We are on the path to freedom, moving toward the true happiness that much of Father Thomas's teaching points to by encouraging us to change the

Contemplative Life

direction in which we have been looking for happiness. An aspect of the human condition that we don't often talk about is our basic core of goodness as human beings. The programs for happiness, our unexamined shadow side, and being caught in the grip of addiction block us from the awareness of our goodness, masking who we really are. In his book *Divine Therapy & Addiction,* Father Thomas reminds his readers to always support others who are beginning to confront addiction:

> "...The most essential thing... is to affirm their basic goodness. In biblical language, this means we are made in the image of God. This image can never be erased by any activity whatsoever. God's presence and light within us supports us every nanosecond of time. All of human misery is simply layers of junk that covers this and so it's sometimes easy to identify the junk as ourselves, instead of recognizing that junk is our enemy disguised as misguided or distorted activity, not our true self that remains a brilliant jewel even though it's at the bottom of a pile of garbage... If they get to the bottom of the pile of this junk, they will find their own immeasurable beauty: God's gift that can never be destroyed by any misconduct whatsoever."[71]

Our basic core of goodness, our true self, is untouched, untarnished by whatever life brings us.

Contemplative Discernment Method to Surface Addictions

1. Start with a prayer, inviting the Holy Spirit into your discernment process around addiction. Ask the Holy Spirit "What is before me?" "What is God asking of me?" Pause, observe, watch, and see what arises. Ask for guidance, detachment from the outcome, and freedom with respect to any preference.
2. What is going on in your life right now? What is pressing, unresolved, unclear, or causing concern, pain, or conflict? Make a list without judging, analyzing, or eliminating anything. Each time you enter into the discernment process choose one issue.

3. Clearly state to yourself and to God the name of the addiction you're examining. Write it succinctly using nonjudgmental language. Use a blank sheet of paper or blank screen and write the date at the top. You will likely be doing the discernment process with the same question several times over the course of a few weeks or months. Use this format for your question to state the issue "What are the Advantages and Disadvantages of my addiction to…?" Be specific, include only one issue per discernment question.
Examples:
A. What are the advantages and disadvantages of my addiction to being right? or
B. What are the advantages and disadvantages of my addiction to emotional eating? or
C. What are the advantages and disadvantages of my addiction to avoiding feeling my afflictive emotions?
You can see from these examples that it is not necessary to get into a lot of detail about the addiction. You know what the addiction and behavior are and all that's behind it and many of the details will come out when you write about the advantages and disadvantages. Ask yourself if the question resonates within your heart. If it doesn't, you may need to go back into prayer to reformulate the question.
4. Ponder the issue, allowing the unconscious or hidden issues to emerge into consciousness. Repeat the question a few times, even saying it out loud.
5. Make two columns, one for advantages and one for disadvantages. Leave room at the bottom of the page to record any insights that arise as you are writing advantages and disadvantages and any consent you've reached once you finish the process.
6. Start with the advantages column. Say to yourself "What are the advantages of my addiction to…?" Write whatever comes to mind—thoughts, feelings, emotions or commentaries. Be succinct. Use one or two words or a phrase per line. No need for full sentences. Don't judge or eliminate what comes to mind. Just write it down.
7. Ponder. Repeat the question several times as you write down your responses.

Contemplative Life

8. Use the Welcoming Prayer if anything comes up that stimulates a reaction, emotional response or resistance. Pay attention to any body sensations you become aware of.
9. Write down any insight or new information that surfaces as you go through this process.
10. When you think you have written all your responses to the question, ponder the question one more time. Don't just think with your head. Be open to the Spirit touching your heart.
11. Then let go of any attachment you may have to anything written in the advantages column. At the bottom of your list write the words "I let go of any attachment to these advantages."
12. Now go to disadvantages column. Ask the question "What are the disadvantages of my addiction to …?"
13. Go through the same process. Ponder the question, write your responses, use the Welcoming Prayer if some emotional response is triggered, jot down any insight or new information. When your list of disadvantages feels complete, write the words "I let go of any attachment to these disadvantages."
14. The same comment could surface in both the advantages and disadvantages columns.
15. Go through the discernment process several times before you come to making a choice or a decision. It's helpful to leave some time, a week or so, in between doing the written discernment process as the Spirit will continue to work in you and reveal more to you. Continue with the process until you have no new self-knowledge or insights. Have you reached a consent? (Your consent may be to continue to discern.) Write down your consent.
16. If after going through the process several times you are unable to come to consent other than continuing the process, check to see if the issue is clearly stated or if the question needs to be restated.
17. When you come to make a choice of action, this becomes the consent to God. A decision is an action of the will manifesting intention.
18. The goal is not 100% assurance, but the peaceful confirmation of your choice, a sense of things falling into place, a sense of harmony within yourself, a sense of clarity about this issue.

Going Deeper

Spiritual Counsel

In this difficult yet liberating chapter on addiction, attachment, and aversion, be sure to spend some time with the spiritual counsel. Remember that the spiritual counsel contains wisdom statements meant to encourage you and help you persevere with the practices. Become familiar with the information in the chapter first and then peruse the spiritual counsel from time to time as you begin to work on your discernment around addiction.

1. "The Beatitude of poverty of spirit springs from the increasing awareness of our true self. It is a non-possessive attitude toward everything and a sense of unity with everything at the same time. The interior freedom to have much or to have little, and the simplifying of one's lifestyle are signs of the presence of poverty of spirit"[72] (Thomas Keating). "Blessed are the poor in spirit, for theirs is the kingdom of heaven" (Matthew 5:3).
2. Attachment is the process that "enslaves desire"— "nails" it to specific behaviors, objects or people. When we are attached, addicted, or have an aversion to some behavior, object or person in our lives, that thing begins to possess our thoughts, emotions and desires. Detachment means both an external freeing from the object of attachment or aversion, and an internal freeing from attachment or aversion to thoughts, emotions and desires. "Detachment is the word used in spiritual traditions to describe freedom of desire. Not freedom from desire, but freedom of desire" (Gerald May).
3. There is always some deeper aversion underlying attachment… It may be to something specific, to new life with God, or to feeling the pain and emptiness of our human condition.
4. Heraclitus, a sixth-century Greek said about attachment that whatever it wishes to get, it purchases at the cost of the soul.
5. Addiction, especially to substances, can have greater behavioral, physical, and social effects than attachment or aversion. Yet if we are honest, we can see the spiritual damage of attachment and aversion. Addiction (or attachment or aversion) can actually be a gift because the behavioral, physical and social effects drive us to spiritual action. Treating addiction may require physical treatments, or a twelve-step program.

6. Simplicity is defined as "lack of complexity or difficulty." As our desire is freed through detachment our hearts, minds and lives simplify and can express divine love more fully. In Simplicity there is no aversion to the deeper pain and emptiness of our human condition.
7. "...We must come to love our longing... Our fundamental disease is a most precious gift from God... It is our true treasure, the most precious thing we have. It is God's song of love in our soul" (Gerald May).

Reflection Questions

The reflection questions will help you deepen your understanding and experience of the teaching on addictions, attachments, and aversions. They will also give you the opportunity to pause, take time, and reflect on where you are on this journey. Don't rush through this teaching. We can get stuck sometimes when we encounter a teaching that is difficult or that asks us to face something we might not be ready or willing to face. Notice if you are resisting and reflect on your resistance, remembering that there is nothing wrong with resistance. It helps us to persevere on the journey if we become aware of where we are resisting. Your reflections may contain the content you will choose to share with your group, spiritual companion or friend, in spiritual direction or in your Holy Listening Circle.

1. Select one thought from the spiritual counsel that spoke to you and briefly explain why.
2. Reflect on your experience using the Contemplative Discernment practice around your addiction using these questions:

    a. How was using the discernment practice for you?
    b. Did you experience change over the three or four times you did it?
    c. Was it difficult to face your addiction?
    d. Did you remember to use the Welcoming Prayer when emotions surfaced?
    e. What insights did you record?
    f. Did any hidden motivations surface?
    g. What consent did you come to?

3. What insight are you taking from the challenging work you've done with this chapter?
4. What does it mean to you to be a contemplative or to live a contemplative life? You have noticed by now that this is a reflection question in each chapter. Look back over your notes from previous chapters and reflect on how your answer to this question has changed over time as you continue to integrate more of the practices into your daily life.

To Practice
Centering Prayer
How is your Centering Prayer practice going? Sometimes, especially if we are experiencing unloading of the unconscious, we may resist continuing to sit in silent prayer. Let's look at what Father Thomas says in *Divine Therapy & Addiction* about how Centering Prayer can help us with the addictive process we may be struggling with in this chapter:

> "Centering Prayer…translates the experience of external quiet to the experience of being quiet inside… To deliberately not talk to yourself for twenty minutes at a time undermines the thought patterns or structures that reinforce one's emotional programs for happiness. By not deliberately thinking *any* thought, you begin to undermine the habitual thought patterns of your whole life, which may be reinforcing the addiction you are suffering from… One begins to lose interest in the addictive process or in the addictions. Exposure to silence on a regular basis offers a kind of universal healing…"[73]

Logging
Continue to practice Logging for five to fifteen minutes daily. Logging may be particularly helpful in identifying thought, emotional, and behavioral patterns that we may now recognize as addictions. Be sure to review your Logging at the end of each week or month to help raise your awareness of any patterns that God may be revealing to you for attention. What insights come to you?

Spiritual Reading
Continue to practice Spiritual Reading for one hour per week, either

doing it all in one day or spending ten to fifteen minutes a day four to five times a week. You may want to take a break from the book you have been using for Spiritual Reading and use a book such as *Addiction & Grace* by Gerald May or *Divine Therapy & Addiction* by Thomas Keating.

Lectio Divina
Practice Lectio Divina three times per week using Scripture passages of your choosing. If you haven't settled on what Scripture to use for Lectio or if you are at a place where you want to try something new, I suggest that Romans 7:7 through Chapter 8 may be helpful as you work on this chapter on addictions.

Active Prayer
Use your Active Prayer daily when your mind is not occupied in conversation, work or some other activity requiring concentration. If you are at all troubled by obsessive thinking, especially as a result of looking at addictive patterns in your life, in addition to your Centering Prayer practice, the Active Prayer may help you to break the automatic rerunning of these obsessive thoughts.

Welcoming Prayer
Use the Welcoming Prayer daily. Working with this chapter on addictions may stir up afflictive emotions more than usual. Don't be discouraged by this and know that you have a tool to help you allow the emotions to surface so they can move through you and be healed.

Sabbath-Keeping
Find a time that fits into your life each week to set aside for Sabbath, whether it be a day, an afternoon or a few hours. Be intentional and prepare ahead of time so that you can devote the time to spiritual concerns, rather than the concerns of daily life. Consider how you can spend the time being rather than doing.

Contemplative Discernment on Addictions, Attachments and Aversions
Repeat the discernment practice two or three times over the course of several weeks using the question you developed for your addiction. Pay special attention to any insights you have and whether you have reached consent. Always start with a clean sheet of paper (or blank screen) and

put the date at the top. If you are struggling to reach consent, check to see if the issue is clearly stated or if the question needs to be restated. If you reach consent early and want more experience with the practice pick another issue from the list you created. While the discernment practice is meant to be a tool you learn for times when you need to enter into a discernment process, using this practice to work on your addiction may continue for a longer period of time.

Resources for Further Study

Anonymous (2018). *Alcoholics Anonymous.* New York, NY: Alcoholics Anonymous World Services, Inc.

de Mello, A. (1992). *Awareness: The Perils and Opportunities of Reality.* New York, NY: Doubleday.

Keating, T. (2009). *Divine Therapy & Addiction: Centering Prayer and the Twelve Steps.* New York, NY: Lantern Books.

May, G., M.D. (1988). *Addiction & Grace: Love and Spirituality in the Healing of Addictions.* New York, NY: HarperOne.

CHAPTER ELEVEN
Forgiveness

*"... Be kind to one another, compassionate,
forgiving one another as God has forgiven you in Christ."*
Ephesians 4:32

IT'S NOT ALWAYS EASY TO KEEP A STEADY COMMITMENT TO THIS WORK of inner transformation, but the fact that you're still reading this book is a great sign! Maybe you're picking it up again after letting it gather dust for a few months. That's okay. Sometimes we need more time to process what we're experiencing or to take a break from the hard work of self-awareness and transformation. But how do we go about approaching this work with hope? How do we remind ourselves that we are on the path to freedom and happiness? Even with all the self-reflection Centering Prayer and the other contemplative practices lead us to, and the conscious unearthing and letting go of our emotional programs for happiness, we may still find ourselves blocked from experiencing love. By "experiencing" I mean both giving and receiving.

What does forgiveness have to do with experiencing love? The two go hand in hand so we start with what Jesus refers to as the two great commandments—to love God and love your neighbor as yourself (Matthew 22:37-39). As much as we may desire to follow Jesus's example and live with hearts open to love, as human beings we carry the baggage of the past in unresolved hurt, shame, conflict, anger, resentment, and woundedness, which often causes us to continue to suffer. And as a result, we may shut down our heart and block the two-way flow of love in our lives, giving and receiving. We have likely heard many times about the healing power of forgiveness and have been told that we *should* forgive. But forgiveness can be easier said than done. We may have tried to forgive or thought we had forgiven, only to continue to be plagued by afflictive emotions and commentaries—an indication that we may not have yet fully forgiven others and, possibly, ourselves. As a

Julie Saad

result, we're not free to experience the love we have been so freely given through the grace of God.

Do you relate to these patterns? They might not fit your experience exactly, but if you take a few moments to reflect on your life, you may recognize some parallels to your own experience. This type of honest reflection helps us not take for granted the ability to forgive and be forgiven. If we want to break patterns of unforgiveness, we will need to cultivate the practice of forgiveness in our daily lives. As we begin to forgive more freely, we will be better able to love and be loved.

The Upper Room, a global ministry dedicated to supporting Christian spiritual life, publishes a quarterly journal which offers a broad range of topics within the Christian ecumenical traditions. In 1992 they devoted the entire journal to the topic of forgiveness. Much of what was included resonates as much for us today as it did then. Marjorie J. Thompson wrote an article called "Moving Toward Forgiveness." In it she gives us a definition of forgiveness which is helpful to our discussion on forgiveness and love:

> "To forgive is to make a conscious choice to release the person who has wounded us from the sentence of our judgment... It represents a choice to leave behind our resentment and desire for retribution... Forgiveness involves excusing persons from the punitive consequences they deserve to suffer for their behavior."[74]

So much of the time we don't see that we have a choice in what we hold onto in the way of judgment and resentment, especially if we have been hurt or are angry. Can you start to see the freedom you might experience if you were to choose to let go of judgment and resentment and forgive? And how forgiveness can start to heal our ability to experience the flow of love in our lives; how it opens us to freely be able to love God and love our neighbor as Jesus suggests? Thompson goes on to say,

> "Forgiveness constitutes a decision to call forth and rebuild that love which is the only authentic ground of any human relationship... It is only because God continually calls forth and rebuilds this love with us that we are capable of doing so with one another."[75]

Forgiveness is a choice and a decision we make to live life more freely. That does not mean it's easy.

Henri Nouwen says, "The great tragedy of human love is that it always wounds. Why is this so? Simply because human love is imperfect, always tainted by needs and unfulfilled desires."[76] This may be true, but what we often don't realize is that living a life of forgiveness—both forgiving and allowing ourselves to be forgiven—opens the door to a more perfect love. One of the hardest things to accept is that we are, each in our own way, broken. No matter how well-intentioned we might be, none of us is perfect and we inevitably hurt each other out of our brokenness, our woundedness, our humanness. We will hurt each other again and again, especially those we love and have close relationships with. It's just part of being human.

Thankfully, our spiritual journey is a lifelong journey. And so it is with forgiveness. Forgiving is not a one-time event that we can say we've done and we're over it. For some of our bigger hurts, such as when we've been traumatized or abused, the process of forgiveness will not be easy and will take time. It's important to remember that it's a process where we have an intention for healing. Healing is God's work, not ours, and we may not know what we need in order to experience healing. It's helpful to not have an agenda or expectations for what our healing experience should be. For example, if we expect that the other person or the relationship will change, we may be disappointed. What is more likely to change is something within ourselves—we become more accepting of the faults of others, or we see our own human condition more clearly so have more compassion for others, or we recognize that someone else cannot truly harm our true self. When we are able to let go of the outcome, we will come to discover we have made progress along the path to forgiveness and healing.

Why Forgive?

When Nelson Mandela was being released from prison where he was held as a political dissident for twenty-seven years, he said, "As I walked out the door toward the gate that would lead to my freedom, I knew if I didn't leave my bitterness and hatred behind, I'd still be in prison."[77] When we hold onto anger, resentment, and revenge fantasies we are inextricably linked to the person who we perceive caused us pain and suffering. We are tied to the past, to the memory of trauma or hurt.

With our energy going out, day after day, to the memory with its accompanying afflictive emotions and commentaries, we are not free to live in the present moment. Our identity gets wrapped up in being the one who was harmed—the victim—and we are not free to be who God created us to be.

In the previous chapter on addictions, Father Thomas reminded us how essential it is to our healing journey to remember the brilliant jewel within us that is our true self, our basic core of goodness. When we cling to our wounded self, we give away our power to the people who have hurt or offended us. Just as our addictions and our unexamined shadow side block us from the awareness of our goodness and who we really are, the same is true when we cling to our hurt and anger. Forgiveness is another aspect of taking responsibility for our emotional life that Father Thomas suggests is necessary lest we continue to be influenced by it to the end of our lives. It's important to remember and to live into the truth that just as no behavior we engage in impacts our basic core of goodness, no one else's behavior can impact it either. Before anything happens to us in life—before we do anything, before anyone does anything to us—we are God's beloved creation. And yet, while we might be intellectually aware that we are God's beloved, we're still fixated on our own actions and those of others.

Forgiveness is both a practice and a prayer that offers us a new way of responding, freeing us up to experience love, the most basic human desire. As a practice, it takes willingness and honesty and requires our participation. As a prayer, we recognize we are not in this alone and ask God to journey with us and show us the way.

Why We Resist Forgiving

Forgiveness is a journey into our pain. We all must take this journey in order to release our pain and be free. Sometimes the memory of the hurt, abuse, or trauma is so painful we think our only option is to try to forget it, to suppress the pain. As we learned in the Welcoming Prayer and the teaching on the human condition, the only way to be free of pain is to go through it. The more we suppress our feelings and deny the accompanying commentaries, the longer we suffer. Because we don't know how to forgive, we may convince ourselves that if we successfully suppress the pain for a period of time that we have succeeded in forgiving. When we are committed to consenting to God's presence and action within, God faithfully reveals to us what is keeping us from

Contemplative Life

being free. If we are not ready to face what's being revealed, God's love is so generous that another opportunity will present itself at another time. Becoming more aware of why we resist forgiveness will help us to be more willing to forgive.

It's not uncommon to think of forgiveness as a sign of weakness. And so, it's helpful to reframe our notion of weakness. Let's look at what Saint Paul says about weakness, "…He said to me, 'My grace is sufficient for you, for power is made perfect in weakness.' I will rather boast most gladly of my weaknesses, in order that the power of Christ may dwell with me. Therefore, I am content with weakness, insults, hardships, persecutions, and constraints, for the sake of Christ; for when I am weak, then I am strong" (2 Corinthians 12:9-10). When we are suffering and vulnerable, especially when we feel something is being inflicted on us by someone else, we may feel weak, but the paradox of the contemplative life is that this is when our heart is most open to the grace of the Spirit. This is when we are most willing to consent to the presence and action of God within. We will not get through life without being hurt, persecuted, abused, or traumatized. We also will not get through life without being the offender at times. When we can face life's challenges knowing that God's grace is freely given, our human weakness makes way for God's strength in us.

We have so often heard the phrase "forgive and forget" that we resist forgiving because the offense is so egregious it shouldn't be forgotten. So, for our purposes here, let me be clear: forgetting is not a component of forgiveness. Quite the opposite is true. Before we can move into forgiveness, we need to give voice to the offense and our hurt. Remembering what happened and how we felt, in some cases, protects us from further abuse and helps us to be clear about our boundaries. Forgetting may be possible once we've been healed, but we keep in mind that sometimes even in the healing process we are left with scars.

We might think that forgiveness means that we condone the behavior or that the person is getting away with something. It is not up to us to mete out justice. We can trust that in some way the person will answer for what they have done, but it's not something we have any control over. What we don't often realize is that we don't forgive only for the well-being of the other person. We forgive for ourselves, to be freed from being bound to the person and to the pain we experienced.

It is a normal human response to want to put conditions on our willingness to forgive and even to desire some sort of revenge. The person doesn't deserve to be forgiven, or our woundedness is too deep, or we expect an apology, or the offense is ongoing. Sometimes our anger and resentment are so strong and have been a part of our lives for so long that we think we have a right to feel this way. We can't see that our resentment is like a chain around our neck, a chain that keeps us bound to the past. We have a right to be angry and aggrieved when we have been hurt, but conditions, resentment, and revenge will never give us any kind of satisfaction. The desire for conditions and revenge keeps us stuck in the grievance and blocks our willingness to forgive. In order to forgive we must make the decision to give up conditions and revenge-seeking.

If we are holding onto resentment, we will have a hard time seeing the divine light in the other person. This will be close to impossible if we have experienced severe abuse or if the harm caused was intentional. However, in most cases, the hurt we experienced may not have been fully intentional but was more likely unconscious. Forgiveness will come easier if we can see the divine light in the other person and let go of our judgment that the harm was intended. It may help to reflect on situations where we have hurt someone unintentionally and felt remorse for our actions. When we can see our own shortcomings, we remember that we are all wounded human beings who are capable of hurting each other. Richard Rohr so beautifully addresses seeing the divine light in the other and in ourselves in one of his Daily Meditations:

> "The longer you gaze, the more you will see your own complicity *in* and profitability *from* the sin of others, even if it is the satisfaction of feeling you are on higher moral ground. Forgiveness demands three new simultaneous 'seeings:' I must see God in the other; I must access God in myself; and I must experience God in a new way that is larger than an 'Enforcer.'"[78]

We may think it's too late to forgive because the person who harmed us has died. For a number of years, I struggled with depression and was unable to get relief from it despite being in therapy and on medication. I went on an intensive retreat at St. Benedict's Monastery in Snowmass, Colorado, wondering why I even bothered to go, as bad as I felt. One morning on the way back to my room from mass at the monastery I had a strong sense that I needed to forgive my mother. My mother had already died by that time, and I was at a loss as to what to do about what felt like an admonition. I had a cassette tape in my car of a Forgiveness Prayer workshop given by Mary Mrozowski, the creator of the Forgiveness Prayer practice. I sat in my car and listened to the tape over and over and started practicing the prayer throughout the rest of the retreat. The oppressive depression I had been experiencing for years was lifted. I remember Father Thomas saying to me on that retreat, "We can pray that your depression has been healed, but if not, it doesn't interfere with the prayer." My work with the Forgiveness Prayer continued even after I returned home. After some time, I started being able to remember so many of the good and loving memories I had of my mom, rather than just the angry and bitter treatment I received from her during the last ten years of her life after my dad died and she was alone and lonely. We don't realize sometimes the effect our inability to forgive or our resistance to forgiving can have on our wellbeing—our mental, emotional, spiritual, and physical health.

How We Can Forgive

As with all our contemplative practices, we start with a prayer to the Holy Spirit for assistance on this journey of forgiveness. How we can forgive starts by determining who in our lives we need to forgive. I doubt you've gotten this far into this chapter without thinking about who in your life you need to forgive. But please take a few minutes now to really think about it. Some offenders are more obvious than others. Some may be people who are currently in your life, your loved ones, friends, or colleagues. Others may be from long ago. Start with yourself, then think of family members, close friends, coworkers, acquaintances, neighbors, even strangers, institutions, enemies, and finally, and maybe most puzzling, God. Because we sometimes think we have forgiven someone when we really have suppressed our feelings and memory of what happened, spend some time thinking about how you have been wounded and by whom and notice if there is still any energy (which often appears in the form of feelings) around some event or time in your life. If there is, that person needs to be added to the list.

The next step in how we can forgive is to tell the story of how you were hurt, wounded, or abused. You can either talk about it with a trusted friend or spiritual companion or you can write about it. Tell yourself the truth. Sometimes we replay this story in our minds and carry the burden of our suffering alone. If this is a story you've told before, look for where you have identified yourself as a victim. You may very well have been victimized, but who you are is so much more than a victim. The problem with stories we may have told over and over is that we start to embellish the truth based on the reaction our story evokes or the feedback we get from others. If our identity is wrapped up in being a victim, it will be more difficult to become willing to forgive. The other side of this is that sometimes we diminish what happened to us and how we were hurt as a way of burying the feelings. When we bury our feelings, they don't go away, but are often magnified, also making forgiveness more difficult. Denying that we were hurt causes us to relive the experience over and over. When we accept that we have been hurt and are suffering, we start the process of transforming our pain through forgiveness.

True forgiveness requires a deep and honest look into the reality of the situation, asking ourselves what it is we need to forgive, what happened to cause our pain, and how we have been hurt. As you've become accustomed to in your Logging practice, start by describing the facts of what happened, followed by how you felt, and more importantly, how you feel now. Pay particular attention to what you are sensing in your body. If the feelings are painful, use the Welcoming Prayer to help you stay grounded. Stating the facts helps us make sense of what happened and telling the truth about our hurt and loss lessens its power over us.

Once we have some clarity about who we need to forgive and for what, the next step is to choose to forgive. It is only by the grace of God that we discover we have forgiven and are now free. Because it is a process that often occurs over time, sometimes over a long period of time, it is not so much an event as it is a discovery that something has changed in us—that we are more free and at peace. On the road to this discovery, we practice the Forgiveness Prayer, which again, is not a one-time event, but an ongoing practice of opening ourselves to God's grace.

The Forgiveness Prayer

The Forgiveness Prayer is a guided meditation. Once you learn where the meditation leads, you will be able to do it on your own without being led through all the steps. It starts with a relaxation exercise, but if you're ready to move into the prayer in the moments following your

Centering Prayer practice, you may not need the relaxation exercise. To begin, read through the guided meditation below. Then, in your imagination, follow it as best you can. You also may wish to record it and listen to it rather than read it. As you start to move out of the relaxation exercise into the forgiveness prayer you reach a point where you invite a particular person into the prayer. Having spent some time creating a list, the person you choose to forgive will likely appear in your prayer. However, since this is a prayer guided by the Spirit, be open to receiving whoever shows up. The Spirit knows well who you need to forgive today and what needs to be healed. Try not to get distracted by trying to make a choice or resisting working with whoever shows up. Forgiveness and healing are a gift from the Spirit.

Now, sit comfortably and begin.

Relaxation Exercise

Take some deep breaths and just breathe in and out. Begin to focus your attention. Take your mind's eye, that intuitive eye, and bring your attention to the top of your head and begin to relax your scalp. Relax. And you can silently say the word "relax" to transmit the message to your body that now is the time to relax. Relax. Relax your scalp and the muscles of your face. Bring your focus, your inner eye, to the muscles of your face and begin to relax the muscles of your face.

Allow your tongue to float in your mouth, not touching the roof of your mouth or the floor of your mouth. Let it float there. And what that does is bring your body, mind, and spirit into balance. Float your tongue. Relax.

Bring your attention to your throat area, softly and gently using the word relax. Take your inner eye and bring your focus to the back of your neck and gently relax…relax…relax.

Bring your attention to your shoulders. Relax your shoulders and your upper arms. Let them hang there, loose. Relax. And that inner eye, bring it into focus like a laser beam, powerful, penetrating. A great light. Now bring that focus to your lower arms and relax…relax.

Bring your attention to your upper back and relax the muscles of the upper back. And just move your gaze and focus down the spine and up, gently moving down and up. And relaxing the muscles connected with the spine. Relax.

Bring your attention and focus to your glutes. Relax the muscles of your glutes. Bring your focus and attention to your abdomen and relax the muscles of your abdomen. Gently relax. Relax.

Bring your focus and attention to the thighs of your legs relaxing those muscles, gently relaxing the muscles past your knees, to the calves of your legs. Relax. And allow the stress and discomfort to leave your body through your toes, becoming very relaxed.

Bring your attention and your focus to the chest area. And just allow that light to move in a circular motion around your heart space, resting, open, relaxing.

Forgiveness Prayer Meditation

Enter the heart space, that space in the center of the chest. Be one with that focus, that light. And enter the heart space, moving through a passageway that is warm and dark and safe, and move down the passageway, relaxed and safe, moving deeper and deeper through this passageway, moving slowly, relaxed.

At the end of the passageway is a doorway filled with light. Move toward the doorway filled with light. And give yourself permission to move through the doorway filled with light, moving through the doorway out into a meadow that is filled with light and sunshine. And a soft breeze that just moves across your face. And using all your senses of smell and touch and taste and sight, move down this pathway allowing the sun to warm you on the path to your sacred place, the sacred place that's filled with the light of the Spirit.

Enter into your sacred place and rest in the presence of the Spirit, allowing yourself to be held, to be nurtured, resting in the presence of the Spirit, using all your senses. Be present to the Spirit and in just a few moments a person will appear. And when that person appears invite that person into your sacred place. Use the person's name. Allow that person to enter into your sacred place.

You and the person in the presence of the Spirit experiencing a very safe place, begin to share with the person how you have been hurt or traumatized, and be very specific, sharing your feelings, your thoughts and your experience of how you have been hurt. Allow yourself to be open and to share your pain, your experience in your relationship with this person. Take as much time as you need. Do not hurry this part.

Once you have fully shared your experience and your pain, tell the person that you forgive them by saying "I forgive you _____ (say the person's name). I forgive you, I forgive you, I forgive you."

Ask the person how you have offended them, hurt, traumatized them. Ask "How have I hurt you?" And just wait for an answer. "How have I offended you?" Again, wait for an answer. Ask for forgiveness by saying "Forgive me. Forgive me for offending you. Forgive me. Forgive me."

Allow the person to leave your sacred place but leave the door open if the person needs to return. Allow the person to leave, as you continue to rest in the presence of the Spirit of the grace of God, resting, resting.

Prepare to leave your favorite and sacred place. It will be easy to return if you choose. Feeling refreshed, move down the path towards the door filled with light and give yourself permission to move through the doorway into the passageway feeling safe and warm and light and just move into the chamber of your heart and allow yourself to emerge into a normal state of consciousness and slowly open your eyes.

At the end of the prayer you may wish to make some notes about what happened and how you felt. What did you experience during the meditation? Do you feel any freer? Do you feel a sense of relief? Do you feel any residual anxiety? Use your Logging practice to continue to notice any changes you may be experiencing in your emotional life, your commentaries, and in your relationships over the coming days and weeks. If you were stuck in the identity of being a victim, notice if you are making new choices and if your story about what happened has changed. If you ran into obstacles or still feel blocked, know that you have started the process. Remember that forgiveness is a process, not a one-time event. You will usually have to repeat this prayer practice many times until one day you discover that you have experienced forgiveness. Forgiveness happens deep in our hearts.

Don't be surprised if you experience the process of forgiveness as a loss or find yourself grieving. When we are hurt by someone we love and trust we may experience a loss of our trust and faith in the person or the relationship. Sometimes we even lose our innocence because our previous expectations of other human beings had been naïve. We also may experience a loss of what might have been had we not experienced the hurt, abuse, or trauma. It might be helpful to do an inventory of what you have lost as a result of what happened, so you have a greater awareness of why you are grieving. When we experience any kind of loss, we will naturally start a grieving process. It's what helps us to release the pain, heal, and move on with our life.

When we put the process of forgiveness into the hands of the Spirit we open ourselves to the unknown and unexpected. We often have a notion of what we need to work on, what needs our attention. But God absolutely knows. Once when I was co-facilitating a forgiveness prayer workshop, while the other facilitator was leading the guided meditation,

Julie Saad

I followed along with the other participants. I thought I was going to be inviting my uncle into my sacred space because he and I had some ongoing miscommunication about his care in an assisted living facility and I was mad at him. But when I went into my sacred space, my sister showed up. I was surprised because I had not been thinking about her. Because I knew to expect surprises, I went with it and didn't try to control who should be there. In the course of the meditation, I realized how much I missed my sister. I live in Colorado, and she lives in Illinois and I hadn't seen her for a couple of years. When I got home, I called my brother and asked him if he and his wife would be willing to host me and my sister and her husband over Memorial Day weekend. He agreed. We had a really good time together and have many photos commemorating our visit. About six weeks later my brother was killed by a drunk driver. That weekend was the last time we were all together. I have always been grateful for that divine intervention as it came through my Forgiveness Prayer.

Sometimes the part of the prayer where we ask the other person how we have harmed them can be difficult, especially if we were victims of abuse or trauma. The day before I flew to Illinois for the sentencing hearing for the man who killed my brother, I was at St. Benedict's Monastery in Snowmass, Colorado for a meeting. I asked Father Thomas if I could meet with him. He knew about the tragic loss of my brother, and I told him the man had pleaded guilty and was going to be sentenced the next day. He asked me if I knew anything about this man. I told him that the only thing I knew about him was what I saw in the local newspaper that he was a former marine, an Iraq War veteran. He asked me if I had ever heard about moral injury. He gave me a DVD to take home and watch. It was a PBS documentary called "Almost Sunrise" about the journey of some veterans who did a trek across the United States to raise awareness about moral injury. Father Thomas was in the film for about five minutes towards the end. I'm sure Father Thomas was trying to help me see the burden this young man must have been under from his war experience and that he was likely suffering. I remember thinking that nothing the justice department could ever do to this man would match what it must be like to know you caused someone else's death by your reckless behavior. I knew I would never get over my brother's death if I couldn't forgive the offender. Even before I ever did the Forgiveness Prayer with him in mind, I was praying for the willingness to forgive him and I knew that it would come when the time

Contemplative Life

was right. The next time I co-facilitated a Forgiveness Prayer workshop I invited this man into my sacred space. When we got to the part of my asking him how I've harmed him, in my imagination I heard him say, "You absolutely have done nothing to harm me. I am so sorry for what I did and how it affected your life. I don't even feel worthy of asking you for forgiveness." Somehow forgiveness came. Forgiveness is not an act of the will. It comes when we strike the balance between human cooperation and willingness, and divine grace and mercy.

How do we know we have forgiven? For each of us it will be different. It may feel as if a weight has been lifted. We may experience an inner peace or sense of wellbeing. We may find we no longer hold any resentment or desire for revenge and instead wish the other person well. We find that the story has changed, and it is now a story about the great lesson we learned and how we were healed. We are able to apply this learning in our present moment relationships and interactions. We can freely choose how we respond to all that life brings us.

Once we have forgiven, we consider whether reconciliation and reparation are necessary or even possible in the relationship. When we have experienced abuse or trauma, unless we have some sort of familial relationship with that person, we aren't likely to want that person in our lives anymore. If both parties have a desire to continue the relationship, reconciliation means restoring the relationship. It may be restored to what it was before the offense occurred or it may reach some new level of intimacy. Even though reconciliation is not always possible, forgiveness is always possible. In this case we make a conscious decision to release the relationship without wishing that person any harm. Reparation means making amends for whatever harm was caused. As you discovered in the Forgiveness Prayer guided meditation, we each have a part in any conflict in a relationship. Reparation is about each person taking responsibility for their part, which is not easy when we have suffered because of the conflict. Reparation would only be necessary if both parties agree that something else is needed to make things right, to reset the balance.

Forgiving Ourselves

The question most frequently asked in Forgiveness Prayer workshops is: "How do I forgive myself?" Once we have learned the Forgiveness Prayer and practiced being a forgiving person, we start to recognize our own deep need to be forgiven. We all carry so much shame for the things we have done in our lives or perceive we have done. Shame is probably the feeling we most try to suppress and not experience. I think it's because it is almost always unwarranted. When we do something that hurts someone else or that we regret, it's normal to feel guilty. It is not normal to hold onto it for so long that we start to feel shame. How do we learn to feel this way about ourselves? We spend most of our lives thinking that what we do is who we are, never understanding that our true self is, as Father Thomas reminds us, a brilliant jewel; that we are loved before we *do* anything; that nothing we do or that anyone does to us can affect or mar this jewel of who we are.

We start the process of forgiving ourselves by recognizing that we are suffering because we haven't forgiven ourselves, or more likely, we don't know how to forgive ourselves. Notice what story you tell yourself about what you have done and notice if you berate yourself about it. You don't have to be a victim to your mind and emotions. Look at the facts of what happened that you think you need to be forgiven for. What was your motivation or intention? Did you intend harm? Remember to ask the Spirit to guide you in this exploration. If you have done something to hurt someone else and have feelings of regret, admit to yourself what you have done and take responsibility for it. You can use the Forgiveness Prayer to bring the person into your sacred space and tell them how you have harmed them and ask for forgiveness. At some point, if the person is still in your life, you may need to go to them directly to apologize and make amends. Rely on the guidance of the Spirit to do this work. Consider the possibility that you could actually do more harm than good before you act on the impulse to make amends. Sit with it for a while and be sure that you are being guided by the Spirit and not by your own guilt and shame.

If you have done or are doing something to harm yourself, admit that and take responsibility for it. One of the hardest things some of us need to face is when we have experienced repeated disappointment, injustice, or abuse that we have turned in on ourselves and then experience self-hatred and low self-esteem. We blame ourselves, which then feeds our shame and humiliation. These worst of the afflictive emotions trigger commentaries that are often reinforced by negative messages we hear from others, most likely the abuser. We must admit and accept responsibility for how we have treated ourselves and rely on God's mercy to find our way to forgiving ourselves. "…Because the tender mercy of our God by which the daybreak from on high will visit us to shine on those who sit in darkness and death's shadow to guide our feet into the path of peace" (Luke 1:78-79).

Use the Forgiveness Prayer and invite yourself into a dialogue of what you have done or think you have done, how you have been harmed, and ask for forgiveness. We are so much harder on ourselves than we would ever be with someone else who has harmed us. "I...urge you to live in a manner worthy of the call you have received, with all humility and gentleness, with patience, bearing with one another through love" (Ephesians 4:1-2). For all the same reasons we forgive others in our life, we forgive ourselves. It is how we grow and heal, how we find purpose in our suffering, how we live into who God created us to be. It is how we free ourselves from the past so we can live in the present moment and hear the call we are always receiving to live and love and serve.

Forgiving God

In the film "Almost Sunrise" that I mentioned earlier about military veterans experiencing moral injury, what Father Thomas says to one of the veterans in the film that made the biggest impression on me is: "I wonder if you can forgive God." Depending on what your relationship is with God at this time it may be difficult to even consider that God has done something to you that you need to forgive God for. Of course, all that we know about our God of love is that God never does anything to harm us and only looks out for our good. But who hasn't come across hard times or circumstances and blamed God for what God did or did not do to help us? Especially when I was struggling with depression, I used to beg God to help me disperse this cloud hanging over me and I would get angry when no help seemed to come. Imagine what it must be like for someone fighting in a war who is forced to do things that would otherwise be morally reprehensible. Or imagine a child who is being abused by a parent, the person in their life they most depend on for survival. How could God put someone in a position like this? The truth is that God doesn't put us in these kinds of positions, but we may think God is at fault. What is relevant in these situations is that we perceived God to be doing something to hurt us and the Forgiveness Prayer can help us to repair this relationship just as it helps us repair our human relationships.

Follow the same guidelines as you would with a person. Do some writing about how you perceive God has hurt you. Don't be afraid to be honest with yourself and let God have it. God is big enough to take on all our hurt and anger and still love us. Do the guided meditation and invite God into your sacred space (where God already dwells!)

The point of Centering Prayer and the contemplative journey is to deepen our relationship with God. We do this by reducing the obstacles that get in the way of intimacy. Denying that we are hurt or angry with God is an obstacle. And we forget that God already knows that we feel hurt and angry and is waiting for us to acknowledge it and be free of it.

Going Deeper

Spiritual Counsel

Forgiveness is a difficult topic for most of us. Remember that the spiritual counsel section is meant to help you with wisdom statements, quotes or Scripture passages that offer sustenance and encouragement. Notice if you are resisting using the Forgiveness Prayer. This may be a time for you to slow down and spend more time with the teaching and your reflections about what you are experiencing. Become familiar with the information in the chapter first and then read through the spiritual counsel section. Notice if any statements stand out for you or that you find particularly meaningful.

1. "An unforgiving heart of itself blocks the mystery of divine grace. It cannot freely receive what God freely gives. Our openness to God and our openness to one another are thus intrinsically linked" (Weavings). "Be kind to one another, compassionate, forgiving one another as God has forgiven you in Christ" (Ephesians 4:32).
2. "When I am honest with myself, I can see that most of what I normally think, worry, and even agonize about has to do with human relationships. What makes me happy or sad is closely linked to what I think or feel about other people…the great tragedy of human love is that it always wounds simply because it is imperfect, always tainted by needs and unfulfilled desires" (Weavings).
3. "Those who are closest to us are also those who cause us the deepest pain. Our real anguish comes from those who love us

but cannot love us in the way our heart desires" (Weavings). "If anyone says, 'I love God,' but hates his brother, he is a liar; for whoever does not love a brother whom he has seen cannot love God whom he has not seen" (1 John 4:20).

4. "In our own ways, we are all broken. Out of that brokenness, we hurt others. Forgiveness is the journey we take toward healing the broken parts. It is how we become whole again"[79] (Desmond Tutu).

5. "Without forgiveness, we remain tethered to the person who harmed us. We are bound with chains of bitterness, tied together, trapped. Until we can forgive the person who harmed us, that person will hold the keys to our happiness; that person will be our jailor. When we forgive, we take back control of our own fate and our feelings. We become our own liberators. We don't forgive to help the other person. We don't forgive for others. We forgive for ourselves"[80] (Desmond Tutu).

6. "Because we are human, some of our interactions will go wrong, and then we will hurt or be hurt, or both. It is the nature of being human, and it is unavoidable. Forgiveness is the way we set those interactions right. It is the way we mend tears in the social fabric"[81] (Desmond Tutu). "…He makes his sun rise on the bad and the good and causes rain to fall on the just and the unjust" (Matthew 5:45).

7. "…Forgiveness frees the person who inflicted the harm from the weight of the victim's whim—what the victim may demand in order to grant forgiveness—and the victim's threat of vengeance. But is also frees the one who forgives. The one who offers forgiveness as a grace is immediately untethered from the yoke that bound him or her to the person who caused the harm. When you forgive, you are free to move on in life, to grow, to no longer be a victim. When you forgive, you slip the yoke, and your future is unshackled from your past"[82] (Desmond Tutu). "…Forgive us our trespasses as we forgive those who trespass against us" (Luke 11:4).

Reflection Questions

You may be ready to work on forgiveness or you may be in a place where you still find it difficult to even consider. Please don't be hard on yourself. You are where you are. Know that God and the community you are journeying with are also with you. The reflection questions may help you to articulate where you are and what you are struggling with or resisting more clearly to help you know where to go from here. Be honest with yourself and do your best to share your reflections with your group, spiritual companion, or friend, in spiritual direction or in your Holy Listening Circle.

1. In what ways am I seeking power and control, affection and esteem, and security in my relationships with others? Am I able to let go of my desire to change the other person?
2. What has the Forgiveness Prayer taught me about relationships?
3. In what ways do I resist forgiving others? In what ways do I resist forgiving myself?
4. Reflecting on forgiveness, what insight are you taking from the teaching in this chapter and your practice with the Forgiveness Prayer?
5. What does it mean to you to be a contemplative or to live a contemplative life? Look back at your answers to this question from previous chapters and reflect on how your understanding has changed over time.

To Practice
Centering Prayer

Now more than ever you will be fortified and nurtured by your regular Centering Prayer practice. Listen to what Father Thomas says in *Open Mind, Open Heart* about the value of attending to our spiritual life:

> "We need to refresh ourselves at this deep level every day. Just as we need exercise, food, rest, and sleep, so also we need moments of interior silence because they bring the deepest kind of refreshment."

I encourage you to avail yourself of this deep refreshment only the Spirit can provide.

Logging

Continue to practice Logging for five to fifteen minutes daily. Hopefully by now you have been practicing Logging regularly enough that it can help you describe what you need to forgive and to notice any changes in you and your relationships as you practice the Forgiveness Prayer. Be sure to review your Logging at the end of each week or month to help raise your awareness of any patterns that God may be revealing to you for attention. How is this practice helping you with other practices? What insights come to you?

Spiritual Reading

Continue to practice Spiritual Reading for one hour per week, either doing it all in one day or spending ten to fifteen minutes a day four to five times a week. In the last chapter I suggested that you use *Addiction & Grace* for Spiritual Reading. As always, it's up to you what you use. Is there another book that's calling you? You might want to consider using this chapter or the spiritual counsel for your Spiritual Reading.

Lectio Divina

Practice Lectio Divina three times per week using Scripture passages of your choosing. You may want to use some of the Scripture passages in this chapter and read them in your Bible in context. Sometimes the story before or after the particular selection can provide deeper meaning.

Active Prayer

Use your Active Prayer daily when your mind is not occupied in conversation, work or some other activity requiring concentration. Remember that the active prayer becomes an aspiration. We aspire to no longer be controlled by our afflictive emotions, commentaries and interior dialogue, but to move more deeply into our hearts and into the heart of God. We start to experience the fruits of our aspiration when we have repeated our active prayer enough that it starts to come to us automatically. Are you noticing your Active Prayer coming to you more automatically?

Welcoming Prayer

Use the Welcoming Prayer daily. The very thought of forgiveness may stir up feelings you haven't experienced for a while. Some of us tend to repress feelings, thinking we have worked through them or that we have already forgiven someone. Try to be diligent about doing body scans and noticing energy shifts in your body as you work with this chapter. Remember the Welcoming Prayer is a tool to help you allow the emotions to surface so they can move through you and be healed.

Sabbath-Keeping

Find a time that fits into your life each week to set aside for Sabbath, whether it be a day, an afternoon or a few hours. Be intentional and prepare ahead of time so that you can devote the time to spiritual concerns, rather than the concerns of daily life. Consider how you can spend the time being rather than doing.

Contemplative Discernment

We use the Contemplative Discernment practice as needed. As you work with this chapter on forgiveness, you can use the discernment practice to help you know if there is anything else you need to do once you've done the Forgiveness Prayer several times. Do you need to make amends? Are you and the other person interested in reconciliation? Is any reparation needed?

The Forgiveness Prayer

Use the Forgiveness Prayer several more times over the course of a few weeks or even months. If you feel that you have resolution with the person you originally invited into your sacred space, continue to do the prayer to see if anyone else surfaces. You likely have many people in your life that you need to forgive, and this prayer will serve you when the time is right. At this point it's important to practice this prayer enough that when you need to forgive someone you will remember that you have this tool.

Resources for Further Study

Tutu, D. and Tutu M. (2014). *The Book of Forgiving: The Fourfold Path for Healing Ourselves and Our World*. New York, NY: HarperCollins Publishers.

Meninger, W. (1996). *The Process of Forgiveness*. New York, NY: The Continuum Publishing Company.

Monbourquette, J. (2000). *How to Forgive*. Cincinnati, OH: Novalis.

"Forgiveness." (March/April 1992). *Weavings*, Volume VII, Number 2. Nashville, TN: The Upper Room.

Arico, C., Fitzpatrick-Hopler, G., Begeman, P., Keating, T., Koock, T., Meninger, W. (2005). *Forgiveness: The Contemplative Life Program 40 Day Practice*. Contemplative Outreach, Ltd.

CHAPTER TWELVE
Contemplative Life

"...Your life is hidden with Christ in God."
Colossians 3:3

Participants in Contemplative Outreach retreats held on the grounds of St. Benedict's Monastery in Snowmass, Colorado are invited to sit with the monks at their public services—vigils before dawn followed by a meditation hour, mass and lauds in the morning, vespers in the evening, with an occasional evening meditation hour followed by a contemplative mass. Monastic life holds a space for retreatants to enter into the rhythm of the monastery. Life slows down. Worldly concerns are on hold. We're not bombarded by all of the information available to us in the outside world. We have the opportunity to experience what it's like to live for a time within a more intentional daily rhythm.

In addition to experiencing the daily rhythm of the monastery, we witness the spirituality of the Trappists monks. The founder of the Denver Chapter of Contemplative Outreach and my spiritual mother and mentor, Sister Bernadette Teasdale (1934-2020), often reminded those of us who served with her that we are "an extension of their spirituality in the world." It was important to Sister Bernadette that we understood the connection between what we were doing—practicing, teaching and supporting others in Centering Prayer—and its roots in the Christian contemplative tradition as modeled by the monks at Saint Benedict's Monastery. Father Thomas also felt that connection was important. The "Guidelines for Contemplative Outreach Service" that he authored state:

> "We maintain a spiritual relationship with St. Benedict's Monastery in Snowmass, Colorado… our spiritual home and a place of retreat and renewal where new insights for our spiritual journey may be revealed."[83]

Julie Saad

The Trappists are a Catholic order of monks and nuns who originated out of the Benedictine tradition, went through a reformation in the eleventh century in Citeaux, France (Cistercium in Latin) when they became known as Cistercians, and another reformation in the seventeenth century in La Trappe, France when they came to be called Trappists, but also continue to be known as Cistercians.

Sister Bernadette had a close relationship with Father Thomas and learned about the Trappist charism through the example of his life. In turn, she modeled this way of life to those of us who served with her. A charism is a gift of the Holy Spirit given for the benefit of all, "…to equip the holy ones for the work of ministry, for building up the body of Christ" (Ephesians 4:12). The charism of a religious order contains the gifts that inspired the founder. Each of us also have charisms. The Trappists follow the "Rule of Saint Benedict," which is a practical guide for living the Gospel that dates back to the sixth century, created by Saint Benedict of Nursia. The Trappist charism in simple terms is a life dedicated to prayer, work, study, community, and hospitality, committed to the values of silence, solitude, humility, simplicity, and service. When I worked as a volunteer with Sister Bernadette I never thought of her as modeling the Trappist charism per se, but she clearly had a way of doing things that became very familiar to all of us. (If you knew her this comment would make you laugh!) Everything we did together started with Centering Prayer. Lectio Divina was practiced regularly in classes, days of prayer, and on retreats. We held liturgical services (mass) at the Center once or twice a month and at any events we held headlined by a priest. Her most noted charism was hospitality. Classes, retreats and events started with a work plan aimed at making participants feel welcome and at home. Most every volunteer learned how to make coffee and snacks, in other words, we learned our way around the kitchen. Think about the places in your life where you feel most at home and part of the reason is likely that you are comfortable in the kitchen. We may think of hospitality as having to do with feeding people, but it has even more to do with building community and making people feel welcome. At the end of every event, you would hear her say "all hands on deck," meaning if we all help (including the participants) the work is easier. When we work together, we are bonding and building community. I've heard many volunteers say that the reason they volunteer is because they enjoy spending time with the friends they have made from this ministry. Sometimes when I was working at a class or event, I would think we

Contemplative Life

had way too many volunteers working for the number of participants coming. But having so many volunteers available to talk to people insured that everyone was personally welcomed, "chatted up" as Sister Bernadette used to say, and made to feel special.

In addition to our commitment to praying and working together we also spent time learning together. We watched Father Thomas's *Spiritual Journey Series* videos, read and discussed his books, and were lucky enough to have him in person for conferences once or twice a year. We hosted other contemplative speakers and teachers and maintained a bookstore with titles of interest to contemplative life. What most of us didn't realize is that we were being formed in contemplative life and service. And we were attracted to what was being offered and what we were experiencing. I remember Father Thomas telling a story about one of his brother monks, Brother Bernie, who was always doing nice things for him. In the beginning Father Thomas was irritated with him because Brother Bernie would do things that he never expected and didn't ask for. In the end Father Thomas said, "Well, this must be the way God treats people." This is what Sister Bernadette was teaching us—how to be a channel of God's love in the world for whomever we encountered.

Those of us who are not called to monastic life but have a committed practice of Centering Prayer, may be called to contemplative life. Even though we may have commitments to family, work, and community we can find ways to incorporate elements of this contemplative way of life into our life in the world. We can look to teachers like Brother Wayne Teasdale, Rory McEntee and Adam Bucko (authors of *The New Monasticism)*, Joan Chittister, and Christine Valters Paintner who have talked about how those of us who are not called to monastic life can nonetheless live in monasteries without walls, or as monks in the world.

Margaret Guenther, an Episcopal priest, retreat leader and spiritual director, wrote a book called *At Home in the World: A Rule of Life for the Rest of Us*. I love that she acknowledges that the rest of us may not be able to commit to the structure of monastic life, but that doesn't mean that we can't commit to a Rule of Life that fits our life circumstances and provides us with the structure and support we need to live a contemplative life. She guides us through finding aspects of spiritual practices and values that we can commit to no matter our station in life, whether we are married, single, parents, church members or not, professionals, students, or retirees. Depending on the realities of our life situation we may not be able to follow something as structured as the Rule of Saint Benedict, but when we consider what God is calling us to and what we are realistically able to commit to, we can create a Contemplative Rule of Life to fit our life.

From beginning to end, the Contemplative Living Experience (CLE) program explores what it means to live a contemplative life. Our journey culminates in formally defining what that means and how to do it by creating a personalized written statement known as the Contemplative Rule of Life. Prior to participating in the CLE program, whether in person or through reading and working with this book, we tend to fit our lives into the rhythm of the culture in which we live, but now we're learning to set our own cadence. We've taken a hard look at how much of our lives we live unconsciously. We've committed to opening our awareness to self-knowledge—"waking up" as Anthony de Mello would say. The purpose of this program is to transform our lives, so we learn how to live in the present moment, with intention, as we become more aware of God's presence in all aspects of our daily life.

At the end of each chapter of this book, we've explored the same reflection question, "What does it mean to you to be a contemplative or to live a contemplative life?" You may have noticed that an answer to that question is never given. The practice of Centering Prayer and living with the intention of consenting to the presence and action of God within awakens in us what it means to live a contemplative life. The answer will be different for each of us. In my study of Lectio Divina, I came across a book written by M. Basil Pennington, one of the founders of the Centering Prayer practice, called *Living in the Question*. The notion of living in the question rather than always searching for answers fascinated me. In it, he says,

> "It is paradoxical how much living in a question can bring clarity to our present experience. We see everything in a new perspective. We plumb the meaning of each thing more deeply. Each relationship takes on new meaning… The elements of our daily routine have more meaning… Living in the question…is a grace, giving a time of heightened realization, a fuller, more vital time of life."[84]

What Pennington describes as "living in the question" is what we do in the Contemplative Discernment practice. Once we learn to discern, we become more comfortable living in the question, and we find that just about everything in life is open for discernment.

Contemplative Service

Before we start the process of discerning and creating a Contemplative Rule of Life, let's look at the movement of how a contemplative practice like Centering Prayer leads to living a contemplative life, which in turn leads to a life of contemplative service. In this section you will find a series of questions appearing in bold print. Take your time pondering the questions, living in the questions.

What's the point? Yes, what is the point of living this life you've been called to? Or are you still pondering whether you've been called to this life?

Why do you practice Centering Prayer? When we start this journey, we're often motivated by the desire to feel better, to be more centered, focused and relaxed, to have spiritual consolations, to deepen our relationship with God. As our practice matures, our motivation changes. It moves us beyond our felt experiences to something deeper.

Have you been moved to something deeper? If so, to what?

What is the purpose of living a contemplative life? You have been exploring what it means to you to live a contemplative life. You may still be questioning what it means to be called to live a contemplative life, but at some point, you chose this path of discovery.

Can you remember and describe how you came to choose this path?

What is happening to you personally as you move along the path of this spiritual journey? We know this journey changes us. We have likely been told by others that we have changed.

How have you changed? How have the changes you've experienced affected others in your life?

When we talk about healing, what is being healed? Are you being healed? We often refer to this journey as a healing journey, precipitated by what Father Thomas calls the divine therapy.

In *Fruits and Gifts of the Spirit,* Father Thomas asks,

> "What are you really doing when you sit down in Centering Prayer and open yourself to God's presence and action within you? You are opening to God's

presence and consenting to God's activity. God's activity is the work of the Holy Spirit in your particular embodiment in this world."[85]

Pay attention to what Father Thomas says about the work of the Holy Spirit in your particular embodiment. The incarnation is the embodiment of Christ in the person of Jesus. But the incarnation also is the embodiment of Christ in you. As such, we are reminded of something Father Thomas has always talked about and encouraged us to keep in our awareness: we all have a basic core of goodness. But because of our human condition we may be blocked from being in touch with our basic core of goodness and may not even be sure we have one, even though Scripture points us to this fact of our lives: "God created [human]kind in his image; in the image of God he created them... God looked at everything he had made and found it very good" (Genesis 1:27, 31). "Do you not know that your body is a temple of the holy Spirit within you, whom you have from God...?" (1 Corinthians 6:19).

Are you aware of your basic core of goodness? If you are the embodiment of Christ, it makes sense that you have a basic core of goodness. This journey is about becoming who we are. It is about awakening to who we are.

The final chapter of Father Thomas's book *Open Mind, Open Heart* contains what he calls "Guidelines for Christian Life, Growth, and Transformation." The first three guidelines point us towards what he tried to impart to us about who we are in God:

1. "The fundamental goodness of human nature, like the mystery of the Trinity, Grace and the Incarnation, is an essential element of Christian faith. This basic core of goodness is capable of unlimited development; indeed, of becoming transformed into Christ and deified.
2. Our basic core of goodness is our true self. Its center of gravity is God. The acceptance of our basic goodness is a quantum leap in the spiritual journey.
3. God and our true self are not separate. Though we are not God, God and our true self are the same thing."[86]

As we've learned, our human condition can be an obstacle to any relationship, including our relationship with God. Fidelity to our

Contemplative Life

Centering Prayer practice and consenting to God's activity—the divine therapy—reduces these obstacles and brings us closer to the capacity of unlimited development that Father Thomas talks about. He says that once we start the process of dismantling the false-self system, all the energy we put into maintaining the false self is freed up, creating a vacuum that allows the Spirit to rush in. We start to live from the place of divine energy. This is where consent leads: becoming transformed into Christ is becoming transformed into who we really are.

What would it mean for your life if you accepted your basic goodness? Notice that in Guideline 2 he says that the acceptance of our basic goodness is a *quantum leap* in the spiritual journey. Father Thomas was always very careful in how he selected his written words. The use of the term "quantum leap" was very intentional. It means a huge movement forward or a dramatic or important advance. For most of us, acceptance is a long journey, and we can only get there through healing and grace. Accepting our basic goodness brings us closer to the reality of Guideline 3—that God and our true self are not separate. Healing the wound that makes us feel that we are separate from God is life changing. The experience of oneness with God brings with it an innate desire to serve God in others and in all creation.

How are you called to serve? Contemplative service, rather than being something we volunteer to do, is more of a vocation, a calling, a way of life. It arises from our center, from who we are in God, and is inspired and led by love. I once heard Father Thomas say, as he was nearing the end of his life, that his practice had become "effortlessness." In the film shown at Father Thomas's memorial service created by Contemplative Outreach from interviews with him called *A Life Surrendered to Love*, Father Thomas says,

> "Effortlessness becomes much more the main practice of your contemplative life, which doesn't mean you do nothing. But you don't think up things to do for yourself. You sort of let it happen. So the best means of doing God's will is an interior habit and disposition (it takes a long time to develop) of effortlessness… Another word for it is emptying. Another word might be detachment. Or a phrase that intrigues me is becoming nothing. So if you want to save your life, you will bring yourself to ruin. But anyone who brings himself or herself to

nothing, will find out who they are (Matthew 16:25). Nothingness, really, is who God is, meaning infinite possibilities."[87]

This is the way of contemplative service—effortlessness. When we are under the influence of the Spirit, service isn't something we feel we must do. It becomes a part of who we are and how we are. In *Invitation to Love* Father Thomas wrote,

> "The contemplative journey, of its very nature, calls us forth to act in a fully human way under the inspiration of the gifts of the Spirit. These gifts provide the divine energy of grace…"[88]

Our basic core of goodness is the gift of our life. In addition to the gift of life, each of us is given different gifts suitable to our unique talents and personality. As Saint Paul wrote in his letter to the Corinthians, "Now there are varieties of gifts, but the same Spirit; and there are varieties of service, but the same Lord; and there are varieties of working, but the same God who inspires them all in everyone. To each is given the manifestation of the Spirit for the common good" (1 Corinthians 12:4-7). One of the ways we can enjoy life and serve God is by using the gifts we have been given so that our service is effortless even though, at times, it may be difficult and intense work. This is the fruit of serving from the place of divine energy.

Do I have to wait until I have been completely purified or transformed before I can begin to serve others? We often think this way, but it's seldom (if ever) true. I've always admired the work of Mother Teresa (Saint Teresa of Calcutta), one of the great saints of our time. She was able to serve the poorest of the poor because she saw Christ in every human being. For much of her life Mother Teresa endured what sounds like a Dark Night of the Soul. She experienced what she thought of as spiritual poverty, a deep longing for God while feeling empty and alone. She struggled with her faith and somehow knew that working and acting with love helped others and gave her life meaning. If you think you need to be further along on the journey in order to serve, consider this Scripture passage: "For I was hungry and you gave me food, I was thirsty and you have me drink, a stranger and you welcomed me, naked and you clothed me, ill and you cared for me, in prison and you visited me... Amen, I say to you whatever you did for one of these least brothers [and sisters] of mine, you did for me" (Matthew 25:35, 40). No matter where we think we are on the journey, we can almost always serve "one of these least brothers [and sisters]."

Whom are you called to serve? In the *Mystery of Christ*, Father Thomas talks about the story of Mary and Martha as an example of the union of contemplation and action. He says,

> "The quality of one's service does not come from the activity itself, but from the purity of one's intention... Purity of intention developed through contemplation brings to action the quality of love. Without contemplative prayer, action easily becomes mechanical, routine, draining, and may lead to burnout. At the very least, it fails to perceive the gold mine that ordinary life contains."[89]

We may think that a call to service is to serve in the community, the neediest, the homeless, the poor, the hungry. While service to any of these groups is worthy and necessary, we usually don't need to look any further than our daily life for who we are called to serve. When we have an intention to bring the quality of love to our daily life, we are serving the people we live with, our families, friends, neighbors, coworkers, grocery store clerks—really everyone we meet.

The gospel message about serving whatever community we are called to serve is "Give as gift what you have received as gift" (Matthew 20:8). Father Thomas says that we do this by transmission, which is the result of how we have been transformed in Christ in our unique and personal journey. It is when we are living our lives out of our practice that what we do flows out of the divine relationship, out of the love that God is. This is how Father Thomas describes transmission in *The Mystery of Christ*:

> "Contemplative prayer enables us to see...the opportunities for spiritual growth that are present day by day in ordinary life. If one is truly transformed, one can walk down the street, drink a cup of tea or shake hands with somebody and be pouring divine life into the world. When the love of Christ is the principal

motivation, ordinary actions transmit divine love... Transmission is the capacity to awaken in other people their own potentiality to become divine."[90]

We see more and more that the contemplative life is not a private journey. Yes, our own healing and transformation are the first step, but they unfold in the greater context of service to the awakening of God's love in the consciousness of the entire human family. It is out of this lens of transmitting God's love in our ordinary daily life that we continue our exploration of living in the questions and creating our personal Contemplative Rule of Life.

Commitment

As you reflect on how you were called to contemplative life, consider all the factors that have led you into choosing this life. **What inspired you to pick up this book? What inspired you to commit to reading about a program called the "Contemplative Living Experience?"** The CLE program is designed to assist in your transformation from being a person who has a contemplative practice to one who is living a contemplative life. If you have been incorporating the practices into your life as recommended (or as close to that as fits into your life) you're probably beginning to realize the value of making choices in collaboration with God.

This is your spiritual journey, your life's journey, and how you live it is up to you. However, the CLE program involves several processes that require a degree of commitment on your part. Commitment helps us to live our lives consciously and with intention. It empowers us to be faithful to living out of our heart's desire. It unfolds day-by-day as we grow and change, and as our life circumstances change. Rather than endlessly searching for a path, we recognize that the path has been found. Now is the opportunity to integrate what we've learned and what we've been called to into our daily lives. Sometimes when we think of making a commitment, we may feel bogged down by what we think we "should" do, but a commitment to contemplative life can be life-giving, and can give us a renewed energy with purpose.

Let's pause here and ask ourselves:

> **What is the desire of my heart? Am I ready to commit to this path?**

Who am I at this time in my life?

Do I believe I am my mind? body? spirit? intelligence? emotions?

Am I aware of a larger Self?

Am I my roles or my self-image?

Who am I called to be?

Who am I in God?

Why is God creating me, in other words, of all God's creation, why is God creating me?

Do I see myself as co-creator with God of my life?

What is it about my current life that gives me the deepest, most abiding sense of meaning?

Am I manifesting God?

What do I hold sacred in my life?

Which relationships in my life contribute to my sense of meaning?

What are my deepest intentions in life?

Contemplative Rule of Life

Historically, in the Christian tradition different monastic or religious orders have followed what is called a "Rule of Life," as we've already explored in looking at the charism of the Trappists. Saint Augustine created a rule which came into being when he wrote down advice for his followers when he couldn't be with them. The Rule of Saint Benedict was created in the sixth century and is followed by many vowed and lay religious. It is a guideline for living in community or in solidarity with a religious order. Even anchorites like Julian of Norwich had a rule. In the sixteenth century the founder of the Jesuits, Saint Ignatius of Loyola, developed what he called "The Spiritual Exercises" which included prayer, meditation and other contemplative practices. Some might think of Alcoholics Anonymous or other twelve-step programs as living by a Rule of Life, the twelve steps. These rules have a certain rhythm to them and help establish a balance to life. Like the word commitment, sometimes we can turn a "rule" into something that we "should" do that is not life-giving. Let's look at creating a Contemplative Rule of Life, not as something we "should" do, but as a guideline that fits the rhythm of our life and that can be flexible as our life circumstances change. Most of us who don't live in a monastery or other intentional community lead lives very different from each other. What fits into the rhythm of my life will probably not fit for yours. Also, what fits for your life today may not fit as life changes in the next few years. Your Contemplative Rule of Life will be fluid and evolve as you change, and your life circumstances and commitments change. Remember that we tend to fit our lives into the rhythm of the culture in which we live rather than intentionally setting our own cadence. The less our rhythm conforms to the culture the freer we will be.

Take this opportunity to look at the current rhythm of your life and notice what you're doing each day unconsciously or out of habit. Is it serving you? Where does God fit in? Do you give God your best time or only what's left over? Is there any left over? I remember hearing a story about Mahatma Gandhi, whose daily meditation practice was very important to him. But during a very busy time, people around him wondered if they should spend a full hour in meditation when there was so much work to be done. Gandhi was reported to say something like, "Yes, you are right. We are far too busy to meditate for one hour. We will meditate for two hours." When we give God our best time in Centering Prayer and our other contemplative practices, we will find we have as much time as we need to take care of our daily life.

Let's look at a few more questions:

What are your current life circumstances and responsibilities? What are your priorities? What is missing from your current rhythm? Take time with these questions and be honest with yourself and realistic.

What responsibilities do you have to family and community? When we live with others or are part of a community, we need to look at how much time and attention we put into our relationships. Are you tending your relationships? When you spend time with family and friends are you fully present? Do you really listen? What about your coworkers? How do you exercise hospitality, the caring and nurturing of others?

How do you meet your needs around work? We all need to work at something that gives life meaning. What sustains you and gives your life purpose? Is it some form of contemplative service? Do you have work that nourishes you rather than drains you? If your work drains you what else do you have in your life that nourishes you like hobbies, avocations, creative outlets? Do you spend enough time in these other activities so that you are being nourished? How do you balance your work with your other needs and responsibilities in life?

What do you need physically, emotionally, spiritually? Some of us spend a lot of time taking care of others, especially those of us who have children or aging parents. It is so much harder to be a caretaker when we are not taking care of our own needs. Are you exercising in ways that you enjoy and support your physical health? How is your diet? Do you nurture yourself by preparing meals and enjoying them with family and friends? Do you spend time with people who listen to you and support you? Do you seek out counseling or spiritual direction when you need to? Are you taking time for solitude, Sabbath-Keeping, rest? Do you have a sacred place that renews and refreshes your spirit? When is the last time you were there?

This is the time to look at all the spiritual practices you've learned and decide which ones fit for you that you can integrate into your life. You may want to set aside a time each month, for example, to review all the practices and see if you have room for something now when you might not have before, or if you have a need for it now and forgot about it. Be aware that if we don't use a practice for a period of time, we will likely forget about it. That's totally normal! But I encourage you to try to incorporate all the practices as you begin this journey. If you commit to them, they will eventually become effortless.

Writing Your Contemplative Rule of Life

Your Contemplative Rule of Life should contain consistency since you are being intentional and may be changing old, unconscious habits. It should also focus on things that matter to you. When you look back over the questions throughout this chapter, you will see that you have started the process of identifying what matters to you. Your Contemplative

Rule of Life should be practical and realistic. You don't want to create something you can't possibly live up to and then feel that you have failed. This is not another New Year's resolution! Look at this as a living, working document that you will review periodically to make sure it still fits for you. Update it when needed. Your Contemplative Rule of Life should be life-giving and not constrict you. At the same time, it should stretch you, challenge you, and encourage you to continue to grow in love.

Here are some suggested steps to help you formulate a Contemplative Rule of Life:

1. Start with a clean piece of paper (or blank screen) and as with all our practices begin your Contemplative Rule of Life with a prayer. What do you want to say to God about your commitment to contemplative life? Write your prayer at the top of the page.
Here is an example of a prayer I wrote before writing my first Contemplative Rule of Life: "Loving Spirit, guide me into gentleness and effortlessness in daily life so that I may be the peace your love offers. I wait in loving attentiveness to your Word. May I do your will always."
2. Look at what you want to include in your life daily, weekly, monthly, and annually. For example, in your daily life you may want to commit to Centering Prayer twice a day, the Active Prayer phrase, Logging, and the Welcoming Prayer. Daily commitments might also include exercise, healthy meals, and time with family. Weekly commitments might include Sabbath-Keeping, doing something fun, meeting with a prayer group, liturgy or worship, regular contact with family and friends, and doing something creative. Monthly might include reviewing other contemplative practices like Discernment or the Forgiveness Prayer, getting a massage, taking care of finances, finding time for solitude, and spiritual direction. Annually might include an intensive retreat, a vacation, and visiting family.
3. Review the questions from the previous section to help you discern what to include in your Contemplative Rule of Life, paying attention to your relationship with God, your life

Contemplative Life

circumstances and responsibilities, family and community, work, and self-care.
4. Keep your Contemplative Rule of Life short, preferably the length of one typed page. Any longer and you may risk creating something that is not realistic or doable.

We talk about this Contemplative Rule of Life as being a commitment, but by now you have already chosen it. It doesn't take much more to commit to it and you've likely realized there's no turning back. Do you remember the moment you first became aware you were being transformed? If not, don't worry. Most of us don't. We just become aware one day that we are different, that we have changed, are more grounded and loving, less reactive, more humble, joyful, at peace with our decisions and life in general. Remember the gospel message "By their fruits you will know them" (Matthew 7:16). When we awaken to the embodiment of Christ within us, the fruits of the Spirit manifest in our lives, not just so that we experience them individually, but we all experience them in relationship with one another, in community. When we live and are guided by the Spirit, we are promised the fruits of the Spirit. "…The fruit of the Spirit is love, joy, peace, patience, kindness, generosity, faithfulness, gentleness, self-control" (Galatians 5:22-23).

Going Deeper

Spiritual Counsel
The spiritual counsel statements in this chapter are geared towards commitment and service. Those of us who struggle with commitment may need to take more time to explore what commitment means to us and why we resist. Spending time with these wisdom statements, quotes and Scripture statements may assist us in becoming aware of what blocks us. Remember that the spiritual counsel statements are meant to encourage you and help you go deeper with the material. I recommend that you read the chapter first to become familiar with the teaching and then notice if one or two of the statements stand out for you or speak to you in some way. Spend time reflecting with those. Then from time to time as you are working with the material review the spiritual counsel to see if any others attract you.
1. Spiritual commitment focuses our intention to "be with" our spiritual life and practices in a tangible way for a period of time.

The conscious intention allows the unconscious to be purified and transformed. Unresolved pain, anger and fear from past experiences with relationships and commitments (held in the unconscious) affect our ability to freely and consciously commit to our relationship with God now. Prayer (such as the Welcoming Prayer and our other contemplative practices) will free us for a fuller relationship with God, other people and ourselves.

2. At times in our spiritual life, we are offered the choice: whether to channel-surf, run after a new experience or method, or to remain waiting upon God in prayer. Commitment to spiritual practice cultivates waiting upon God.

3. It is often the failure of our own efforts, plans and sense of control over our own intentions and desires that allows the breakthrough of grace, mystery and new life into our lives. "For who knows God's counsel, or who can conceive what the Lord intends?... Thus were the paths of those on earth made straight, and people learned what pleases you, and were saved by Wisdom" (Wisdom 9:13, 18).

4. Our relationship with God needs to be expressed in our life through simplicity, discernment, forgiveness and service. Otherwise, our attachments/aversions, our self-will and our relationships with others are isolated from God and controlled by the unconscious programming of the false self, and any commitments we make will be buffeted by the winds of discouragement, woundedness, ignorance or burnout.

5. "...It is commitment to the journey and fidelity to the practice that leads to transforming union, not spiritual experiences. Such experiences, of course, may help to bring us to this commitment... We are initiated into the narrow path that leads to life, which is the way of pure faith"[91] (Thomas Keating).

6. Contemplative service is a manifestation of an interior call—a prompting from the Spirit. It is the way one consents and responds to the movement of the Spirit in the interactions of everyday life, according to one's gifts and calling within our family, work, community and our global society.

7. Service is more than volunteering. It is a specific form of volunteering with the intention of being transformed in and through the experience. Service is more than helping or doing a task. It is a way of being—a disposition of the heart, with no

beginning and no end. Service is a deep form of stewardship for God's people and God's creation, arising out of an experience of Oneness. It is a call from God to serve the Divine Indwelling in others and as such, is both motivated and inspired by Divine Love.

Reflection Questions

The teaching throughout this chapter is meant to bring you to deep self-reflection. You have already worked with reflecting and writing on the many questions contained in the material. The questions in this section may help you to simplify, summarize or bring together what you have already been reflecting on. This may be some of the content you will choose to share with your group, spiritual companion or friend, in spiritual direction or in your Holy Listening Circle.

1. Am I aware of any feelings, emotions, thoughts, commentaries or body sensations about my Contemplative Rule of Life? If so, did I remember to use the Welcoming Prayer?
2. Having expressed my commitment, what spiritual practices am I more drawn to, or empowered to use?
3. What are my gifts, and how might I consent and respond to the promptings of the Spirit to provide contemplative service?
4. You spent time in this chapter working on your "Questions on Commitment." Reflect on your experience with these questions: Who am I at this time in my life? Who am I called to be? What is it about my current life that gives me the deepest, most abiding sense of meaning?
5. Reflecting on what it means to you to be a contemplative or to live a contemplative life, what are your thoughts and feelings about committing to a Contemplative Rule of Life?

To Practice
Centering Prayer

Why do you do Centering Prayer? Earlier in the chapter I said as our practice matures, our motivation changes. It moves us beyond our felt experiences to something deeper. What is that "something deeper" for you? Listen to what Father Thomas suggests in *Open Mind, Open Heart*:

"It is not so much what we do but what we *are* that allows Christ to live in the world. When the presence of God emerges from our inmost being into our faculties, whether we walk down the street or drink a cup of soup, divine life and love is pouring into the world."[92]

Logging

Continue to practice Logging for five to fifteen minutes daily, remembering to review your Logging weekly or monthly to discover any patterns or insights.

Spiritual Reading

Continue to practice Spiritual Reading for one hour per week, either doing it all in one day or spending ten to fifteen minutes a day four to five times a week.

Lectio Divina

Practice Lectio Divina three times per week using Scripture passages of your choosing.

Active Prayer

Use your Active Prayer daily when your mind is not occupied in conversation, work or some other activity requiring concentration.

Welcoming Prayer

Use the Welcoming Prayer daily either by doing a body scan and welcoming and letting go of what you discover, or when you notice you are experiencing afflictive emotions, troubling thoughts, and commentaries.

Sabbath-Keeping

Find a time that fits into your life each week to set aside for Sabbath, whether it be a day, an afternoon, or a few hours. Be intentional and prepare ahead of time so that you can devote the time to spiritual concerns, rather than the concerns of daily life. Consider how you can spend the time being rather than doing.

Contemplative Discernment
Use Contemplative Discernment as needed for something you need help deciding or a decision you are not at peace with, or to continue to work on addictions, attachments, and aversions.

The Forgiveness Prayer
Use the Forgiveness Prayer as needed, particularly when you notice conflict, pain, hurt, or dis-ease in relationships.

Resources for Further Study

Bucko, A. and McEntee, R. (2015). *The New Monasticism: An Interspiritual Manifesto for Contemplative Living.* New York, NY: Orbis Books.

Chittister, OSB, J. (1990). *Wisdom Distilled from the Daily: Living the Rule of St. Benedict Today.* New York, NY: Harper & Row.

Guenther, M. (2006). *At Home in the World: A Rule of Life for the Rest of Us.* New York, NY: Seabury Books.

Fitzpatrick-Hopler, G. (2006). *Contemplative Service: The Contemplative Life Program 40 Day Practice.* Contemplative Outreach, Ltd.

Paintner, C. (2021). *Sacred Time: Embracing an Intentional Way of Life.* Notre Dame, IN: Sorin Books.

Teasdale, W. (2003). *A Monk in the World: Cultivating a Spiritual Life.* Novato, CA: New World Library.

CHAPTER THIRTEEN
Community

> *"As a body is one though it has many parts,*
> *and all the parts of the body, though many, are one body,*
> *so also Christ."*
> 1 Corinthians 12:12

PART TWO OF THIS BOOK STARTS WITH WHAT I CALL THE "PRACTICE chapters." The theme for the first practice chapter is "awareness of God's presence and action." It contains a guided meditation called Stepping Stones which gives us an opportunity to reflect on the course of our life, awakening us to God's presence and action in the people, events, and circumstances throughout our life—whether we were aware of it at the time or not.

We've been reflecting on what it means to be a contemplative and to live a contemplative life throughout this book. Where has your reflection led you? Do you have a greater awareness of God's presence and action, not only in your life, but in all of life? Abbot Joseph Boyle, the abbot at St. Benedict's Monastery in Snowmass, Colorado from 1985 until he died in 2018, often said that there were two books of Scripture, one is the Bible and the other is nature. I always felt that what he was trying to help us understand is that God is not only revealed to us in Scripture but we should also go out in the world and look around with awe at all of creation, and with the eyes and ears of mystery and wonder see that God is in all and all is in God. Choosing a contemplative life opens us to beginning to understand this, experience it, and witness it.

The final chapter of Father Thomas's book *Intimacy with God*, called "From the Inside Out," is a beautiful reflection on how this simple practice of Centering Prayer in daily life leads not only to our own transformation but bonds us with community and impacts the world in which we live. I encourage you to read the whole chapter, but here's an excerpt that will give you a glimpse of the significant impact Centering Prayer has on our sense of community:

> "Centering Prayer... bonds us with everyone else in the Mystical Body of Christ and indeed with the whole human family. There is really no such thing as private prayer. We cannot pray at this deep level without including everyone in the human family, especially those in great need. We also feel the need to express this sense of bonding and unity with others in some form of community...
>
> "Bonding with others takes place as the love of the Spirit is poured forth in our hearts. We feel that we belong to our community, to the human family, to the cosmos. We feel at home in the universe. We feel that our prayer is not just a privatized journey but is having a significant effect in the world. We can pour into the world the love that the Spirit gives us in prayer."

The many people who have journeyed together in the Contemplative Living Experience (CLE) program attest to the importance of the bonding that takes place when we pray together and share our faith and life journeys with one another. This is the space in which we have permission to be who we are, even when we're flawed, wounded, and messy. There is a love poured forth that heals our wounds, allows our true self to shine forth, and encourages us to continue to consent to God's presence and especially God's action in our lives—the action that Father Thomas calls the divine therapy.

Later in this chapter we'll talk about forming "contemplative living communities" which are an outgrowth of the CLE program. I went through the Nine-Month Course (the course the CLE program is patterned after) in 2002 and became part of a contemplative living community. We have been meeting monthly ever since. We started out with eight people in the group and over time one person died, two moved away, we added one new member, and two children were born to a couple in the group. These are some of the people I have become closest to over the years and who know me as well or better than most of my friends and family. In fact, I think of them as family.

Once I had to call on one of my "brothers" in the group, my friend Bill, to help me work through something I uncovered in the nine-month "Writing to Heal" course I took in 2014, which covered a range of topics from "Uncovering the Wound" through "Realizing the Gift," and "Transforming Pain," and finally offered some measure of healing. The teacher, Mark Matousek, always encouraged us to follow the writing. In other words, if something came up in the writing that stirred a strong reaction, we were instructed to write more about it. I was writing about my dad and how I never questioned his love for me, probably the closest I had ever felt to unconditional love. Reflecting on my dad's love brought tears to my eyes. He died in 1993. As I followed the writing, I began to realize that I had never felt that kind of love in my eleven-year marriage. My marriage had ended twenty-seven years prior to my taking the Writing to Heal course, so this writing stream caught me by surprise. Because I had worked on healing the pain around my divorce through therapy, Al-Anon, and my Centering Prayer practice, I thought my healing was complete. Apparently not! I started thinking about the secrets I still held about what went on in this marriage and the amount of shame I was still carrying because they remained hidden within me. So, I started detailing the secrets. I ended up writing 2,000 words. Mark had recommended we try to keep our writing under 1,000 words, but I knew I needed to get this out. As soon as I finished writing, I knew intuitively that this piece of writing needed to be read and that I needed to read it out loud to a man. I asked Bill if he would be willing to listen to me read. My ex-husband was an alcoholic who I'm not sure ever made it into any sort of recovery. Bill is a recovering alcoholic. Since Bill and I were both familiar with working the steps in a twelve-step program, we approached this as a fifth step in which we admit "...to God, to ourselves and to another human being the exact nature of our wrongs." The key to healing at this point in a twelve-step program is to be honest and forthright about what we have kept secret, often even from ourselves, by writing it down and sharing it with another human being. The experience of the reading on my part and the listening on Bill's part ended up being a healing experience for both of us. One of the things I remember Bill saying after listening to me read my 2,000 word story is "I was that guy." It was an opportunity for both of us to reflect on where we came from and where we are today. Talking about what I had written helped me to see my marriage from a point of view other than my woundedness and shame, something I wouldn't have been able to do on my own. I had made the decision to be vulnerable and allow Bill to witness my human condition. His response allowed me to see (through him) my ex-husband's human condition. Once I let down the walls of defensiveness and self-righteousness, all that was left was compassion and forgiveness. Only then was I able to really let go and experience healing from this woundedness.

When we have experiences like this in relationship and in community, we begin to see how interconnected we are. Throughout his teaching, as in the final chapter of *Intimacy with God*, Father Thomas reminds us that Centering Prayer and contemplative life are not just for our personal gratification. Centering Prayer is not a relaxation exercise or a mindfulness practice; we deepen our relationship with God when we pray. We consent to God's presence and action within not only while we're doing Centering Prayer, but also in our daily lives in all that we do, in all that we are, and in all that we experience. The grace of God heals us and transforms us, but none of us lives in a vacuum. Whatever we experience and however we are transformed affects every interaction we have so that we "can walk down the street, drink a cup of tea or shake hands with somebody and be pouring divine life into the world."[93]

When I'm teaching Centering Prayer, especially to those who have some experience with the practice, I try to impress on them how important this simple way of life and prayer is—that what we are doing is affecting the world. It reminds me of something I've heard Sister Joan Chittister say when she hears people despair about how much pain and suffering there is in the world and wonder how my little life can be of any help. She realistically knows that no one of us can ease so much suffering but encourages us to "do something." We all can do something. If I am patient and less judgmental towards my loved ones, if I am kind to the grocery store clerk, if I greet everyone I meet with a nod and a smile, if I check in on an elderly neighbor, if I send a sympathy card to someone who is grieving, if I encourage a teenager who is struggling with self-confidence, I am *doing something* and I am pouring divine life into the world.

We began the practice chapters with a guided meditation, and we now come full circle with another guided meditation. Let's see where this one takes you. Allow yourself to be surprised!

Sacred Place: A Guided Meditation

This guided meditation begins with a relaxation exercise to help you get into a meditative state. At the end of the practice, you will be asked to do some writing about your experience in your notebook or digital journal. You may wish to record the guided meditation on your phone or another device and then quietly listen and respond. If you are not able to do that, read the guided meditation slowly and quietly and simply follow the instructions. With your notebook handy, begin the guided meditation.

Close your eyes and take a few deep breaths, receiving the Spirit on your in breath and letting go of any heavy energy on the out breath... breathing in deeply and breathing out deeply... breathing in and out once more.

Feel your feet grounded to the earth... and relax... Feel the light energy moving into the soles of your feet... then into your ankles and just relax... With your internal eye, see the light move up the calves of your legs and then up into the thighs of your legs... Let your internal eye focus on this golden light moving into the area of your glutes and then, into your lower spine... Relax, taking a deep breath... Relax...

Now see the light energizing your spine as a golden column of love energy moving up your back toward your neck... Relax... Relax... And feel the warmth of this energy moving into your neck and then up into the back of your head... Relax... See the light energy moving up to the crown of your head and feel its warmth throughout your head... Relax as you feel this warmth.

Now move with your internal eye down the front of your face and feel that warm energy within your face... and cheeks and chin... Feel the energy moving down into your neck, and then your chest, feeling the warmth and seeing the light of this energy pulsing within you.

Follow this energy into your chest, allow it to be the segue... Picture a walkway that takes you into an open meadow, or picture a safe and sacred place where you can feel the breeze of the morning... Look around... What do you see?... Perhaps trees... a pond in the distance... fields of flowers just beginning to blossom... And now look over to the side and see a bird for a moment or two... Gently open your eyes and begin to write a story about this bird. Take seven or eight minutes to write your story and at the end of this time, plan to return from your sacred place.

So now, at the end of seven or eight minutes of writing, as you draw your story to a close, close your eyes again and walk slowly away from this sacred place, knowing you can return whenever you wish... feeling once again the morning breeze as you walk away… Sensing the light energy that warms your soul and come back to your chest or your heart, feeling that warmth of the Spirit in this present moment… And when you are ready, gently open your eyes.

If you are meeting with a group, you may wish to share your story with your group or with a trusted spiritual companion or director. How is God present for you today? How has the story you wrote, inspired by seeing a bird in your sacred space, awakened you to the presence of God in your life?

Forming Community

The CLE program is meant to be experienced in community. Those of us who practice Centering Prayer and have discovered within ourselves the desire to go deeper into our own hearts and into the heart of God may also find ourselves opening to new and meaningful human connections along the way. Sharing what's on our heart, being honest and vulnerable, laughing and crying together, the healing that comes from being heard, becoming known in a way we may never have been previously, being present to each other, holding space for each other's joy and pain—all of this makes the community CLE experience truly extraordinary. Often people start to feel a sense of grief about the program ending as they get toward the last month or two. The transformation that happens in community opens us up to forming deep and lasting friendships—the type of companionship most of us yearn for on the spiritual journey.

Part of Father Thomas's vision for Contemplative Outreach was to form small faith communities, much like the early Christian church, to support and nourish each other in the practice of Centering Prayer and in living lives rooted in the contemplative dimension of the Gospel. The many Centering Prayer groups that meet weekly around the world are one way that vision has taken hold. Another is through small groups that form at the end of the CLE program that have come to be known as contemplative living communities. By the end of nine months in the program, participants are accustomed to meeting once a month and appreciate the comradery, support, and accountability the commitment to this program affords them. A natural outcome of the CLE program is that small groups form and continue to meet monthly after the program is complete.

Over the years, the facilitators of the CLE program established guidelines for the formation of these contemplative living community small groups. Guidelines are meant to be suggestions, not requirements, to help groups get started. They seem to be helpful to most groups starting out with the understanding that the group will evolve as it allows the Spirit to move within the community. Guidelines are set out for membership, for a monthly meeting format, and for adding new members.

Guidelines for Contemplative Living Communities Membership:

1. An established daily practice of Centering Prayer, preferably two twenty to thirty minute prayer periods per day.
2. Completion of the CLE program or its equivalent, i.e., having worked through this book, or having watched *The Spiritual Journey Series* video course, or having been on a Contemplative Outreach ten-day intensive retreat (including *The Spiritual Journey Series*).
3. A commitment to living a contemplative life as expressed in your personal Contemplative Rule of Life.
4. A commitment to supporting other community members by participating in monthly meetings and sharing the responsibility of facilitating group meetings.
5. A commitment to participate in an annual intensive retreat (if you are able).
6. An agreement that each member takes full responsibility for the meeting so there is no leader or hierarchy in the contemplative living community. The role of facilitator rotates among members. The facilitator for the day keeps the agreed upon times, leads the prayer, and presents the topic for discussion.

Guidelines for Monthly Contemplative Living Communities Meetings:

1. Meetings are held monthly with the members deciding the meeting place. It is suggested that meeting dates and facilitators be set at least four months in advance.
2. Time Frame: in-person gatherings should last a minimum of four hours and a maximum of seven hours (depending on the size of the community). If you are meeting on Zoom you may

want to shorten each meeting time and meet more often, like twice a month for two hours.
3. Group size: three to eight members is ideal.
4. Agenda for the Day
   o Two twenty to thirty minute periods of Centering Prayer—one at the beginning of the meeting and one at the end.
   o Check in and check out periods.
   o Topic of Discussion.
   o Lunch or dinner break of at least thirty minutes.
5. Check In: The facilitator for the day will advise the time available to each member for check in. Between five and fifteen minutes are recommended for each member. Check in is a form of faith sharing and gives each member an opportunity (without comment or interruption) to articulate their contemplative journey experience since the last meeting as it relates to their faithfulness in living out their commitment to their Contemplative Rule of Life.
6. As each member takes this opportunity to articulate their contemplative journey experience since the last meeting, the rest of the community listens for the movement of the Spirit in each person's sharing. Suggestions, questions, or comments will be given only if asked for by the person sharing (as time allows).
7. Topic of Discussion: A topic relating to contemplative living in everyday life is presented by the facilitator. The facilitator may choose to do a fifteen to twenty minute presentation related to personal experience with a book, DVD, or other teaching that has affected their life, and then open the meeting up for discussion. The group may also decide on a format where they read a book together and discuss, watch a DVD, or review specific teachings on the contemplative practices.
8. Check out: Bring closure to the day with a brief sharing of each member's experience of the meeting.

Guidelines for Adding New Members:

1. The group may decide to be a closed group, not accepting new members.
2. If the contemplative living community is open to new members, the following guidelines are suggested:
   - The potential new member expresses an interest in joining the group to an existing member.
   - The group member takes the request to the next contemplative living community meeting for the group's consideration.
   - The potential new member is given all materials regarding membership and is assisted in creating a Contemplative Rule of Life prior to attending the first meeting.
   - The potential new member makes a commitment to attend five consecutive meetings and to follow the membership and meeting guidelines.
   - The potential new member and the group then discern together whether the group is a good fit. New membership is offered only if the group reaches consensus.

So many options are available for forming community these days. If forming a contemplative living community is not possible or desirable, you may continue to meet regularly with the group you journeyed with through this program. You also may wish to look into opportunities for community through Contemplative Outreach. You can go to their web site www.contemplativeoutreach.org where you will find "Centering Prayer Free Online Support Groups" and a link to the "Online Meditation Chapel." You will also find links to contacts for communities in the U.S. and Internationally and a calendar of retreats and workshops offered by various Contemplative Outreach chapters or groups.

Some other contemplative groups you might find of interest with the potential to find community are:

- The World Community for Christian Meditation (WCCM) at www.wccm.org
- Shalem Institute for Spiritual Formation at www.shalem.org
- Center for Action and Contemplation at www.cac.org

Julie Saad

- Center for Christogenesis at www.christogenesis.org

Going Deeper

Spiritual Counsel

This final spiritual counsel offers you some wisdom statements about community and the oneness of all creation.

1. "...That they may all be one, as you Father are in me and I in you, that they also may be in us... that they may be one, as we are one" (John 17:21-22).
2. "To live in the Spirit is the fulfillment of every law and commandment, the sum of every duty to each other, and the joy of oneness with everything that is"[94] (Thomas Keating).
3. "In a Centering Prayer community we become one not just with the people in the room and all those truly seeking God; we also become one with everything that God has created: with nature, with art, with relationship, with the service of others. This bonding effect gives us an inner desire to form community and to be faithful to it..."[95] (Thomas Keating).

Reflection Questions

1. If you have been meeting with a small group in a Holy Listening Circle, since this is the end of the formal program, it is time to close the group. The format for closing is for each person to share for five minutes on the following question:

    What has participation in the CLE program meant to you and how has it changed your life?

    Each person's sharing is followed by three minutes of silence before the next person shares. After everyone has shared, the group will say goodbye to each other.

    If your small group decides to continue meeting and perhaps form a Contemplative Living Community, spend some time discerning together where you will hold your first meeting and what your format will be.

Contemplative Life

2. In Chapter Four you were asked to reflect on and write your answer to the question: What are you committing to and what is it you would like to see changed in your life as a result of participating in the CLE program? Look back at how you answered this question and reflect on how you answered it compared to your experience now, after completing the program.

Closing Ritual

You may wish to formally close the program by doing a closing ritual together. Here's a suggested format, but you may design the ritual in your own way.

1. Choose one or more persons to lead the closing ritual and guide the group in the readings and reflections.

2. Song:

    Play a recording of the Taizé song *"Veni Sancte Spiritus"* or another contemplative piece of music that's meaningful to your group.

3. Opening Reflection:

    As we gather here together, we recognize we have, each of us, come a long way as we have experienced the CLE program. We have prayed with and for each other. We have let ourselves be vulnerable. We have intimately shared our frustrations and our hopes. As we bring our participation in the CLE program to a close, let us once again share our prayer, knowing we already are our true selves.

4. Sharing:

    Reflecting on your Contemplative Rule of Life, please share what you would like to say to God and to this community about your commitment to living a contemplative life.

5. Blessing with holy oil:

   Traditionally oil is used in the rites of many of the world's religious traditions to bless us into life and to bless us into death. We will celebrate God's life in us and the transformation of the false self. We celebrate the transformation to new life we have shared with each other. (If you are holding this closing ritual online each person can bring their own oil, either a favorite essential oil or a few drops of olive oil, so you can each bless yourself as the facilitator reads the blessing.)

   Prayer—Let us pray together:

   Creator God, you who have loved me from the beginning of time, you who have planted your Word in my heart and imagination, anointed me with love, called me by name. Deepen in me the desire to live with you always. Anoint my mind and my imagination with the healing oil of your love. Let your blessed oil of love bathe me. Purify me from head to heart. Bless my eyes and ears so that I may more clearly hear and see the beauty of all creation. Oh God, help me to believe the truth about myself, no matter how beautiful it is! (Adapted from *Seasons of Your Heart* by Macrina Wiederkehr.)

   Each of you may dip your finger in your oil and anoint your own forehead (making the sign of the cross if that feels right to you) while the facilitator offers this blessing: May this oil remind you of the new life within you. (Alternatively, a facilitator can bless each person with oil and say the blessing.)

   We hope that as you go forward, living a contemplative life, you may sense God's presence in a deeper way. As you commit yourself on this journey, our prayer for you is that you will experience the vibrancy of your true self in the presence of the divine within you.

6. Closing Prayer—Let us pray together:

   All good and gracious God, we are walking into mystery. We face the future not knowing what the days and months bring or how we will respond. Be with us as we journey. Deepen our ability to see life through your eyes. Fill us with hope and an abiding trust that you dwell in us amidst all our joys and sorrows. We thank you for the unique gift of each person living in this community who has journeyed with us over our time together. We praise and thank you for being our faithful companion on this journey. Amen.

Resources for Further Study

Best, M. (2008). *Community, Oneness in Contemplation: The Contemplative Life Program 40 Day Practice.* Contemplative Outreach, Ltd.

Keating, T. (2017). *Intimacy with God: An Introduction to Centering Prayer,* Chapter 12 "From the Inside Out." New York, NY: The Crossroads Publishing Company.

AFTERWORD

*"So whoever is in Christ is a new creation:
the old things have passed away;
behold, new things have come."*
2 Corinthians 5:17

Reflecting on the journey of creating this book, I'm reminded of a painting class I took soon after I retired. I was still in those early months of retirement and just letting myself "be" for a while, seeing what might surface as I considered what I was going to do next in my life. I had never painted before and had no idea what I was doing in this class. But I had a great teacher and the camaraderie of a class full of serious but fun amateur artists each week. I found it difficult to paint while at home by myself because I was never sure what to do next, so I did most of my painting in class, spending many weeks on each painting. Over time, I realized I was developing a relationship with each of my paintings as they unfolded before my eyes. I remembered each step in the process—mixing paint to get the right color, learning how to see perspective, how to foreshorten a raised knee, how to paint light and shadows. After developing such deep relationships with my paintings, I wondered how professional artists put their creations up for sale!

This book has been like that for me, a relationship that has developed over time. When I first had the idea to write a book, I had no idea where to even start. But I had such a strong desire to share these teachings with others within Contemplative Outreach who have not had the opportunity to take the Contemplative Living Experience program in person that I just started writing. After I wrote a couple of chapters I told my cousin Jay, to whom this book is dedicated, that I had started writing a book. Jay was a journalist, writer, editor, and storyteller. He told me he would be happy to read the first chapter and give me feedback. I sent him the first two chapters and his encouragement was effusive. I was stunned. One of his comments was, "I think this book is going to have a much wider audience than you think it will!" With that kind of encouragement, I launched into the chapter on the human condition. I agonized every day because it was so hard to summarize this seminal teaching, especially when my false self kept feeding me this self-doubt: "Who are you to think you can summarize Thomas Keating's teaching?"

After four months of writing, I took a break and went on a ten-day private retreat at St. Benedict's Monastery in Snowmass, Colorado. Being on a private retreat at the monastery gave me the opportunity to engage in the rhythm of the monastery—getting up at 4:00 a.m. every day and going to vigils and then staying in the chapel for an hour of Centering Prayer. I returned to the chapel at 7:30 for mass and attended vespers each evening. One day after mass in the morning, I met another woman who is an experienced author and was at the monastery to work on a book. It hadn't occurred to me to work on my book, but I had my computer with me, so why not? I set to work on the human condition chapter and after a few days I finished it! The guest master, who was a friend of mine, said that the words were probably spoken to me from the sacred valley surrounding the monastery. The next day I wrote the chapter on Centering Prayer without even looking at my notes.

The day I got home from my retreat I received a phone call from my sister-in-law telling me I needed to come to Illinois right away because my brother had been in a terrible motorcycle accident. I repacked my dirty clothes and headed for the airport. It took me fourteen hours to get to Champaign, the whole way not knowing how my brother was. As I traveled, I wrapped myself in the prayer shawl I had taken on retreat with me and said the Welcoming Prayer over and over. When I got to the hospital my sister put her arms around me and said, "It's just you and me now." Our brother was still on life support because he was an organ donor, but he was gone. I was devastated. No one else on the planet shared my life story like my little brother. Steve was only eleven months younger than I, so when we were little kids people thought we were twins. We were pretty much inseparable. After I moved to Denver there seemed to be more than physical distance between us, but later in life we became close again. I remember him saying to me one time, "I wonder how we got so close lately."

In the year or so that followed Steve's death I didn't care much about anything that I cared about before he died, and I quit writing.

When I look back at times like these, I'm amazed at how God works in my life. (I'm not sure why I'm continually amazed since it happens often enough!) A year after Steve's death I was invited by Contemplative Outreach to help with a project Father Thomas had initiated. He wanted to inspire people to go "back to basics," he said, and find a way to make *The Spiritual Journey Series*, especially the human condition teaching, more widely available. The Contemplative Outreach team who worked on this project decided to do a year-long online course through our partners at Spirituality & Practice. Because I had experience with facilitating classes using the original *Spiritual Journey Series* videos, I took on the task of editing the original videos to remove any dated language and content and I wrote a companion narrative for each video segment. This became my weekly work for a full year. The experience gave me the opportunity to be more immersed in Father Thomas's teaching than ever and to be disciplined about writing every week. As that project came to a close, I started thinking about my own book again. My desire to return to it was beginning to stir.

Later that year I bumped into Kate Sheehan Roach in the hallway at a Contemplative Outreach conference in Denver. We had met before, but I didn't really know her or what kind of work she did. For some unknown reason I started telling her about my book and my struggles with it since my brother's death. I even said to her, "I don't know why I'm telling you all this." She replied, "I do" as she handed me one of her business cards and, wouldn't you know it, she's an editor. I called her about a month later and hired her to be my editor. She has been enormously helpful in keeping me focused, motivated, and excited about what I have to offer. After working with her for several months, I started to see the book really taking shape.

Then the COVID-19 pandemic started. By March of 2020 we were going into lockdown. It seemed as if the world suddenly stood still. I had a dawning realization that this was big, and it wasn't going away any time soon. So many people all over the world were suffering and dying. So much unknown. Spreading so fast around the world. We could no longer deny the oneness of the human family, that we live in a global society. What affects one affects all. When one suffers and is hurt, we all suffer and hurt. As I was adjusting to being in isolation with all the fear and anxiety for my safety and those I care about, I was also experiencing anger and sadness over the way the United States was responding and what was happening to so many people—loss of jobs and income, inability to make rent and mortgage payments, getting sick with the virus, friends or family in the hospital not being able to visit them, loved ones dying alone. It seemed like most of the time I was overwhelmed with emotion and wondered how I would get through another day. I finally decided to stop watching so much television, start taking my dog for long walks, find ways to be with people outside, and in a sense, surrender to the reality of the pandemic. I was reminded of something Father Thomas says in *Open Mind, Open Heart*: "By consenting to God, you are implicitly praying for everyone past, present, and future. You are embracing the whole of creation."[96] In the midst of a pandemic lockdown there wasn't much more I could do.

As I was adjusting to being in lockdown and isolation I returned to working on the book in earnest. I could only attend so many Zoom retreats and I needed something substantive to focus my time, attention, mind, and emotions. I was at the point in the book where the practices I was working on were not widely taught throughout Contemplative Outreach and so I needed to do more research. I was becoming more immersed in the teaching and, in the process, reflecting more on the impact of the teaching and the practices on my life. Once the chapters were mostly written and we started editing, I went back to the questions that have haunted me since I started facilitating and teaching Centering Prayer and contemplative life: "Am I living this? Am I walking my talk? Do I have any idea what I'm talking about? Or am I a spiritual phony?" Some of that is my false self talking, and some of it is an honest, conscious examination of my life, my motivation, and my ability and willingness to be present.

This is where I draw a parallel between writing this book and the relationships I found myself developing with my paintings. I am in deep relationship with this teaching and this book. I sometimes worry that publishing this book will invite people into my life in ways I'm not really ready for. But the truth is, I don't know of any other way to teach this kind of material except through my own experience, which necessarily involves using my life and my pain as my primary example. But this journey is never over. There isn't really a destination, other than maybe what I think of as "Into the Heart of God." Even though God is in my heart and I am in God's heart, and even though I trust what Julian of Norwich says to be true, "All shall be well, and all shall be well, and all manner of things shall be well," and even though I try my best to do as Father Thomas suggests and take responsibility for my emotional life—I still struggle, I get lonesome, my mind catches onto something I can't let go of, and I still "do what I hate" (Romans 7:15).

What encourages me and keeps me going is recognizing that all along this never-ending journey I am cultivating and experiencing the fruits of contemplative life. In the beginning of this book, I shared about my experience in Al-Anon. During those years I felt I was as "militant" about working the steps as anyone in AA because it was "life and death" to me just as it was to anyone who was serious about recovery. *The Promises* of working the twelve steps from the book *Alcoholics Anonymous* (widely known as "the big book") illustrate what I experienced in my own recovery in Al-Anon:

> "We are going to know a new freedom and a new happiness.
> We will not regret the past nor wish to shut the door on it.
> We will comprehend the word serenity and we will know peace.
> No matter how far down the scale we have gone, we will see how our experience can benefit others.
> That feeling of uselessness and self-pity will disappear.
> We will lose interest in selfish things and gain interest in our fellows.
> Self-seeking will slip away.
> Our whole attitude and outlook on life will change.
> Fear of people and economic insecurity will leave us.
> We will intuitively know how to handle situations which used to baffle us.
> We will suddenly realize that God is doing for us what we could not do for ourselves."[97]

I used to read these promises every day. They were an aspiration for me, a prayer. All the people who came before me in Al-Anon and AA believed in and experienced these promises, and I trusted I would too. These are the sort of things that you don't check off as they occur, but that you discover once they become your lived experience.

Father Thomas often points to the fruits and gifts of the Spirit and even wrote a little book about them. The fruits of the Spirit are "love, joy, peace, patience, kindness, generosity, faithfulness, gentleness, self-control" (Galatians 5:22-23). When we have a committed practice of Centering Prayer, we become more sensitive to the Spirit working within us and soon discover that we are a manifestation of the fruits of the Spirit. Like the promises, they come to us over time, and we can trust that the Spirit is alive in us and working to heal and transform us.

Experiencing the promises of the twelve steps and the fruits of the Spirit revealed to me that the obstacles that were keeping me from being who God created me to be and living the life I was meant to live were gradually being dismantled. This is the way of most spiritual paths. We start with self-examination and do the work on ourselves in order to experience healing and the fruits of doing the work. But there is a greater purpose here. It's the underlying reason I wrote this book and do this work.

Before he died, Father Thomas had been working on a document that we in Contemplative Outreach know as the "Vision, Theological Principles and Guidelines for Contemplative Service." The original document was written long ago and has been revised over the years. One of Father Thomas's final gifts to us was to write commentaries on each of the principles and guidelines since he knew his time on earth was getting short, and soon we would be unable to consult with him directly about what they meant. In his commentary on the first theological principle he says,

> "The fundamental purpose of Centering Prayer and Contemplative Outreach is to further the knowledge and experience of God's love in the consciousness of the human family."

I have read this commentary many times, but while I was in the middle of writing this book it became like a beam of light awakening in my consciousness. So many people in our world have a concept of God as a punishing overseer who is watching our every move. God is indeed watching our every move, but not with any intention other than to join us in love in whatever we are experiencing in life. Father Thomas says many times in his teaching that what we are doing by having a faithful Centering Prayer practice and consenting to being transformed is having a significant impact on the world. Whenever I'm teaching about Centering Prayer or contemplative life, I ask my students if they're aware that what they are doing is having a significant impact on the world. It's something I've reflected on for years, discerning what Father Thomas might mean by this, but also what it means to me. I think it's about letting go of the false self energy, transforming our very being into divine energy. It's what Teresa of Ávila says about Christ having no body now on earth but ours. It's being able to see Christ in every human being the way Mother Teresa modeled.

Listen to some of the things Father Thomas says about this throughout his teaching. I want you to hear it in his words, so you get a sense of how important a point this was that he was trying to get across to us:

> "When the presence of God emerges from our inmost being into our faculties, whether we walk down the street or drink a cup of soup, divine life and love is pouring into the world."[98]

> "In a Centering Prayer community, we become one not just with the people in the room and all those truly seeking God; we also become one with everything that God has created: with nature, with art, with relationships, with the service of others… We are invited first to share in our own redemption by accepting our personal alienation from God and its consequences throughout our lives, and then to identify with the divine compassion in healing the world through the desire of the Spirit within us. 'The unspeakable groanings of the Spirit,' as Paul calls them, are our desire to bring peace and knowledge of God's love into the world. The love that is the source of those desires is in fact being projected into the world and is secretly healing its wounds. We will not know the results of our participation in Christ's redemptive work in this life."[99]

> "We feel that our prayer is not just a privatized journey but is having a significant effect in the world. We can pour into the world the love that the Spirit gives us in prayer."[100]

> "Divine love makes us apostles in our inmost being. From there comes the irresistible presence and example that can transform the world."[101]

> "If one is truly transformed, one can walk down the street, drink a cup of tea or shake hands with somebody

and be pouring divine life into the world… When the love of Christ is the principal motivation, ordinary actions transmit divine love. This is the fundamental Christian witness; this is evangelization in its primary form."[102]

"…He has penetrated the very depths of our being, our separate-self sense has melted into his divine person, and now we can act under the direct influence of his Spirit. Thus, even if we drink a cup of soup or walk down the street, it is Christ living and acting in us, transforming the world from within. This transformation appears in the guise of ordinary things—in the guise of our seemingly insignificant daily routine."[103]

I always felt that Father Thomas was trying to teach us what it means to live the contemplative dimension of the Gospel. I admit through most of my spiritual journey I didn't know what that meant. I remember hearing him say one time "Just teach people the silence." The silence teaches us everything. His teaching explains what happens when we commit to a life of contemplative prayer and as we start to experience what he taught (not just read about it), we integrate it into our lives, or more likely, God does the integrating. How many times have I heard Father Thomas talk about the "restructuring of consciousness" and pondered what that means? And then I would have an interaction with a loved one that left me feeling unloved only to discover that "feeling unloved" was something I created out of my emotional programs and could then immediately let go of the feeling and all the accompanying commentaries. Even five years ago that would not have come so quickly. Of course I'm not unloved! Or the "transforming union," which is "…a way of being in the world that enables us to live daily life with the invincible conviction of continuous union with God."[104] Do I have an invincible conviction? Conviction, yes, but God is still working on me to get to the invincible part. What about "unity consciousness?" Sometimes. "The unitive way is the awareness of the abiding presence of God, a presence that is not undermined by what we feel or think, by what others do, or even by tremendous tragedy."[105] When I am able to be present, I experience the abiding presence of God. And I am human and at times I get tired and cranky and fan the flames of my emotional programs, leaving me feeling separate and alone.

For me, a life committed to contemplative prayer is the path into the heart of God—into the heart of love. Making this commitment changes everything. Over the years as I would hear the message from John's Gospel "He must increase; I must decrease" (John 3:30), it always resonated with me, but I didn't know why until I digested and assimilated Father Thomas's words in *Invitation to Love*:

> "According to John of the Cross, the same fire of divine love that is experienced painfully in the night of spirit becomes gentle and full of love in the transforming union. The 'I' of self-centeredness diminishes to a very small 'I.' The great 'I AM' of Exodus looms in its place. Thus, the divine plan is to transform human nature into the divine, not by giving it some special role or exceptional powers, but by enabling it to live ordinary life with extraordinary love."[106]

I can't think of anything else I would rather do.

ACKNOWLEDGEMENTS

Who would have ever thought that writing a book was a community experience? I'm the author after all, aren't I? I should have known! I remember when David Frenette was writing his book, *The Path of Centering Prayer*, I was helping him with classes and retreats he was giving using the material from his book because he wanted feedback on how people were receiving the teaching before it went into the final manuscript. I've had a similar experience in the writing of this book. So many people have helped me in countless ways. David was my spiritual director for several years and one of my mentors and friends. He is one of the architects of the original Nine-Month Course which inspired the writing of this book. It's hard to recount and express the gratitude I've always felt in my heart for what I learned from him, mostly just from being in his presence.

Of course, none of this would have been possible without the life and teaching of Thomas Keating and his determination to renew the contemplative dimension of the Gospel in modern times. I had the opportunity to spend time with him and get to know him personally, although I have to say I was always in awe of him. I like to tell this story about my relationship with him because it makes me laugh at myself. Because I was in awe of him, I couldn't bring myself to ask to have a meeting with him even though I was dying to. He always had a close relationship with Sister Bernadette Teasdale from the Center for Contemplative Living in Denver and talked to her often. When Sister Bernadette retired and I became the Contemplative Outreach coordinator in Denver, I still could not ask Father Thomas if I could meet with him. One day while I was in my room in the retreat house at St. Benedict's Monastery, someone knocked on my door and handed me a note from a phone call that came into the kitchen in the retreat house. It was from Father Thomas. It said that he could meet with me at 2:00 that afternoon, *if I thought it would be helpful!* That simple message changed my relationship with him. It's not that I ever stopped being in awe of his teaching and his incredibly gentle presence, but I no longer hesitated to meet with him or call him if I thought it would be helpful!

My cousin, Jay Walljasper, to whom this book is dedicated, was an early cheerleader. I thought I was writing a manual for Contemplative

Outreach to use to help groups in other places put on the Contemplative Living Experience program. It was Jay's comment to me that he thought this book would have a wider appeal than I thought it would that changed the course of the book. I always admired his writing ability and read many of the articles he wrote over the years. To have him compliment my writing and offer to help me was such a gift.

My friend Diane Ahonen has listened to me talk about all my feelings of inadequacy all these years that I've been teaching at the Center in Denver and teaching the Contemplative Living Experience program. When Rose and I first started talking about doing the program at the Center rather than a retreat center, we knew we would need to hire a cook rather than ask volunteers to cook. I have watched Diane cook for everyone she knows over many years and even though she never did it professionally I had a feeling she could handle what we were looking for. And by all accounts she really enjoys doing it! One of the things we have gotten the most positive feedback from participants about over the years is the meals, especially the Friday evening dinner when we come together for dinner and conversation after not seeing each other all month. I always get very nervous when I'm giving a presentation and she would be the first one to hear it on Friday mornings while she was making that evening's apple or berry crisp and I was sitting at the counter reading my notes out loud. She lives closer to the Center than I do, and we both have dogs so I would stay at her house and when she wasn't cooking at the Center, she was taking care of the dogs. How do you ever thank someone for that kind of friendship?

I told you in the Afterword about how my editor, Kate Sheehan Roach, came into my life at the Contemplative Outreach conference in 2019. I didn't realize at the time that our "chance" encounter was an answer to prayer. After I finished my work on *The Spiritual Journey Series* online course, I was struggling to stay motivated to work on the book. I remember about a month before I met Kate in one of my conversations with God, who I was sure was telling me to write this book, I said that I thought I needed help. But I didn't know where to go. So, I just sort of left it to roll around in my consciousness for a while, knowing that something would turn up. Kate's personal practice of Centering Prayer and her involvement with Contemplative Outreach for so many years was truly a godsend, not to mention what a great editor she is. She was a master at figuring out how best to work with me which is not necessarily the way she works with all her authors. We've done a lot of rounds of editing together, and it really does feel like something we do together, and her guidance just makes the book get better and better. I am most grateful that this journey together has resulted in a friendship that will live on long after the book is published.

Sister Bernadette Teasdale was the founder of the Center for Contemplative Living in Denver. I first met her in 1994 and she became a spiritual mother to me. I had a lot of "growing up of my faith" to do at that time in my life and I attribute it to Father Thomas's teaching under her guidance. Her door was always open, and she had such a big heart. At times she was a force to be reckoned with because she had such a big, outgoing personality, but she always came from a place of love. I'm so grateful to have known her and to have been shepherded on this path by her.

If God has elves, Bernie Jacques was the elf that was sent to me. He always had a mischievous side, which I loved about him, but is probably the person who most modeled the lay contemplative life for me. He was almost twenty years older than I, but we became such good friends—prayed together, taught together, and served together. He died in 2009 and I continue to miss his presence in my daily life.

My friend Dan Davis was a reader of the early chapters, long before I knew what I was doing. We've been friends for over twenty years, from the time we formed the contemplative living community we both continue to be a part of. We've been through a lot together! He's one of those people whose encouragement early on gave me the motivation to keep going. I chose four people to read the manuscript once it was in final draft form and Dan was one of them. I always say that he's probably read every spiritual book that was ever written in many different religious and spiritual traditions. He provided great general comments and suggestions, but what I valued most was that instead of doing a quick read through he spent time with the book and made personal notes along the way as he was reading about how the material was affecting him.

Bob Albrecht and Bill Hershberger are also part of our contemplative living community and not only read the draft but also heard many stories of the book's journey. Bob and I served and taught together in many different capacities at Contemplative Outreach of Colorado. He is such a steady force in my life, a wonderful compliment to my tendency towards drama! Bill is the friend I referred in Chapter 12 who I trusted enough to share my writing about the secrets in my marriage. I have always felt he is a kindred spirit and someone who is there for me in a way few people are in life. I'm so grateful for their friendship and for listening to me and encouraging me through it all.

Jane Vennard, who wrote the foreword to this book, is my spiritual director. She has heard so much about my spiritual journey but also about my journey writing this book. Before I started working with Kate, she was the one who was holding me accountable to keep writing. Even before she read any part of the book, I think she knew I was onto something. She was one of the readers of the final draft and I incorporated most of her suggestions into the final manuscript. I'm so honored that she agreed to write the Foreword. I'm most grateful for the spiritual companionship we have developed over these many years.

Father Carl Arico, who was on the first Lama Foundation retreat in the 1980s with Father Thomas and served as the vice president of Contemplative Outreach for many years, sent me an email one day and told me it wasn't like he was looking for something to do, but if I thought it would be helpful, he would be happy to read my book. After he read it, we had a long conversation about the book, full of feedback and stories as only Father Carl can tell. It was most helpful to have the perspective of someone who was close to Father Thomas for so many years and has taught most of the practices in this book.

My fourth reader of the final draft was Rose Meyler. Rose taught me how to teach the Welcoming Prayer and the Forgiveness Prayer and eventually mentored me in teaching and facilitating the Contemplative Living Experience program. I have known Rose since the mid-1990s when we both started serving Contemplative Outreach in Denver and soon became friends. It was important to me that someone who knows the program as well as she does read the manuscript. Always a faithful mentor, her gentle suggestions and feedback were just what I needed to make sure the teaching is accurate. I'm grateful for all the time we spent together teaching and bringing this material to life for people and for her friendship.

My friend and fellow CLE facilitator, Bob Mischke, when I was trying to decide what to do about proofreading said to me "You know, I'm pretty good at that. My mother was an English teacher." He offered to proofread and has found some of those niggling things that some people wouldn't notice, but if you are a natural editor like I am, would drive you crazy. Bob was one of my early teachers of Centering Prayer and we soon became friends from serving together in Denver.

Other friends who read early chapters and offered helpful feedback are Sue Kahalekulu, Tom Smith, and Pamela Begeman. When I was so unsure of myself and what I was doing writing a book their support helped to keep me going. Sue is a volunteer at the Center and one of the facilitators of the CLE program in Denver. Tom and I serve on the Contemplative Outreach governing board and have become friends over the years. Pamela and I have worked together for several years on the Contemplative Outreach online courses. She is one of the first people who kept saying to me, "See? You are a writer!"

Tara Steckler is one of my friends from Contemplative Outreach who gave me a message from God that came to her in prayer that I was going to write three books. She always hesitated to give people these messages and I always tried to encourage her to just do it. I'm grateful for the message I received and for our friendship.

The monks at Saint Benedict's Monastery in Snowmass, Colorado have been a constant in my life from the first time I went there on retreat in the early 2000s. I think I recognized right off that this was as close as I was going to get to the source of what we were trying to do in Contemplative Outreach. They are living the contemplative life. Of course, their contemplative life looks very different from the way I live it, but the connection has always been real and palpable for me. How many times did I thank them for being there and doing what they do because without them I couldn't do what I do? And the response was always thanking me for what I was doing because without that they couldn't do what they do. I have known so many of them over the years: Brother Aaron, Father Micah, Brother Thomas, Brother Michael, Father Ed, Brother John, Brother Dean, Brother Gabriel, Brother Chuck, Brother Raymond, and Brother Benito. I know there are more whose names I have forgotten but have not forgotten their spirit. Father William Meninger, one of the co-creators of the practice of Centering Prayer, came to Denver many times over the years to teach us about *The Cloud of Unknowing*, the enneagram, and Julian of Norwich. Father Thomas, of course, lived at Saint Benedict's Monastery for many years and was generous with his teaching schedule and meeting with retreatants and visitors. Abbot Joseph Boyle whose welcoming presence is an example for me of how Jesus must have treated people. And now, after Abbot Joseph's passing, Abbot Charlie Albanese, whose gentle and calm presence carries on what was started in Snowmass so many years ago. I'm grateful to them for holding the space for contemplative prayer throughout the centuries.

A program like CLE could not be carried out without the many volunteers who so graciously give their time and energy to pass on what they learned and experienced in the program through their own transformation. The other facilitators over the years included Rose Meyler, Joanne Warner, Joan Shanks, Nancy Burns, Pat Wittkopf, Sue Kahalekulu, Tara Steckler, and Bob Mischke. Others who helped with set up, welcoming, and preparing meals included Joe O'Leary, Fred Spafford, Sister Joan Wageman, Jan Letson, Irene Martin, Nancy Ruane, and Shawn Dehne. So many others supported the program by being prayer partners for the facilitators and participants. We always felt held by the community.

To the many volunteers and friends at Contemplative Outreach in Denver, it is with you that I grew up in the spiritual life. I have felt supported and loved by you for more than twenty-five years.

My family has been a constant in my life, largely due to my mother's modeling of how important family was to her. Even though I wandered away from my family in my young adult years, they have always been my foundation. Perfect? No. But as my life has unfolded my gratitude deepens for what they taught me, how they allowed me to find my own way and learn my own lessons, and how they held me in love. My parents, George and Jean Saad, were married for 46 years, until my dad died in 1993. My mother lived another 10 years without him and never got over missing him. We watched them go through a lot of ups and downs through those years and continue to love each other and us through it all. My sister Carrie Eizik has always been a model for me of expressing creativity—what I think of as making what's going on inside of me visible. She is an artist extraordinaire, a painter and so much more. She also is a writer and editor and has always shown interest in this book, asking me how it's going, encouraging me to keep at it, and commiserating with me about the process of editing! As my big sister she has shown me the way in so many things in life and I probably never let her know enough how grateful I am to have her in my life. My brother Steve Saad died in 2016 after being hit by a drunk driver. He was eleven months younger than me—Irish twins some say—and so much a part of my life I never imagined life without him. I've never had another relationship in my life that was as easy as my relationship with him. It reminds me of what Father Thomas said about his beloved friend Brother Bernie: "This must be the way God treats people."

NOTES

[1] Johnston, W. (Translator and editor). (1993). *The Cloud of Unknowing* (p. 40). New York, NY: Image.
[2] Keating, T. (2006). *Open Mind, Open Heart* (p.175). New York, NY: The Continuum International Publishing Group Inc.
[3] Johnston, W. (1973). *The Cloud of Unknowing and The Book of Privy Counseling* (p. 48). New York, NY: Doubleday.
[4] Merton, T. (1969). *Contemplative Prayer* (p. 5). New York, NY: Image Books.
[5] Laird, M. (2006). *Into the Silent Land* (p. 1). New York, NY: Oxford University Press, Inc.
[6] Delio, I. (2013). *The Unbearable Wholeness of Being* (pp. 74-75). Maryknoll, NY: Orbis Books.
[7] Anonymous. (1984). *Alcoholics Anonymous*. New York, NY: Alcoholics Anonymous World Services, Inc.
[8] Laird, M. (2006). *Into the Silent Land* (p. 17). New York, NY: Oxford University Press.
[9] Bourgeault, C. (2010). *The Meaning of Mary Magdalene* (p.55). Boston, MA: Shambhala Publications, Inc.
[10] Keating, T. (2014). *Invitation to Love* (p. 118). London: Bloomsbury Publishing Plc.
[11] Keating, T. (1987). *The Mystery of Christ* (p. 39). Warwick, NY: Amity House, Inc.
[12] Laird, M. (2006). *Into the Silent Land* (p. 117). New York, NY: Oxford University Press, Inc.
[13] For a full detailed explanation of Thomas Keating's teaching on the human condition see the video series *The Spiritual Journey, Part 2, Models of the Human Condition* published by Contemplative Outreach, Ltd. or Thomas Keating's book *Invitation to Love*.
[14] Keating, T. *The Spiritual Journey Series, Part 2, Models of the Human Condition*, p. 9. Contemplative Outreach, Ltd.
[15] Matousek, M. (2014). "Writing to Heal." The Shift Network.
[16] Williamson, M. (1992). *A Return to Love* (pp. 190-191). New York, NY: HarperPerennial.
[17] Tutu, D. and Tutu, M. (2010). *Made for Goodness* (pp. 5, 7). New York, NY: HarperOne.
[18] Keating, T. (2005). *Manifesting God* (p. 106). New York, NY: Lantern Books.
[19] Keating, T. (2006). *Open Mind, Open Heart* (p.12). New York, NY: The Continuum International Publishing Group Inc.
[20] https://www.youtube.com/watch?time_continue=33&v=I1VFKlpbol8
[21] Keating, T. (1987). *The Mystery of Christ* (p.39). Warwick, NY: Amity House, Inc.
[22] Source Unknown.

[23] Adapted from "The Shalem Pamphlet on Group Spiritual Direction" by Rose Mary Dougherty, www.shalem.org.
[24] de Mello, A. (1992). *Awareness*. New York, NY: Doubleday.
[25] Keating, T. (1987). *The Mystery of Christ* (p.39). Warwick, NY: Amity House, Inc.
[26] Mulholland, Jr., M. (2000). *Shaped by the Word* (49-63). Nashville, TN: Upper Room Books.
[27] Laird, M. (2006). *Into the Silent Land*. New York, NY: Oxford University Press.
[28] Some of the material contained in this section was developed by the Contemplative Outreach Lectio Divina Service Team.
[29] Keating, T. (2017). *God is Love: The Heart of All Creation* (pp. 136-137). Contemplative Outreach, Ltd.
[30] Keating, T. (2017). *God is Love: The Heart of All Creation* (p. 139). Contemplative Outreach, Ltd.
[31] Mulholland, Jr., M. (2000). *Shaped by the Word* (49-63). Nashville, TN: Upper Room Books.
[32] Mulholland, Jr., M. (2000). *Shaped by the Word (p. 20)*. Nashville, TN: Upper Room Books.
[33] Keating, T. (2017). *Intimacy with God* (p. 98). New York, NY: The Crossroads Publishing Company.
[34] Mulholland, Jr., M. (2000). *Shaped by the Word* (p. 22). Nashville, TN: Upper Room Books.
[35] Keating, T. (2017). *Intimacy with God* (pp. 100-101). New York, NY: The Crossroads Publishing Company.
[36] Keating, T. (2002). *The Spiritual Journey: Part 1 – The Basic Course* (tape transcription, p. 30). Butler, NJ: Contemplative Outreach, Ltd.
[37] Keating, T. (2000). *Fruits and Gifts of the Spirit* (pp. 6-8, paraphrased). New York, NY: Lantern Books.
[38] ibid (p. 28).
[39] Mulholland, Jr., M. (2000). *Shaped by the Word* (pp. 35-36). Nashville, TN: Upper Room Books.
[40] Keating, T. (2002). *The Spiritual Journey: Part 4 – The Divine Therapy* (tape transcription, p. 77). Contemplative Outreach, Ltd.
[41] Keating, T. (2017). *Intimacy with God* (pp. 187). New York, NY: The Crossroads Publishing Company.
[42] Keating, T. (2014). *Reflections on the Unknowable* (p. 126). New York, NY: Lantern Books.
[43] Keating, T. *Lectio Divina Series: Centering Prayer & Lectio Divina* (available on YouTube). Contemplative Outreach, Ltd.
[44] Mulholland, Jr., M. (2000). *Shaped by the Word* (p. 20). Nashville, TN: Upper Room Books.
[45] Keating, T. (2002). *The Spiritual Journey Series: Part 1 – The Basic Course* (tape transcription, p. 30). Contemplative Outreach, Ltd.
[46] Keating, T. (2006). *Open Mind, Open Heart* (p. 58). New York, NY: The Continuum International Publishing Group Inc.

[47] Some of the material contained in this section was developed by the Contemplative Outreach Welcoming Prayer Service Team.
[48] Most of the references to Mary Mrozowski come from a transcript of a retreat she gave in Denver October 15-17, 1993.
[49] Keating, T. (1992). *The Spiritual Journey: Part 2 – The Human Condition* (tape transcription, p. 50). Contemplative Outreach, Ltd.
[50] Keating, T. (2006). *Open Mind, Open Heart* (p. 169). New York, NY: The Continuum International Publishing Group Inc.
[51] Keating, T. (1992). *The Spiritual Journey: Part 2 – The Human Condition* (tape transcription, p. 52). Contemplative Outreach, Ltd.
[52] Keating, T (2006). *Open Mind, Open Heart* (p. 23). New York, NY: The Continuum International Publishing Group Inc.
[53] Ibid, (p. 141).
[54] Moyne, J. and Barks, C. (2001). *Unseen Rain*. Boston, MA: Shambhala Publications, Inc.
[55] Haughey, J. (1989). *Converting Nine to Five* (p. 47). Eugene, OR: Wipf and Stock Publishers.
[56] Ibid, (p. 23).
[57] Nouwen, H. (2013). *Discernment: Reading the Signs of Daily Life* (p. 8). New York, NY: HarperCollins Publisher.
[58] May, G. (1988). *Addiction & Grace: Love and Spirituality in the Healing of Addictions* (p. 163). New York, NY: HarperCollins Publishers.
[59] Kidd, S. (1990). *When the Heart Waits* (p. 14). New York, NY: HarperCollins Publishers.
[60] Nouwen, H. (2013). *Discernment: Reading the Signs of Daily Life* (p. 8). New York, NY: HarperCollins Publisher.
[61] Ibid, (p. 18).
[62] May, G. (1988). *Addiction & Grace: Love and Spirituality in the Healing of Addictions* (p. 163). New York, NY: HarperCollins Publishers.
[63] Keating, T. (2006). *Open Mind, Open Heart* (pp. 33-34). New York, NY: The Continuum International Publishing Group Inc.
[64] May, G., M.D. (1988). *Addiction & Grace: Love and Spirituality in the Healing of Addictions* (pp. 38-39). New York, NY: HarperOne.
[65] Keating, T. (1987). *The Mystery of Christ* (p. 39). Warwick, NY: Amity House, Inc.
[66] Keating, T. (2002). *The Spiritual Journey Series: Part 2 - Models of the Human Condition* (tape transcription, p. 47). Contemplative Outreach, Ltd.
[67] Abrams J. and Zweig, C. (1991). *Meeting the Shadow: The Hidden Power of the Dark Side of Human Nature*. New York, NY: Penguin Group (USA) Inc.
[68] Keating T. (2012). *Invitation to Love* (pp. 11-12). London: Bloomsbury Publishing.
[69] May, G., M.D. (1988). *Addiction & Grace: Love and Spirituality in the Healing of Addictions* (p. 139). New York, NY: HarperOne.
[70] Ibid, (pp. 38-39).

[71] Keating, T. (2009). *Divine Therapy & Addiction: Centering Prayer and the Twelve Steps* (pp. 53-54). New York: NY: Lantern Books.
[72] Keating, T. (2006). *Open Mind, Open Heart*, (p. 163). New York, NY: The Continuum International Publishing Group Inc.
[73] Keating, T. (2009). *Divine Therapy & Addiction: Centering Prayer and the Twelve Steps* (pp. 153-154). New York, NY: Lantern Books.
[74] Thompson, M. (1992). "Moving Toward Forgiveness" (p. 19). *Weavings*, Volume VII, Number 2, Nashville, TN: The Upper Room.
[75] Ibid.
[76] Nouwen, H. (1992). "Forgiveness: The Name of Love in a Wounded World" (p. 13). *Weavings*, Volume VII, Number 2. Nashville, TN: The Upper Room.
[77] Source unknown.
[78] Rohr, R. (2017). "The Scapegoat Mechanism" from Richard Rohr's Daily Meditations, April 30, 2017, cac.org.
[79] Tutu, D. and Tutu, M. (2014). *The Book of Forgiving* (p. 3). New York, NY: HarperOne.
[80] Ibid, (p. 16).
[81] Ibid, (p. 4).
[82] Ibid, (p. 21).
[83] www.contemplativeoutreach.org: About, Vision, Guideline #10.
[84] Pennington, M.B. (1999). *Living in the Question: Meditations in the Style of Lectio Divina* (pp. 2-3). New York, NY: Continuum.
[85] Keating, T. (2000). *Fruits and Gifts of the Spirit* (p. 28). New York, NY: Lantern Books.
[86] Keating, T. (2006) *Open Mind, Open Heart* (p. 158). New York, NY: The Continuum International Publishing Group Inc.
[87] Keating, T. (2018). *A Life Surrendered to Love*. Contemplative Outreach, Ltd.
[88] Keating, T. (2014). *Invitation to Love* (p. 147). London: Bloomsbury Publishing Plc.
[89] Keating, T. (1987). *The Mystery of Christ* (pp. 50-51). Warwick, NY: Amity House Inc.
[90] Keating, T. (1987). *The Mystery of Christ* (p. 25). Warwick, NY: Amity House Inc.
[91] Keating, T. (2014). *Invitation to Love* (p. 140). London: Bloomsbury Publishing Plc.
[92] Keating T. (2006). *Open Mind, Open Heart* (pp. 55-56). New York, NY: The Continuum International Publishing Group Inc.
[93] Keating, T. (1987). *The Mystery of Christ* (p. 25). New York, NY: Amity House.
[94] Keating, T. (2008). *The Heart of the World* (p. 92). New York, NY: The Crossroads Publishing Company.
[95] Keating, T. (2017). *Intimacy with God* (p. 184). New York, NY: The Crossroads Publishing Company.
[96] Keating, T. (2006). *Open Mind, Open Heart* (p. 32). New York, NY: The Continuum International Publishing Group Inc.
[97] Anonymous. (1976). *Alcoholics Anonymous* (pp. 83-84). New York, NY: Alcoholics Anonymous World Service, Inc.

[98] Keating, T. (2006). *Open Mind, Open Heart* (pp. 55-56). New York, NY: The Continuum International Publishing Group Inc.
[99] Keating, T. (2017). *Intimacy with God* (pp. 185-186). New York, NY: The Crossroad Publishing Company.
[100] Ibid, (p. 187).
[101] Keating, T. (1987). *The Mystery of Christ* (p. 12). Amity, NY: Amity House
[102] Ibid, (p. 25).
[103] Ibid, (p. 87).
[104] Keating, T. (2014). *Invitation to Love* (p. 117). London: Bloomsbury.
[105] Keating, T. (2000). *Fruits and Gifts of the Spirit* (p. 8). New York, NY: Lantern Books.
[106] Keating, T. (2014). *Invitation to Love* (p. 115). London: Bloomsbury.